Olympism: The Global Vision

The collection starts from the premise that Olympism and the Olympic Games make sense only when they are placed within the broader national, colonial and post colonial contexts and argues that sport not only influences politics and vice-versa, but that the two are inseparable. Sport is not only political; it is politics. It is also culture and art.

This collaboration is a first in global publishing, a mine of information for scholars, students and analysts. It demonstrates that Olympism and the Olympic movement in the modern context has been, and continues to be, socially relevant and politically important. Studies focus on national encounters with Olympism and the Olympic movement, with equal attention paid to document the growing nexus between sports and the media; sports reportage; as well as women and sports.

Studies published here seek to assert that the Olympic movement was, and is, of central importance to twentieth and twenty-first century societies. Finally, the collection demonstrates that the essence of Olympism and the Olympic movement is important only in so far as it affects societies surrounding it.

This book was previously published as a special issue of The *International Journal of the History of Sport*.

Boria Majumdar, a Rhodes scholar, is a Research Fellow at La Trobe University, Melbourne. He has taught at the Universities of Chicago and Toronto and has written extensively on the history and politics of sport in India and across the world. Deputy Executive Academic Editor of the *International Journal of History of Sport* and Executive Academic Editor of *Sport in Society*, some of his books include *Twenty-Two Yards to Freedom: A Social History of Indian Cricket* (2004), *Goalless: The Story of a Unique Footballing Nation* (2006) and *The Illustrated History of Indian Cricket* (2006).

Sandra Collins is a lecturer of Japanese History and Culture at San Francisco State University. She was most recently a Visiting Scholar for the Center of Japanese Studies, University of California, Berkeley as she finished her manuscript for The Missing Olympics: 1940 Tokyo Games. Japan, Asia and the Olympic Movement (forthcoming, Routledge). She has published several works on the role of Japan in the Olympic Movement. She received her Ph.D. from the University of Chicago in modern Japanese History where she began her research on the cancelled 1940 Tokyo Games. She was also was an inaugural Post-Graduate Research Scholar for the International Olympic Committee and a Fulbright-Hays Scholar at the University of Tokyo Institute for Socio-Cultural Information Studies.

Sport in the Global Society

General Editors: J.A. Mangan and Boria Majumdar

Olympism: The Global Vision
From Nationalism to Internationalism

Sport in the global society
General Editors: J.A. Mangan and Boria Majumdar

The interest in sports studies around the world is growing and will continue to do so. This unique series combines aspects of the expanding study of *Sport in the Global Society*, providing comprehensiveness and comparison under one editorial umbrella. It is particularly timely, with studies in the aesthetic elements of sport proliferating in institutions of higher education.

Eric Hobsbawm once called sport one of the most significant practices of the late nineteenth century. Its significance was even more marked in the late twentieth century and will continue to grow in importance into the new millennium as the world develops into a 'global village' sharing the English language, technology and sport.

Other Titles in the Series

Olympism: The Global Vision

From Nationalism to Internationalism

Edited by Boria Majumdar and Sandra Collins

Routledge
Taylor & Francis Group

LONDON AND NEW YORK

First published 2008 by Routledge
2 Park Square, Milton Park, Abingdon, Oxon, OX14 4RN

Simultaneously published in the USA and Canada
by Routledge
270 Madison Avenue, New York, NY 10016

Routledge is an imprint of the Taylor & Francis Group, an informa business

Typeset in Minion by KnowledgeWorks Global Limited
Printed and bound in Great Britain by MPG Books Ltd, Bodmin, Cornwall

British Library Cataloguing in Publication Data
A catalogue record for this book is available from the British Library

Library of Congress Cataloguing in Publication Data

ISBN10: 0-415-42537-9 (hbk)
ISBN13: 978-0-415-42537-7 (hbk)

CONTENTS

Series Editors' Foreword

SPORT IN THE GLOBAL SOCIETY was launched in the late nineties. It now has over one hundred volumes. Until recently an odd myopia characterised academia with regard to sport. The global *groves of academe* remained essentially Cartesian in inclination. They favoured a mind/body dichotomy: thus the study of ideas was acceptable; the study of sport was not. All that has now changed. Sport is now incorporated, intelligently, within debate about *inter alia* ideologies, power, stratification, mobility and inequality. The reason is simple. In the modern world sport is everywhere: it is as ubiquitous as war. E.J. Hobsbawm, the Marxist historian, once called it the one of the most significant of the new manifestations of late nineteenth century Europe. Today it is one of the most significant manifestations of the twenty-first century world. Such is its power, politically, culturally, economically, spiritually and aesthetically, that sport beckons the academic more persuasively than ever - to borrow, and refocus, an expression of the radical historian Peter Gay - 'to explore its familiar terrain and to wrest new interpretations from its inexhaustible materials'. As a subject for inquiry, it is replete, as he remarked of history, with profound 'questions unanswered and for that matter questions unasked'.

Sport seduces the teeming 'global village'; it is the new opiate of the masses; it is one of the great modern experiences; its attraction astonishes only the recluse; its appeal spans the globe. Without exaggeration, sport is a mirror in which nations, communities, men and women now see themselves. That reflection is sometimes bright, sometimes dark, sometimes distorted, sometimes magnified. This metaphorical mirror is a source of mass exhilaration and depression, security and insecurity, pride and humiliation, bonding and alienation. Sport, for many, has replaced religion as a source of emotional catharsis and spiritual passion, and for many, since it is among the earliest of memorable childhood experiences, it infiltrates memory, shapes enthusiasms, serves fantasies. To co-opt Gay again: it blends memory and desire.

Sport, in addition, can be a lens through which to scrutinise major themes in the political and social sciences: democracy and despotism and the great associated movements of socialism, fascism, communism and capitalism as well as political cohesion and confrontation, social reform and social stability.

The story of modern sport is the story of the modern world-in microcosm; a modern global tapestry permanently being woven. Furthermore, nationalist and imperialist, philosopher and politician, radical and conservative have all sought in sport a manifestation of national identity, status and superiority.

Finally, for countless millions sport is the personal pursuit of ambition, assertion, well-being and enjoyment.

For all the above reasons, sport demands the attention of the academic. *Sport in the Global Society* is a response.

J.A. Mangan
Boria Majumdar

Series Editors
Sport in the Global Society

Preface: The IOC Olympic Studies Centre

Philippe Blanchard

My first conscious contact with Olympism dates back to 1992, on the occasion of the Albertville Winter Games. Until then, I had seen only the sporting images shown on television. Albertville was for me a revelation, as the constituent elements that I had until then neglected came out of the shadows:

- the aspiration of a territory;
- the devotion of the athlete to his discipline;
- the expectations of participating nations;
- the joy and artistic explosion.

Being part of the preparations for these Games naturally led me to take an interest in previous editions of the Games and to await the next. In my contact with communities of athletes, volunteers, historians and collectors, I would discover the foundations of universality and timelessness that are part and parcel of Olympism.

At the same time, this multiplicity of contacts confronted me with a multiplicity of points of view, all with a personal narration. Thus each person I met had his own story of the Games, telling such-and-such an anecdote or speaking of such-and-such an athlete.

I understand today that this narrative work is part of an appropriational approach, each person wanting his own part of the Games: the value of the Olympics also lies in their history, and this history must therefore be accessible.

To this end, the International Olympic Committee (IOC) created the Olympic Studies Centre (OSC) in 1992 in order to facilitate access to historical information, the life of the IOC and the stories of Olympians or Games organizers.

Since 1994, the OSC has been located at the Olympic Museum. It is today composed of four complementary sections: historical archives, the IOC library, the information (documentation) centre and the images section.

Through their work and services, these sections fulfil the two main tasks of the OSC:

1. To build up and preserve the patrimony of the Olympic Movement, particularly by managing a collection which is unique in the world:
    *   *Historical archives*: Documents from the IOC administration and Olympic Movement from 1894 to 1984; the correspondence of IOC presidents; relations with the national Olympic committees and international federations; organizing committee documents and so on. (There are 10,000 files, more than one linear kilometre.)
    *   *Library*: monographs and periodicals on the Olympic Movement, the Olympic Games and sport in general (22,000 titles).
    *   *Images*: photographs (1896–2006, 500,000 documents) and films (1900–2006, 30,000 hours) on the Olympic Games and the activities of the IOC and Olympic Movement.
2. Facilitate access to this patrimony for the Olympic family and the academic community, particularly through the following main services:
    *   Loans of monographs, sending of articles (8,000 per year).
    *   Distribution of images (9,200 photos and 300 hours of films distributed in 2005).
    *   Hosting researchers at the OSC (160 visitors from around 40 countries per year).
    *   Reference service (2,600 requests handled per year).

For the last decade the OSC has also aimed to promote research, teaching and publications connected with Olympism.

In 1997, the OSC established a Research Council to help it in the areas of research, the strategic orientation to give to its collections and their distribution internationally. The council's members, all academics known worldwide for the quality of their research on the Olympic Movement, were chosen by the IOC president, who chaired the council.

At the highest level, the IOC recognized its need to work with universities and their representatives. Together, we have developed projects allowing us to expand our historical analyses, study Olympic architecture, follow the effects of national policies on sports promotion or study multicultural approaches to the Olympic phenomenon and disseminate its values outside the Olympic family itself.

In 1999, we sought to encourage the work of researchers by creating, under the aegis of the Research Council, a Postgraduate Research Grant Programme. This programme serves as a link between the IOC and the universities of the world by reaching postgraduate students or young professors in the humanities and social sciences. As researchers, these young scholars will be an important source of future creativity and vitality for the Olympic Movement.

The IOC covers the transport and living costs of these grant-holders to enable them to devote themselves more easily to studying our archives and bibliographic collections.

To date, we have received and analysed 233 files, and 28 researchers from 13 countries have benefited from these scholarships.

With 101 files submitted, the European universities show their vitality in the field of Olympic studies, followed by North America and Asia (42 files each), Latin America (22 files), Africa (17) and Oceania (9 files submitted, chiefly by Australian researchers). Surprisingly, Japan is absent from this list. This distribution is partially reflected in the scholarships allocated: Europe (13), North America (6), Asia (4), Oceania (3) and Latin America (2).

The quality of the candidatures and our university contacts make us confident for 2007, and we should beat the record of 42 files received for this year (2006).

With regard to the content, too, we can see changes, and while the first subject area explored was the history of the various bodies that make up the Olympic Movement, today we find also the economic, social and environmental aspects of the Games explored (host cities and countries), as well as multiculturalism (anthropology and sociology), a topical theme in the run-up to the next Games in Beijing.

I wish to warmly thank the publishers of the *International Journal of the History of Sport* (*IJHS*) for giving us this unique platform with which to highlight the work of all the researchers we have hosted since 1999. Thanks to the *IJHS*, we are pleased to present a selection of this research work. We hope that this publication will help you better to know, understand and even assess the history of the Olympic Games and the Olympic Movement, and that it will be a source of inspiration for many new researchers willing to study in depth the Olympic phenomenon.

Welcome to the results of the Olympic Studies Centre grant holders. The articles published in this publication do not necessarily reflect the opinions of the International Olympic Committee and are solely the authors' responsibility.

The Lausanne Olympic Studies Centre Research Grants Programme

John J. MacAloon

The contributors to this special Olympic issue of *The International Journal of the History of Sport* have been assisted by research grants from the IOC Olympic Studies Centre, located at the Lausanne Olympic Museum. At the request of the editors, I am pleased to provide a brief history of this Postgraduate Research Grants Programme.

The inauguration of the permanent Olympic Museum on 23 June 1993 accomplished a dream that went back to the days of Pierre de Coubertin. Realization of the project depended on the personal resolve of IOC President Juan Antonio Samaranch, on a new stance of active cooperation by the Swiss authorities and on the financial collaboration of international corporations, political entities and individual elites. The opening of the Olympic Museum brought a new level of public institutionalization to match the new fiscal health and political sophistication created for the Olympic Movement during the Samaranch years.

The woeful curatorial state of the Olympic material heritage had been a subject of embarrassment to IOC authorities, staff, and professional observers through most of the twentieth century. [1] To remedy this state of affairs, an Olympic Studies Centre, comprising library, documentation, archival and sound and image components, figured prominently in the design of the Olympic Museum. A mix of trained professional archivists and curators and of existing IOC employees with cultural interests was deployed to staff this new centre. While Olympic sports fans and general tourists were not long in discovering the Olympic Museum – it was named 'European museum of the year' in 1995 – the problem remained of how to effectively notify a worldwide scholarly community of the existence and new capacities of the Lausanne Olympic Studies Centre.

On 29–30 November 1997, the first meeting of the new Olympic Museum Research Council took place in Lausanne. [2] This council was appointed by President Samaranch and ably coordinated by IOC secretary general and Olympic Museum director Françoise Zweifel. The council's mission was to advise the museum and Olympic Studies Centre on all matters of research, conservation, publication and communication germane to the scholarly community. Other constituencies were well represented on the museum's regular board, but outside the fields of physical education, medicine and sports management, neither the IOC nor the museum had access to much substantive expertise in the social and human sciences. Sad but fair to say, the intellectual and educational reputation of the central organs of the Olympic Movement had largely varied in inverse proportion to the academic quality of the universities with which they came into contact.

In the best universities of the world, the coin of the realm is advanced postgraduate research. To make the new facilities and collections more available to younger scholars to conduct such research seemed to me one important way to simultaneously augment quality Olympic scholarship in the human sciences and to improve mutual relations between the Olympic Movement and world-class universities. After vetting the idea with my research council colleagues, I proposed the postgraduate research scholars programme to the Olympic Studies Centre. At our meeting of 28–29 May 1999, the first scholarship winners (including one of the guest editors of the present volume) were selected. Around 30 such awards have subsequently been made.

While only the members of the research council make the final selections, the Olympic Studies Centre professionals actively collaborate by evaluating the likely relevance and usefulness of the collections to the project proposed. Grantees are provided transportation to and living expenses in Lausanne for a period of up to three months. Because of this highly concentrated period of labour, successful proposals typically address very specific aspects of research projects already well under way. As exemplified by the papers in this special issue, grantees largely use their time in Lausanne to elaborate, augment or test their interpretations of their subject matters through acquiring, so to speak, the point of view of the IOC archives (within, of course, certain temporal embargoes conventional in similar organizations).

This grant programme is limited to advanced postgraduate and early postdoctoral researchers with full-time university affiliations, because of the well-known difficulties of acquiring research funding for scholars in these early stages of their careers. Senior scholars capable of significant work are naturally expected to be able to secure their own funding, and the Olympic Studies Centre staff always stands eager to assist them on these terms. Non-scholarly projects, for example those involving purely policy issues or popular 'Olympic education', are supported by other IOC agencies and partners such as Olympic Solidarity, the International Olympic Academy and the national Olympic committees.

The Postgraduate Research Grants Programme has proven to be 'value-added' for both sides of the relationship. By inevitably being drawn into what I have called 'fieldwork in the archives', grant recipients come away not only with new documentary evidence for their projects but also with a keener sense of the daily life and institutional functioning of the International Olympic Committee as a total institution. [3] Olympic Studies Centre personnel are in turn exposed to the latest research agendas in universities around the world and are particularly assisted in evaluating the strength of their own collections by scholars with linguistic and cultural competencies not possessed by the current IOC or Olympic Museum personnel.

High-level, peer-reviewed university scholarship necessarily operates on slower temporal rhythms than other kinds of institutional work. The grants programme has now been around long enough to be able to collect sufficient finished work into this special issue of the *IJHS*. We expect that its 'demonstration effect' will be a powerful one, alerting young researchers from institutions in still wider parts of the world as to the resources available through the Olympic Studies Centre, while illustrating clearly the standards and characteristics most likely to make a research proposal successful in the competition.

I'm sure my colleagues in the inauguration of these initiatives, as well as succeeding members of the research council, join me in thanking in particular Boria Majumdar, *IJHS* deputy executive editor and a former PRGP grantee, Nuria Puig of the Olympic Studies Centre and, of course, guest editor Sandra Collins for their hard work in bringing out this volume. Finally, we recollect with gratitude and fondness the many collaborations in Lausanne over the years with Françoise Zweifel, Fernando Riba, Cristina Bianchi, Ruth Beck-Perrenoud, Yoo-Mi Steffen, Patricia Eckert and Benoît de Chassey among many others.

Notes

[1] See MacAloon, 'Postscript'.
[2] The founding members were: pioneering de Coubertin scholar Yves-Pierre Boulogne; university-based Olympic scholars Profs Karl Lennartz, John MacAloon, Miquel de Moragas and Otto Schantz; and Dr Wayne Wilson, Olympic historian and among the world's most accomplished sports librarians.
[3] MacAloon, 'Postscript'.

Reference

MacAloon, John J. 'Postscript: History as Anthropology'. *International Journal of the History of Sport* 23, nos. 3–4 (May–June 2006): 666–86.

Prologue: The Story of the Homecoming: IOC weds *IJHS*

Boria Majumdar

'History consists of the corpus of ascertainable facts. The facts are available to the historian in documents, inscriptions and so on, like fish on the monger's slab. The historian collects them, takes them home, and cooks and serves them in whatever style appeals to him'. So writes E.H. Carr in *What is History*? [1]

Carr goes on to define history as 'an unending dialogue between the past and the present' and for him the chief function of the historian 'is to master and understand the past as a key to understand the present'. [2] For historians of sport, or to be more specific of the Olympics, Olympism and the Olympic Movement, to accomplish what Carr has mentioned above it is essential to have at their disposal the best and most authentic of sources, i.e. letters, artefacts, photographs, correspondence and private papers containing information on the Games' history from the nineteenth and twentieth centuries. This collection is unique in that for the first time all the contributors to it had unlimited access to the hitherto inaccessible IOC 'official' archive.

Some things are destined to happen. For me personally, this collection was one such. To place a few facts on record: most contributors to this collection don't know each other. I, for example, know only one of my eight colleagues. And I have met my co-editor only once, at a conference at the University of Chicago in April 2005. Yet this collection has come together with consummate ease and can claim to be one of the most eclectic collections on the subject of Olympism and the Olympic Movement. How it all happened is the story this brief prologue will narrate. It happened because the International Olympic Committee, in a rare gesture for institutions of this nature, has accomplished for scholars a valuable resource in the guise of the Olympic Studies Centre at Lausanne, Switzerland. The creation of the centre was not all. The IOC has also taken the initiative in encouraging scholars from around the world to make use of this resource. Funding scholars to dig into this well-maintained archive, the IOC has tried to live up to the declared ideals of the centre, to 'preserve and disseminate the collective memory of the Olympic Movement and to coordinate and promote research, teaching and publications about Olympism'. [3] Yet something remained unaccomplished. And it is this longing for more that helped plan this volume.

Soon after my formal introduction to the staff of the studies centre in December 2004, I casually inquired into the history of the grants programme, written about in some detail here by my colleague John MacAloon. And on hearing the diverse nature of projects accomplished under the umbrella of the programme, I was amazed. Most of these projects, it may be mentioned, have been published. In fact, grant-holders are under compulsion to submit a research report to the IOC on return from Lausanne and are encouraged to publish their findings in the form of scholarly articles. What this process lacked was a common platform for publication. And the editors of *IJHS* are delighted to provide this platform.

Two fundamental ideas lie at the heart of this decision. One was the determination to contribute to the growing corpus of research in this field – a category much developed in recent years. The second was to incorporate writing of high intellectual, aesthetic and imaginative standard, yet that which is easily accessible to the informed and interested general reader. We intended to publish writings on Olympism and the Olympic Movement completely devoid of jargon which, in effect, stand on their own. All the pieces in this collection are products of thorough and meticulous research, impossible without access to the IOC archives at Lausanne. In fact, as mentioned at the start, the fundamental motivation for this collection arises from the interest in developing a dynamic corpus of analytical writing on Olympism and the Olympic Movement enriched by access to hitherto unused archives. This collection also aims to throw open a space to those academics who consider themselves writers, i.e. have an eye for aesthetics and the craft of writing, as well as those professional writers who like to have that last obscure fact which may appear in his/her writing confirmed after a couple of hours at the nearest library. The idea was to try and achieve an empirically rich collection on Olympism, global in scope, focusing on a series of subjects under which the traditional disciplines will interact and enmesh with each other.

The collection starts from the premise that Olympism and the Olympic Games make sense only when they are placed within the broader national, colonial and postcolonial contexts and argues that sport not only influences politics and vice versa, but that the two are inseparable. Sport is not only political; it is politics. It is also culture and art. To deny this is to simplify inexcusably and myopically the position of sport in the modern world. As is perhaps clear by now, the collection could not have been accomplished without the coming together of the leading institution of sport in the contemporary world, the IOC, and the leading academic journal on sport in the globe, the *IJHS*.

Suffice to say that this collaboration is a first in global publishing: it has helped collate a mine of information for scholars and analysts, intellects and academic alike. One important fact the collection hopes to demonstrate is that Olympism and the Olympic Movement in the modern context have been and continue to be socially relevant and politically important. It is the spirit of Olympism that dominates the collection, and there are studies celebrating the aesthetics of this great innovation of mankind. While most studies focus on national encounters with Olympism and the Olympic Movement, equal attention was paid to documenting the growing nexus between sports and the media; sports reportage; and women and sports. The collection has in case studies such as India the never before discussed and written about information on national engagements with Olympism as well as a more theoretical, discursive element that examines the place of Olympism in modern societies, past and present.

Most studies published here seek to assert that the Olympic Movement was, and is, of central importance to twentieth- and twenty-first-century societies. In fact, it is no truism that modern sport serves as a barometer of political relations in the world. Two ancillary points made here are that sport once viewed as imperial cement is now perceived as national mortar; and that sport, while hardly fundamental to global survival, has been a not insignificant element in imperial and post-imperial nationalistic assertion and denial. Finally, the collection seeks to demonstrate that the essence of Olympism and the Olympic Movement does not reside in medals won, records broken or television rights sold as ends in themselves. The Olympics, and its relevant records and statistics, are important only by the way they can affect societies surrounding them. Accordingly, when the Puerto Ricans march in the Olympic opening ceremony even when they don't have a representative in the United Nations [4] or when an unknown Anthony Nesty of Suriname wins gold defeating the favourite Matt Biondi of the US, the significance of such acts stretch far beyond the narrow confines of sport.

Of necessity, a collection of this nature cannot be comprehensive in its range of questions, but it is certainly one of the first attempts to unravel global encounters with Olympism within the precincts of one volume. In view of the complexities of national Olympic encounters, a single volume can only scratch the surface. Thus a collection can only reveal part and not the whole story of how significant and complex each of these encounters have been for individual nation states – politically, economically, culturally and emotionally. Furthermore, the paucity of written material on some of these encounters, as in India, means that it cannot be satisfactorily comprehensive; but, to borrow Tony Mangan's phrase, used elsewhere, 'it certainly attempts to be stimulatingly exploratory'. [5]

The editors wish to make one thing clear at the start: that the virtue of this collection lies in its presentation of the eclectic role of Olympism in colonial and postcolonial global societies. Thus an array of articles that view critical issues of nationalism, commercialism and gender through the lens of Olympism and the Olympic Movement are made available. More, this collection does not seek to ascertain the pre-eminence of one nation's tryst with Olympism over that of others. Rather, it makes the point that claims to understand the true nature of the movement by simply looking at Olympic history in one country or region are simplistic and short sighted.

Until very recently, as K.A.P. Sandiford has argued:

> Social historians neglected sport because in their view as well as that of laymen, it merely involved forms of play. History was a much more serious business, involving work, industry and worship. This narrowness of approach was not confined to historians; it was at one time characteristic of all social science. [6]

This attitude, however, has been rapidly changing since the 1970s. There is today, as is increasingly widely acknowledged, a substantial corpus of literature on the history, sociology and social anthropology of sport. As Sandiford states, 'Historians now know that it is hardly possible to write intelligibly about work without also dealing intelligently with play; and it is universally recognized that sport is one of the most important features of any society's culture'. And with the IOC being the second biggest global body after the United Nations, it is inevitable that studies on Olympism and the Olympic Movement will help further our understanding of the complexities of the modern global world.

In conclusion, this collection is a pointer to the future. Later pointers, it is hoped, will be put in place by the IOC and the *IJHS* in the years to come, resulting in an array of studies on the Olympic Movement. As is understandable, a venture of this kind rests on the strength of imaginative and aggressive collaboration, and this particular effort was no different. Knowing full well the difficulties confronting them, the IOC and the *IJHS* editors evolved an extremely focused collaboration strategy. Inspired collaboration, the collection proves, was worthwhile.

Notes

[1] Carr, *What is History*, 1.
[2] Ibid.
[3] See http://www.olympic.org/uk/passion/studies/index_uk.asp, accessed 24 May 2006.
[4] For details, see Macaloon, 'La Pitada Olímpica'.
[5] Mangan, 'Prologue: Asian Sport', 9.
[6] Sandiford, *Cricket and the Victorians*, 5.

References

Carr, E.H. *What is History*. New York: Knopf, 1962.
Macaloon, John. 'La Pitada Olímpica: Puerto Rico, International Sport and the Constitution of Politics'. In *Text, Play, and Story: The Construction and Reconstruction of Self and Society*, edited by Stuart Plattner. Washington: American Anthropological Association, 1984.
Mangan, J.A. 'Prologue: Asian Sport: From the Recent Past'. In *Sport in Asian Society- Past and Present*, edited by J.A. Mangan and Fan Hong. London: Frank Cass, 2003.
Sandiford, Keith A.P. *Cricket and the Victorians*. London: Scolar Press, 1994.

The Latin American 'Olympic Explosion' of the 1920s: Causes and Consequences

Cesar R. Torres

The experience of Latin American nations in joining the Olympic Movement typifies the difficulties encountered by Baron Pierre de Coubertin in making the movement universal during the first three decades of the Olympic Games. Until 1920, Latin American participation in Olympic arenas was restricted to athletes from six nations. Most of these entries, which until 1912 amounted to fewer than 15 athletes per Games, were the result of decisions taken by individual athletes rather than the expression of collective national efforts. Latin American representation in the International Olympic Committee (IOC) did not fare much better. Despite the fact that 11 Latin American citizens from eight different countries were chosen as IOC members between 1894 and 1922, there was neither visible regional attendance at IOC meetings nor a decisive commitment to establish national olympic committees (NOCs) in Latin America during this period. [1]

Coubertin had long been interested in increasing Latin American participation in Olympic matters. In addition to selecting several Latin American IOC members, during the First World War he established a committee to spread the Olympic ideals throughout the region and dedicated a pamphlet entitled *¿Qué es el Olimpismo?* ('What is Olympism?') to its youth. His efforts did not rapidly win over a substantial number of Latin American hearts. However, that pattern changed in the early 1920s. Suddenly, Latin Americans entered Olympic arenas en masse. Between 1922 and 1924 eight Latin American citizens joined the IOC and five NOCs were either established or recognized in the region. More important, the 1924 Olympics in Paris witnessed the athleticism of over 160 athletes representing eight Latin American nations. The Latin American teams won seven medals, including two gold. Since then, athletes from the region have regularly animated the Olympic Games.

The dramatic change during the 1920s from the negligible role that Latin American athletes and officials had played in the first 30 years of modern Olympic life can be described as an 'Olympic explosion'. The term explosion, which evokes images of a violent expansion, aptly describes a process that deeply stirred the feelings of those involved in the massive Latin American entry into the Olympic Movement. This entry, long-desired and ardently contested by many parties, had multiple causes and lasting consequences.

Olympic scholarship has largely ignored the intricate unfolding of Coubertin's aspiration for Olympic universality in Latin America. The few studies that even address the burst of Latin American activity in Olympic matters during the 1920s emphasize Coubertin's policies of universalizing participation in the Olympic Movement and imply a linear relationship between his undertakings and the sudden growth of regional interest in the movement. [2] For instance, Allen Guttmann contends that 'The dates when each of the world's NOCs was granted official recognition reveals a familiar pattern of ludic diffusion'. Guttmann asserts that the IOC's imprint in Latin America is obviously visible in the fact that 'Argentina, Uruguay, and Mexico formed NOCs in 1923. The creation or IOC recognition of the NOCs of Bolivia, Chile, Brazil, Venezuela, and Colombia followed in the 1930s'. [3] Guttmann's argument implies that Olympism was embraced sooner in the former nations than the latter. However, Chile participated in the 1912 Olympics in Stockholm and Brazil first established a NOC in 1914. Admittedly, as Guttmann argues, the date on which NOCs were officially recognized by the IOC reveals 'something' about the pattern of ludic diffusion. In significant ways, however, those official dates obscure 'much' about the internal logics and intricacies of the processes at work in Latin American nations. The causes underlying the incorporation of the Olympic Movement into the fabric of the Latin American nations are not simply unidirectional.

A fuller account of the processes through which Latin America during the 1920s 'exploded' into the Olympic Movement reveals a more complex pattern of diffusion. To understand the dynamics of the process requires a survey of Latin American sporting cultures at the end of the First World War; an appreciation of Coubertin's new strategies of globalization developed during the war; and a recognition of the crucial role that an alliance between the IOC and the Young Men's Christian Association (YMCA) and the 1922–23 tour of Latin America by IOC representative Count Henri de Baillet-Latour played in expanding the region's connections to the Olympic Games. A closer look at the causes and consequences of the Latin American 'Olympic explosion' reveals that both responses to the external pressures of the IOC and the YMCA and internal conflicts over control and demand for access to modern sport shaped the incorporation of Latin America into the Olympic Movement.

Latin American Sports and the IOC after the First World War

In the first two decades of the twentieth century Latin America experienced marked changes. Although the success of the liberal economic policies as well as changing international conditions intensified a number of significant political, social and cultural challenges in the region throughout the early 1900s, life in Latin American nations was not as dramatically disrupted during the First World War years as it was in Europe. Throughout this period, Latin Americans continued to engage, more or less customarily, in their preferred cultural practices, including modern sports. This was especially so in the growing Latin American urban centres which were increasingly influenced by the region's integration into global markets and the rise of mass communication.

By the early 1900s, modern sports had not only arrived but had also been subjected to a complicated process of cultural adaptation and appropriation. The first tide of ludic diffusion that had some recognizable effect came to Latin American shores from Great Britain around the mid nineteenth century. British capitalists on the continent brought their sports – from football to rugby, from cricket to field hockey, from tennis to golf – and a specific ethos to abide by when practising them. The novel activities were first adopted by the local elites and then rapidly embraced by people from all walks of life. The success of modern sport in Latin America largely lies in the discourses constructed around them. Joseph L. Arbena has argued that even as early as the 'mid-1800s sport was increasingly tied to the spread of so-called modern, European culture'. [4] In the process, by contrast, indigenous and folk physical forms were condemned as hindrances to modernity.

A second tide of ludic diffusion, this time from North America, furthered the obliteration of indigenous and folk physical forms from the Latin American cultural landscape. The increasing role that the United States began to play in Latin American affairs around the 1900s also meant the arrival of its sports, most notably baseball, basketball and volleyball. Much like their British predecessors, American sports were seen as engines of progress and enthusiastically embraced by the elites as well as the masses. On occasion, these European and North American imports were questioned by politicians or members of the elite. In one instance, in spite of the support in local sport circles, the proposal to subsidize a team to the 1908 Olympics in London was rejected by the Argentine Congress. [5] However, by the early 1920s this kind of resistance was clearly receding. In Argentina, exuberant YMCA officials proclaimed that football, tennis, rowing and golf clubs 'now realize an effervescent Sunday program that caters to all classes of Argentines'. In Mexico, the YMCA declared that 'There are scores of base ball and football clubs which are practicing their sports'. [6] While sport clubs flourished in the region's cities, incipient national and regional sport bureaucracies struggled to consolidate themselves, and civic leaders touted the benefits of sport, Latin American politicians discovered or convinced themselves that sports produced powerful images of common national identities. In Mexico, according to Arbena, government officials 'contemplated in sport a mechanism for reestablishing Mexican credibility in the international community'. [7] Sooner rather than later in the 1920s, images of athletic nationalism pervaded Latin America's urban mass cultures.

At the same time as sport was consolidating itself as an integral feature of Latin American life, the havoc caused by the cannons roaring in Europe jeopardized the survival of Coubertin's Olympic Movement. Although Coubertin agonized that the Olympic Games might be exterminated by the war, he rejected Havana's bid to host the 1920 Olympics. For the IOC leadership, the Caribbean city seemed unready to host such an important event. [8] Despite his rejection of a Latin American host, during the First World War Coubertin came to realize more than ever that if his Olympic Games were not just to survive but to become an event of global proportions, international participation in Olympic affairs had to be increased. From the IOC's perspective, participation, at least in the case of Latin America, did not include organizing an actual Olympic Games.

The IOC-YMCA Partnership and the 1922 Latin American Games

In Coubertin's mind, the prospect of Olympic rejuvenation was further endangered when he learned that the United States military, concerned about the allied troops in the immediate post-war period, planned with the assistance of the YMCA an Inter-Allied Games or, as they were popularly known, a 'Military Olympics'. Although the event was generally perceived as a positive enterprise, it generated anxiety in Olympic circles. Apprehensive about the impact of the new international competitions on his Olympic enterprise, Coubertin wrote on 25 January 1919 to Elwood S. Brown, an American who at the time was athletic director for both the American Expeditionary Force and the International Committee of the YMCA, protesting against the 'action of the YMCA in deciding to hold Olympics in France in 1919'. [9] Coubertin's action would prove providential for the IOC and its ambition to achieve universality.

Brown rapidly answered, assuring Coubertin that the Inter-Allied Games 'is not a rival of the Olympic Games in any sense'. [10] His reply not only had a soothing effect on the worried Coubertin but also served as the starting point of a fruitful relationship. In mid-1919 Coubertin wrote to and met several times with Brown. [11] The evidence indicates that it was the latter who suggested combining efforts in order for the two institutions to spread their goals. Referring to the YMCA's achievements and progress with regard to the organization of regional Games, in early 1920 Brown called to the attention of Coubertin 'that the plans which I outlined to you in Paris are definitely maturing'. Attempting to further convince Coubertin that the regional Games either already organized or planned by the YMCA did not constitute a threat to the Olympic Games, Brown insisted that a 'most unusual opportunity now exists to give a great impulse to physical training throughout the world, to develop backward areas along the lines of Olympic ideas and ideals, and to contribute definitely to the extension of your Committee's influence'. [12] Coubertin, who had proposed Brown to present the plan in the 1920 IOC Session, must had been pleased with the latter's words. [13]

In 1920 Brown toured South America. One of his goals was to 'conduct the preliminary negotiations and to make the basic arrangements for the South American Games in 1922, on the occasion of Brazil's Centenary Fiesta'. [14] Brown faithfully kept the IOC president informed. The day before embarking for New York Brown summarized his trip, stating that he was 'greatly encouraged over the whole situation in South America'. [15] Indeed, Brown had met with numerous prominent sport and governmental officials, including the presidents of Brazil, Chile and Uruguay. [16] If Coubertin had any doubts about the YMCA, Brown's tour to South America paved the way for the approval of the cooperation agreement later in 1920. At this point Coubertin also unmistakably understood how much this cooperation could help the IOC achieve its goal of universality.

Brown officially presented his proposal to the IOC during its August 1920 Session in Antwerp. The proposal emphasized that the IOC and the YMCA pursued similar goals and underlined the YMCA's worldwide structure. In the case of Latin America, by the early 1920s the YMCA had numerous working chapters. These chapters took a leading role in promoting physical education and sports in Argentina, Brazil, Chile, Cuba, Mexico, Peru, Puerto Rico and Uruguay. If the YMCA outreach capacity was not in itself sufficiently attractive for the IOC to help achieve its goals, Brown suggested a scheme difficult to turn down. He claimed that the IOC goals could be further advanced through the organization of regional Games such as the Far Eastern Games that the YMCA had launched in 1913, as well as the YMCA's proposed Indian Empire Games and South American Games. In return for its offer, the YMCA simply asked the IOC to grant official recognition to and encouragement for the regional Games it organized. [17] This would strengthen and legitimize the YMCA's work in different regions of the world. Enthused by the benefits of the YMCA proposal and bolstered by Coubertin's support for the project, the IOC accepted the scheme unanimously. [18] With the partnership fully endorsed and Brown named South American *chargé de mission*, the IOC and the YMCA embarked on the first project the YMCA had in store, the 1922 Latin American Games.

The early proposals to celebrate Brazil's centenary in September 1922 made reference to a series of sport events that were national in scope. For example, in a 1919 plan Nestor Ascoli, a prominent public figure, proposed to have

'Brazilian championships of Olympic Games' organized by the *Confederação Brasileira de Desportos* (Brazilian Confederation of Sports). Rio de Janeiro's Fluminense Football Club had also indicated interest in organizing the event. Despite these initial proposals, the evidence suggests that the internationalization of the sport events within the centennial celebrations was a YMCA initiative. [19] In May 1920, Brown wrote that he had proposed to the *Confederação* that 'Brazil immediately extend an invitation to Peru, Chile, Argentina and Uruguay to enter the South American Games'. [20]

The scheme gained momentum on 27 August 1920, a few days after the IOC-YMCA agreement had been signed, when Roberto Trompowsky Jr., *chef de mission* of the Brazilian delegation to the Antwerp Olympics, offered a banquet to Coubertin and Brown. During the banquet the IOC announced that it gave support to the 1922 International Games to be organized in Rio de Janeiro. [21] This endorsement did not mean that Coubertin was convinced about the success of the enterprise or that he trusted the Brazilian rhetoric. Foreseeing difficulties, Brown wrote to Coubertin in December 1920 that he was 'fully conscious of the ever present danger, which you speak of – that is, the tendency or rather habit of overstatement, hasty unsound plans'. [22] However, Brown thought that the YMCA officials in South America would be able to help stage a successful Games. Whether Brown was overconfident or ingenious, the preparations for the South American Games tested the nerves, capacity and influence of the YMCA.

Difficulties in staging the contests soon appeared. The first was Brazilian inaction. In late May 1921, Jess T. Hopkins, secretary for physical education of the South American Federation of YMCAs, wrote to Coubertin explaining that 'things are moving slowly in Brazil for the 1922 Games'. [23] This description – a glaring understatement, for things were hardly moving at all – was intended to convey the situation to Coubertin without alarming him too much. Even while Hopkins recommended that the IOC not recognize the event, Brown reported to the June 1921 IOC Session held in Lausanne that the preparations for the 1922 South American Games were proceeding smoothly. Moreover, arguing that Cuba, Puerto Rico and Mexico would be encouraged to participate in the Games, Brown proposed to rename the event the Latin American Games – a move that provided a greater international flavour to the festival. The IOC agreed to the change and Coubertin profusely thanked Brown for his devotion to the Olympic cause. [24]

Backed by the IOC, the YMCA continued its efforts in Brazil. A serious economic crisis forced the Brazilian government to reconsider the entire centennial celebrations. While all preparations for the Games were halted, the chance that the athletic events would be downgraded was ever present. At this point, not only Hopkins but also Brown and the IOC were concerned about whether or not the official Olympic recognition of the Games should be withdrawn. While the Brazilians wanted to retain such recognition, the IOC did not see any reason to honour its commitment if the Games were not truly international. [25]

In mid January 1922, Hopkins met with the *Confederação Brasileira de Desportos* and presented a plan to settle the issue. The new scheme stipulated a number of requirements to be met if the Games were to continue enjoying IOC support. The plan required that the *Confederação* secure governmental recognition for its organizing committee, that the government second the invitation to other countries, that Coubertin be invited and that all technical matters be presented to the IOC technical representatives, all YMCA officials. The YMCA gave the Brazilians a 30 January 1922 deadline to approve the plan. The *Confederação* failed to meet the deadline but requested, and obtained, an extension until 15 March. The Brazilians then failed to meet the second deadline. Although in early January the YMCA did not deem it appropriate to contact the government to pressure the *Confederação*, its view had changed after the second deadline passed. Henry J. Sims, YMCA physical secretary director in Rio de Janeiro, took the matter up directly with government officials, hoping to save the whole enterprise. The YMCA could afford neither the collapse of the Games nor the withdrawal of IOC recognition. [26]

In several meetings with Carlos Cesar de Oliveira Sampaio, mayor of Rio de Janeiro, Sims explained the urgency of the situation and clarified that IOC recognition of the Games would have to be withdrawn 'unless its success is guaranteed by the Supreme Government of Brazil'. [27] The YMCA move proved effective. After conversations with federal authorities, Sampaio assured Sims 'that the Government wanted Olympic patronage and recognition and would take the necessary steps to insure such an outcome'. [28] Sampaio also formed a new organizing committee, secured the funds necessary for the Games and asked the Fluminense Football Club to play a prominent role in the athletic events. Armed with the good news, Brown requested that Coubertin provide approval at once. The baron, however, preferred to postpone the decision until the June 1922 IOC Session to be held in Paris. [29]

With the good news about the Games spreading, the indefatigable Brown appeared at the IOC Session. He explained the difficulties encountered in the preparations for the 1922 Latin American Games but emphasized that all obstacles had been cleared. Brown insisted that IOC recognition of the Games would guarantee the success of the event. Coubertin agreed that the official recognition of the project granted to the Brazilian government more than a year earlier should not be withdrawn. After an intense debate, the IOC maintained its support for the Games. Coubertin also noted that it would not be possible for him to honour the invitation forwarded by the Brazilian organizers and proposed Baillet-Latour to replace him as IOC representative. [30]

As the different delegations paraded on 13 September 1922 during the opening ceremony of the 1922 Latin American Games, Baillet-Latour and Brown must have marvelled at the prospect of Olympic expansion (see Figure 1). Brazilian president Epitacion da Silva Pessoa, governmental officials, diplomats and sport dignitaries witnessed the official arrival of an Olympic-like fanfare. The organizing commission of the Centenary Sport Festivities administered three different sets of Games that constituted the festivities: the Latin American Games, the International Sports

Figure 1 The Argentine delegation parading during the opening ceremony of the 1922 Latin American Games. Courtesy *El gráfico* (Buenos Aires), 20 Sept. 1922, 12.

Championships and the International Military Games. The specific list of sports included in each of the first two events remains unclear. [31] Whatever the details of the organizational structure, Argentina, Brazil, Chile, Paraguay and Uruguay sent athletes to Rio de Janeiro. All the competitors were men. Women were not invited to the inaugural Latin American Games. Notwithstanding the female absence, the centennial sport spectacle celebrated from 27 August to 15 October drew massive crowds. Competition developed as scheduled, although there were organizational problems and questionable refereeing decisions. These disputes prompted protests by participating nations, which in some cases were impregnated with nationalistic overtones. [32] Considering the lack of experience of the regional sport community in international competitions, these inconveniences were hardly surprising.

1922–23: Baillet-Latour's Latin American Tour

Baillet-Latour's presence at the 1922 Latin American Games marked the beginning of an eventful ambassadorial tour for more than six months throughout Latin America. The controversies on the playing field did not deter the activity of the sport officials gathered in Rio de Janeiro (see Figures 2 and 3). They even came from nations that were not taking part in the Games, such as Alfredo B. Cuéllar, a Mexican sportsman

Figure 2 Argentine, Chilean and Uruguayan athletes at the 1922 Latin American Games. Courtesy *El gráfico* (Buenos Aires), 20 Sept. 1922, 13.

and journalist. [33] While representing the IOC at the athletic events and social galas, Baillet-Latour was introduced to regional sport dignitaries. They met formally to discuss the possibility of organizing regularly occurring Latin American Games, a move favoured by the IOC.

The meeting, convened by the *Confederação Brasileira de Desportos*, took place on 19 September. Enthused by the events of the hour and Baillet-Latour's presence, the regional sport officials unanimously decided to create a Latin American Games Committee. The primary goal of this institution was to organize the Games regularly, which in turn would feed the Olympic Games with regional athletes. According to the Chilean newspaper *El Mercurio*, the gathering toasted several times 'for the prosperity of the Latin American nations'. [34] In order to continue its efforts, the second meeting of this novel regional sport bureaucracy was scheduled for October 1923 in Buenos Aires. [35]

The creation of the Latin American Games Committee consolidated the strategy set out by Brown and approved by the IOC in 1920. The administrative impulse of those days in Rio de Janeiro, which also incited the formation of the South American Cycling Confederation, pleased the IOC. While still in Rio de Janeiro, Baillet-Latour testified to this, stating disingenuously to *La Nación*, an Argentine daily, that his impression of the initial Latin American Games was excellent. He also urged

Figure 3 The Brazilian Toledo during the 1922 Latin American Games discus throw competition. *El gráfico* (Buenos Aires), 20 Sept. 1922, 15.

authorities in the region to create NOCs and to affiliate national sport federations to their international parent institutions. The IOC's programme could not have been stated more accurately. [36]

Once the competitions of the 1922 Latin American Games finished, Baillet-Latour continued his ambassadorial tour. With the unfailing assistance of YMCA officials and their vast network of contacts as well as his new acquaintances, Baillet-Latour visited Uruguay, Argentina, Chile, Peru, Cuba and Mexico from October 1922 to February 1923. Peru appears not to have been in his original itinerary but, with the support of the YMCA, Baillet-Latour visited the nation. Hopkins revealed that 'I know that they [the Peruvians] would have felt slighted had you given them only the time available while your boat remained in port'. [37]

Throughout his journey Baillet-Latour met with sport officials, politicians and civic leaders. In those meetings he emphasized how beneficial it was for 'new countries' to take part in the Olympics, insisted on creating NOCs, recruited potential IOC members and promoted the value of sport. In the South American nations, Baillet-Latour advertised the South American Games, a title that given the experience in Rio de Janeiro he preferred over the Latin American Games. In the Central American nations Baillet-Latour encouraged the creation of their own regional Games. Where local conditions were propitious, Baillet-Latour not only insisted on creating NOCs but also hurried their creation. During his stay in Mexico, he engineered the creation of a provisional Mexican Olympic Committee. Unsurprisingly, all its members were proposed by Baillet-Latour. Cuéllar was not among those blessed by the IOC representative. [38]

One of Baillet-Latour's recurrent means of publicizing the IOC's goals and projects for the region was a formal speech, which he adapted to the culture of each nation and publicized widely. During his trip Baillet-Latour maintained correspondence with YMCA officials who were delighted to help him contact people along his way and published newspaper articles on the IOC's internationalist mission. [39] While in Chile, with half the trip ahead, he felt confident of his eventual success. From Santiago he wrote: 'I am very satisfied with my mission in America, I believe to have reached good results and to have left the IOC in a very good situation in those new countries'. [40] At the end of his trip Baillet-Latour believed that he had advanced the IOC's globalization policy and expected to see Latin American fruits ripen in the very near future. Baillet-Latour commented to the Associated Press that 'he expected them [the countries he visited] to be well represented for the first time at the Paris Olympic [sic]'. [41]

Baillet-Latour returned to Europe just in time to report on his ambassadorial mission at the April 1923 IOC Session held in Rome. Surprisingly, he was very critical of the organization of the 1922 Latin American Games, claiming that it reflected the primitive sporting conditions of the participating countries. Baillet-Latour declared that Latin American sport officials were ignorant of rule books, and that athletes and spectators did not have any sporting education. Yet he also lauded the region's athletic potential and complimented the enthusiasm of many sport officials. All things considered, Baillet-Latour believed that Latin America could be effectively incorporated into the Olympic Movement if regional sport bureaucracies were properly assisted. To start this process Baillet-Latour proposed seven new Latin Americans, whom he had met during his trip, for membership of the IOC. The IOC accepted the nominees, and after profusely thanking Baillet-Latour for his productive tour, awarded him a commemorative medal. [42]

The Latin American 'Olympic Explosion'

Paradoxically, at the time of the Rome IOC Session, the Latin American Olympic situation went through a period of deflation. Early in 1923 there was hardly any news about the Latin American Games Committee's second meeting scheduled for October 1923 in Buenos Aires. In spite of the inactivity, the ever optimistic Brown reported in October that 'the Congress will take place in BA [Buenos Aires] next February'. [43] That meeting never took place. However, the Latin American Games Committee's failure to gather did not mean that the region had lost interest in Olympic affairs. The extraordinary mobilization of all kinds of resources generated by the 1922 Latin American Games and Baillet-Latour's ambassadorial tour had immediate repercussions. After Baillet-Latour finished his ambassadorial tour, several Latin American nations started to work on the pressing requirements of the IOC's mandate, the creation of NOCs and the preparation of national envoys to the 1924 Olympics. This, however, aroused old apprehensions and, as well, created new ones. [44]

By the time of the 1922 Latin American Games, the *Confederación Argentina de Deportes* (Argentine Confederation of Sports), born the year before out of a dispute with a short-lived *Comité Olímpico Argentino* (Argentine Olympic Committee), had become the sole sport authority in the nation. After organizing the national team for the Games and welcoming Baillet-Latour in Buenos Aires, the *Confederación* started planning for the 1924 Olympics. Its authorities met with Argentine president Marcelo T. de Alvear, who had presided over the defunct *Comité* and was also an IOC member, and found him well-disposed to request congressional support for the first Argentine Olympic expedition. Significantly, it was not at all clear who would be the beneficiary of that support. Rumours that Alvear desired to form a new and definitive *Comité* materialized in August 1923 when he sent a note to Congress stating that the government considered it appropriate to create such an institution. The fate of the *Confederación* was sealed on 31 December when Alvear signed an executive decree establishing the *Comité*. Old allegiances could not be overlooked.

Ricardo C. Aldao, a distinguished sport leader and member of Alvear's ruling party who had become Argentina's second IOC member in 1923 with the support of the YMCA, was named president of the new *Comité Olímpico Argentino*. Notably, Aldao had arranged with Alvear the creation of the newly founded *Comité*, which swiftly set up a programme to send the first Argentine delegation to the 1924 Olympics. The arrangements for this Olympic debut were fractured by the tensions between the new *Comité* and the old *Confederación Argentina de Deportes*. A major controversy erupted over whether athletes from national sport federations not affiliated to their international counterpart were eligible for the Olympic team. After stormy negotiations and troubling trials the Argentine Olympic delegation was formed with representatives from 11 sports. Despite the mediation of government officials, football, already the most popular sport in Argentina, did not join the Olympic team. Differences between the two institutions and their respective allied federations proved an insurmountable obstacle to fielding an Argentine Olympic football squad in 1924.

Much as in Argentina, in the mid 1920s Uruguayan football was divided. The prospect of Olympic football participation generated similar power struggles to those that raged in Argentina. The *Comité Olímpico Uruguayo* (Uruguayan Olympic Committee), which had been created in October 1923 on the initiative of Uruguayan IOC member Francisco Ghigliani, wished to form a team with the best footballers irrespective of their affiliation. When an agreement between the rival football federations proved impossible, the *Comité* voted not to be represented in the Olympic football tournament. This decision infuriated Ghigliani, who believed that international affiliations should be honoured. Strangely, a football team had been shipped to Europe while negotiations were still being held. To secure the participation of this team, Ghigliani dissolved the *Comité* and registered the team with the French organizers. The IOC member's authoritarian behaviour horrified the leaders of the *Comité* as well as the Uruguayan media – although not the IOC. In spite of the *Comité*'s complaints to the IOC about Ghigliani's contravention of Olympic and moral principles, the Uruguayan football team proceeded to Paris as if nothing had happened.

Akin to the situation in Uruguay, Mexico also experienced problems with its incipient Olympic bureaucracy prior to the 1924 Olympics. In November 1921, Miguel de Beistegui, a Mexican IOC member, announced to Coubertin the constitution of a national committee for the Olympic Games presided over by Carlos Rincón Gallardo, the Marquis of Guadalupe. Coincidentally, Rincón Gallardo was also chosen to preside over the *Comité Olímpico Mexicano* (Mexican Olympic Committee) created by Baillet-Latour in February 1923. Apparently this committee did not do much in the months following Baillet-Latour's departure. A displeased group of sportsmen created the rival *Asociación Olímpica Mexicana* (Mexican Olympic Association) on 27 August. The *Asociación* contacted the organizers of the 1924 Olympics asking to be recognized. The French, eager to increase international participation, did not object. [45]

Members of the *Asociación Olímpica Mexicana* were quickly labelled by YMCA officials as 'athletic *insurrectos*' who ignored not only the established *Comité Olímpico Mexicano* but also amateur rules, which in the eyes of both the IOC and the YMCA was perhaps even more appalling. [46] The crux of the matter had to do with underlying tensions between the YMCA and governmental educational authorities, most notably José F. Peralta, who was both general director of physical education and president of the *Asociación*. To complicate matters even further Carlos B. Zetina, then president of the *Comité*, was also related to the Mexican YMCA. Some members of the press asserted that class also played its part in the dispute. Pedro Mier, a journalist with *El Mundo*, sarcastically asked if Peralta's lack of nobility was the reason behind the IOC's refusal to acknowledge his *Asociación*. More pragmatically, Mier also wondered whether Mexican athletes would compete in Paris. [47]

Several months full of intrigue went by without much change in the Mexican Olympic stand-off. Meanwhile, Peralta, along with the president of the daily *Excélsior*, organized an aggressive fundraising campaign to prepare and send a Mexican team to the 1924 Olympics. Not long before the team embarked for Europe with Cuéllar, the sportsman and journalist that attended the 1922 Latin American Games, as its *chef de mission*, a deal was struck. On the one hand, the *Asociación Olímpica Mexicana* recognized the authority of the *Comité Olímpico Mexicano* and after organizing the 1924 team regenerated itself as the *Federación Atlética Nacional* (National Athletic Federation). On the other hand, the *Comité* recomposed itself and included Peralta as a member. The IOC and the French organizers were immediately informed. [48] Most probably, the arrangement was fuelled by Mexico's national aspirations to organize the first Central American Games in 1926.

After participating in the 1922 Latin American Games, Chilean sport witnessed similar problems to those testing Mexico's Olympic and sport leaders. The *Federación Sportiva Nacional* (National Sporting Federation), created in 1909, had long been considered the sport authority in Chile. However, after the Games, perceptions about the *Federación* noticeably changed. Dissatisfied with the performance of the Chilean athletes in the contests, the press increasingly criticized the bureaucracy. For instance, the daily *El Mercurio* claimed that the *Federación* was incapable of leading national sport because it was neither popular nor respected either in sporting circles or the government. Although the *Federación* denied the criticisms, it embraced some of the press suggestions for reform. By the end of 1922, under the leadership of Jorge Matte, the *Federación* implemented changes to include more national sport federations and democratize the composition of its executive board. Despite these changes, in October 1923 Hopkins reported that an organization rivalling Matte's had emerged. The rival institution was the *Confederación Nacional de Deportes* (National Confederation of Sports). Regardless of this rivalry, Matte, who had become an IOC member earlier in 1923, did not disappoint his colleagues and formed an initial *Comité Olímpico Chileno* (Chilean Olympic Committee) that organized the nation's second Olympic delegation. The presence of Chilean athletes in Paris soothed divisions, albeit temporarily. [49]

Replicating the Chilean process, national involvement in the 1922 Latin American Games divided Brazilian sport. The Brazilian *Comité Olympico Nacional* (National Olympic Committee) and the powerful *Confederação Brasileira de Desportos* (Brazilian Confederation of Sports) had gently coexisted since their creation in 1914 and 1916 respectively. Nonetheless, the problems plaguing the 1922 Latin American Games were seen by displeased parties as an opportunity to criticize the role of the *Confederação* in the event and oppose it. The challenge, however, did not come from the *Comité*.

Instead, the *Associação Paulista de Esportes Athleticos* (São Paulo's Association of Athletic Sports), a member of the *Confederação Brasileira de Desportos*, became the most vociferous critic. The São Paulo press also harshly criticized the Games and called into question the existence of the *Confederação* itself. The long-standing rivalry between Rio de Janeiro and São Paulo helped drive the dispute. While criticism of the *Confederação* escalated, Baillet-Latour visited São Paulo. [50] He did not appease their animosity. After he left, the daily *O Estado de São Paulo* wrote that in the 1922 Latin American Games São Paulo sport was 'the true intellectual, moral and material support of *Carioca* [Rio de Janeiro's] sport that pretends to be the whole of Brazilian sport'. [51] Unsurprisingly, in 1923 both Arnaldo Guinle from Rio de Janeiro and José Ferreira Santos from São Paulo were coopted onto the IOC. Both men were linked to the YMCA.

The Rio de Janeiro-São Paulo tension endangered plans to send a team to the 1924 Olympics. Citing budgetary restrictions, the *Confederação Brasileira de Desportos* had resolved that only shooting, rowing, football and water polo representatives would be sent to Paris. Antônio Prado Junior, a São Paulo sport official, wanted track and field included in the list. After surly deliberations, the *Confederação* complied, but only on condition that the São Paulo Track and Field Federation in charge of forming the team raised its own funds. Prado Junior and *O Estado de São Paulo* organized a successful fund-raising campaign. In the meantime, the internecine disputes led the government to withdraw the subsidy granted to the *Confederação* to send the Olympic delegation, which in turn deregistered the Brazilian entries. Prado Junior, this time assisted by Ferreira Santos, fought to have Brazil reinstated. Their efforts paid off. On 4 May 1924, a small Brazilian delegation embarked for Paris. [52]

Much like Brazil, Cuba and Peru had difficulties sending teams to the 1924 Olympics in Paris. Unlike Brazil, the difficulties in Cuba and Peru arose from pessimistic perceptions of their sporting cultures. Although the appointment of Porfirio Franca to the IOC in 1923 was celebrated in Cuba, many on the island believed that, with the exception of baseball, Cuban sports were in their infancy and, consequently, participation in the Olympic Games was impossible. Against this background, very few Cuban athletes competed in the French capital. [53] In Peru, YMCA officials argued that even if the nation could arrange its first Olympic team, it was not worth the effort. In October 1923, Hopkins affirmed that athletic 'development is so backward in that country that I think they should not attempt to send a team'. [54] This did not mean that all Olympic activity was discouraged in Peru. A few months after the close of the 1924 Olympics, the Peruvian government established a *Comité Olímpico Peruano* (Peruvian Olympic Committee) that replaced an earlier organization. [55]

While Argentine, Brazilian, Chilean, Cuban, Mexican and Uruguayan athletes were busy competing in Paris at the Olympic Games, Latin American sport officials held two meetings proposed by the IOC. The first took place on 3 July at the St Hubert Club and was labelled the Latin American Congress. One of the outcomes of this meeting was the fact that this new group decided to convene again in 1925 in order to adopt a proposed constitution for the Latin American Games Committee and set a date for a second Games. [56] It was also resolved at the July 3rd meeting to change the name of the Games back to the original South American Games. Neither the 1925 meeting nor the Games ever took place.

The second meeting, labelled the Central American Congress, took place on 3 and 4 July, in the same place as the Latin American Congress. It proved more profitable. After discussing several administrative matters, attendees considered a time and place for an inaugural Central American Games. Cuéllar described Mexico's national stadium and argued that the edifice 'would make Mexico the logical place for the realization of the first Central-American Games'. [57] Mexico was indeed the logical place. There was no other proposal. The assembly unanimously voted Mexico City the host of the 1926 Games. At the suggestion of Cuéllar, Cuba was granted the 1930 Games.

In December 1924, a *Junta Nacional* (national board) was created in Mexico to organize the first Central American Games. By mid-1925 the organization of the Games run into severe difficulties. The problems originated in the rift that divided Mexico's Olympic efforts between Baillet-Latour's visit and the 1924 Olympics. To mend the problems, the *Junta Nacional* reorganized itself and set up a comprehensive strategic plan to achieve the Central American Games. In the summer of 1924 the *Junta Nacional* sent José Martínez Ceballos, its secretary, and Enrique C. Aguirre, a YMCA official serving as the Games' technical director, on a two-month tour to promote the Games. In spite of their efforts, only Cuban and Guatemalan athletes competed alongside Mexicans in the Games. El Salvador and Costa Rica sent observers but no athletes. [58]

The 1926 Central American Games were inaugurated by Mexican president Plutarco Elías Calles on 12 October and closed on 2 November. Besides the details of the competitions, the Games as a whole held significant meaning for Mexicans. As Arbena has argued, the event showed 'that Mexico was a potential international leader, at least in its own geopolitical sphere'. [59] The Mexican Olympic structure consolidated itself after the Games. Some of those involved in the organization became members of the *Comité Olímpico Mexicano*. Looking forward to the 1928 Olympics in Amsterdam, Aguirre proclaimed early in 1927 that 'we trust we shall not have as many difficulties as we had in '24'. [60] And they did not. Indeed, Mexico had a strong presence in Amsterdam.

The experience of preparing national Olympic delegations to the 1928 Olympics did not proceed uniformly in Latin America. For instance, in Argentina, Olympic matters had achieved some degree of stability as a result of another presidential executive decree. In 1927, Alvear had unified the rival *Confederación Argentina de Deportes* and *Comité Olímpico Argentino*, a compromise that facilitated the formation of the nation's second Olympic team. Chile had also seen its rivalries tempered. In 1926, the rival *Federación Sportiva Nacional* and *Confederación Nacional de Deportes* created a *Confederación Deportiva de Chile* (Sporting Confederation of Chile). Soon after, a definitive *Comité Olímpico Chileno* was established and worked to send a team to Amsterdam. The Uruguayans managed to send a football team that replicated its 1924 gold medal performance. On the other hand, divisions in Brazilian sport intensified after the 1924 Olympics to the point where arranging a team for Amsterdam proved impossible. Peru could not manage an Olympic debut. Perhaps nourishing the belief that its athletes were not yet ready for the world's stage, Cuba was represented by a lone athlete. Considering that the island was to be the host of the second Central American Games, its one man representation was, at the least, curious. [61]

The IOC called for conferences of the South American Games and the Central American Games during the 1928 Olympics. The South Americans met on 31 July. Once again they decided to create a cycle of South American Games and once again they failed to bring the Games to fruition. At the meeting of the Central American Games, held on 1 August, Baillet-Latour congratulated Mexico on organizing the first Central American Games while at the same time regretting the poor participation in the event. Although Cuba had named a delegate to the meeting, his failure to appear in Amsterdam put the future of the second version of the Games scheduled for 1930 on hold. Eventually, Alberto Barreras's absence was clarified and the Games were successfully organized. [62]

An Assessment

The process of both ludic and Olympic diffusion, so intimately connected, had started long before the 1920s in Latin America, albeit with various degrees of intensity and success in different nations. Early in 1921, Brown recognized this somewhat disorganized but energetic process and used it to justify the IOC-YMCA partnership's intervention in the region. Brown predicted that the 1922 Latin American 'Games will unite in each country concerned the various athletic bodies into one national unit'. [63] If it materialized, Brown's prediction would be instrumental to the IOC's goal for the region. National athletic unity would be crucial for facilitating full and permanent regional inclusion in the Olympic Movement.

It soon became obvious that planting Latin America on the Olympic map would not be an easy task. Referring to the many difficulties in hosting the Games and forecasting future regional problems, a YMCA official declared in an odd combination of military and poetic language that the situation 'was loaded with dynamite. In my judgment, it has proved TNT (To or Not To, after Shakespere [*sic*], but quite a bit after him)'. [64] Added to preexisting conditions, the IOC-YMCA intervention in Latin America generated a torrent of consequences that created a Latin American 'Olympic explosion'. These consequences constitute the rather unprecedented and complex Latin American reaction to the IOC's and YMCA's 1920s Olympic call. Some of the regional responses to the IOC-YMCA policies of globalization were desired while others were not only unexpected but also counterproductive.

On the one hand, the 1922 Latin American Games and Baillet-Latour's ambassadorial tour helped the IOC establish a network of contacts in the region through which it hoped to expand the Olympic cause. This allowed the IOC to identify and select members in several Latin American nations who in turn would push the creation of NOCs, encourage participation in the Olympic Games and enable the establishment of regional Games. Some of these goals were rapidly achieved, others took time to develop and still others never materialized. On the other hand, some of the developments ignited by the IOC-YMCA partnership had unintended and undeniably negative consequences. As soon as Baillet-Latour returned to Europe, there were virulent power struggles to control the embryonic regional Olympic organizations and disorderly but thriving sport structures. Many countries saw the emergence of institutions and individuals that seriously rivalled the institutions and individuals endorsed by Baillet-Latour and the YMCA. In some cases, the power struggles already raged but escalated after the IOC planted a foot in the region. This situation sometimes jeopardized national efforts to send teams to the Olympic Games during the 1920s. In spite of the problems dividing sport in the region, by the late 1920s most of the Latin American nations influenced by the IOC's policy of globalization were in one way or another active in Olympic matters.

From the IOC perspective the IOC-YMCA partnership was successful in Latin America during the 1920s. However, whatever its perceived merits, the partnership had significant weaknesses. An evident and damaging shortcoming was the ambiguity of policy implementation. Olympic rhetoric was usually contradicted by practice. For instance, although Hopkins recommended against using 'big stick methods' and 'hurrying' Latin Americans 'in the process of growing up', [65] that is precisely what the partnership ended up doing. By using an interventionist approach the partnership erected itself as a powerful force in the region and enormously influenced the ongoing political process for consolidation in which many sport agencies were engaged. Since the partnership's goal was supposedly to achieve national sport unity, the power struggles in the mid-1920s were an ironic byproduct of its policies.

Officials in the partnership could not, or did not, want to accept their share of responsibility with regard to this state of affairs. For them, the problems in Latin America stemmed from the inadequate development of national bureaucracies. This is most evident in the tone used by Baillet-Latour in reporting about the 1922 Latin American Games. The future IOC president elaborated on the troubled competitions and, as expected, mentioned lack of organization, ignorance of rulebooks and excessive patriotism as the causes of the problems. Baillet-Latour also compared Latin American sport development to that of Europe. Although he predicted a bright future for the region, the report exuded Eurocentrism. [66] Baillet-Latour's 1924 request that Latin Americans study the constitution of the European NOCs to defuse some of the regional conflicts confirms his world view. For the IOC potentate, it was the European-controlled IOC that would teach Latin America how to organize its sporting affairs. It is not coincidental that Coubertin, following the lead of YMCA officials, condescendingly referred to events such as the 1922 Latin American Games as 'Olympic kindergartens'. [67]

The shape that the IOC policy of expansion took in Latin America in the 1920s was not only paternalistic but also insensitive to the history of national struggles to achieve stable sport institutions and its subtleties. It was applied homogeneously and there was no attempt to reflect whether this policy was the most appropriate for the political and social underpinnings of sport in the different Latin American nations. It could be argued that all the IOC was trying to accomplish in the region was to lay a foundation for establishing and exercising its power. Applied indiscriminately, the policy of Olympic expansion forgot its broader mission and was primarily fuelled by the narrow goal of creating NOCs and increasing participation at the Olympic Games.

On the positive side, the IOC's policies in the region forced Latin American sport and Olympic officials as well as politicians and civic leaders to imagine the kind of sport they wanted, ponder what role sport had to play in the life of their nations, and fight stereotypes of incivility and ineptitude. In the process, Latin Americans became not only integrated into the Olympic Movement but also aware of their misfortunes, needs and potential. The study of the achievements and shortcomings of the 1920s IOC's policies of globalization in Latin America, the regional 'Olympic explosion', reveals a much richer and more complex pattern of ludic diffusion than mere annotations of the dates in which regional NOCs were granted official recognition.

Acknowledgements

The author would like to thank the IOC Olympic Studies Centre, located in the Olympic Museum in Lausanne, for the postgraduate research grant that has allowed him to investigate this area of Olympic history. The author also wishes to thank the Kautz Family Young Men's Christian Association Archives of the University of Minnesota Libraries and the Argentine sport magazine *El Gráfico* for allowing him access to important material for this project. Finally, the author would like to express gratitude to Prof. Mark Dyreson for his valuable advice, and Doug Collier, Pablo Galarza, Beatriz Hambeck and Paulina Suárez Pérez for their unsparing assistance.

Notes

[1] For the information in this paragraph and the next see de Coubertin, *Olympic Memoirs*; Lyberg, *Fabulous 100 Years*; Mallon, *The Olympic Record Book*; Torres, 'Mass Sport Through Education or Elite Olympic Sport?', 'Tribulations and Achievements', 'Like Father, Like Son'; and Wallechinsky, *The Complete Book of the Summer Olympics*.

[2] See Boulongne, 'Pierre de Coubertin (1896–1925)', 285–6; DaCosta, 'Olympic Globalization', 91–105; Guttmann, *The Olympics*, 41, 52; Guttmann, *Games and Empires*, 128, 130; Guttmann, *Sports. The First Five Millennia*, 263–4, 266–7; Kraemer-Mandeau, 'National and International Olympic Movements in Latin America'; Mayer, *A Travers les Anneaux Olympiques*; McGehee, 'The Origins of Olympism in Mexico'; and Müller and Tuttas, 'The Role of the YMCA'.

[3] Guttmann, *Sports. The First Five Millennia*, 266.

[4] Arbena, 'Sports', Vol. 5, 171.

[5] See Torres, 'Ideas encontradas'.

[6] P.P. Phillips, Annual Report Letter, 30 Sept. 1918, 'Argentina. Buenos Aires. Annual Reports. 1902–18'; and Jess T. Hopkins, Visitation Report, 11 Dec. 1918, 'Mexico. Correspondence. 1889–1921', Kautz Family Young Men's Christian Association Archives, (hereafter YMCA Archives), University of Minnesota Libraries.

[7] Arbena 'Sport, Development, and Mexican Nationalism', 352.

[8] See various letters from Dick Grant to Pierre de Coubertin for the period 1915–16 in 'JO Ete 1920. Correspondance Generale. 1914–17', Le Comite International Olympique Archives (hereafter IOC Archives), Lausanne, Switzerland. See also Allison V. Armour, Memorandum, 'Armour, Allison Vincent. Correspondence. 1909–1918', IOC Archives and *La Lucha* (Havana), 22 Dec. 1916, n.p.

 [9] Elwood S. Brown to Pierre de Coubertin, 3 Feb. 1919, 'Young Men's Christian Associations. 1909–27' (hereafter 'YMCA, 1909–27'), IOC Archives. For the role of the United States military and the YMCA in the 'Military Olympics' see Wakefield, *Playing to Win*; and Pope, *Patriotic Games*.

[10] Elwood S. Brown to Pierre de Coubertin, 3 Feb. 1919, 'YMCA, 1909–27', IOC Archives.

[11] See Elwood S. Brown, Memorandum on Trip to South America. March–April–May 1920, 'South America. General. 1893–1970s. South American Federation. Reports and budgets. 1914–87' (hereafter 'South America, 1893–1970s'), YMCA Archives; and Elwood S. Brown to Pierre de Coubertin, 23 Jan. 1920, 'YMCA, 1909–27', IOC Archives.

[12] Elwood S. Brown to Pierre de Coubertin, 23 Jan. 1920, 'YMCA, 1909–27', IOC Archives.

[13] Ibid.; and William M. Sloane to Pierre de Coubertin, 10 March 1920, 'YMCA, 1909–27', IOC Archives.

[14] Elwood S. Brown to Pierre de Coubertin, 23 Jan. 1920, 'YMCA, 1909–27', IOC Archives.

[15] Elwood S. Brown to Pierre de Coubertin, 22 May 1920, 'YMCA, 1909–27', IOC Archives. See also Elwood S. Brown to Pierre de Coubertin, 7 May 1920, 'YMCA, 1909–27', IOC Archives.

[16] Elwood S. Brown, Notes on Trip to South America. March, April and May 1920, 2, 'South America, 1893–1970s', YMCA Archives.

[17] See Latourette, *World Service*, 201–44; Federación Sudamericana de Asociaciones Cristianas de Jóvenes, *Quince Años de Educación Física*, 3–4; Elwood S. Brown to the International Olympic Committee, c. Aug. 1920, 'YMCA, 1909–27', IOC Archives. Brown and the American press usually referred to the Far Eastern Games as the Far Eastern 'Olympics'.

[18] See Procès-Verbaux du 19ème Session du Comité International Olympique, Anvers, 1920, IOC Archives.

[19] See Ascoli, *Projeto de Commemoração*, 59–60; and Elwood S. Brown to Pierre de Coubertin, 23 Jan. 1920 and 2 March 1920, 'YMCA, 1909–27', IOC Archives.

[20] Elwood S. Brown to Pierre de Coubertin, 22 May 1920, 'YMCA, 1909–27', IOC Archives. See also Jess T. Hopkins to Elwood S. Brown, 5 Feb. 1921, 'South American Federation. Correspondence and reports. 1900–50s. Conferences. 1914–50s. Printed material' (hereafter 'South American Federation'), YMCA Archives.

[21] de Franceschi Neto, 'A Participação no Brasil', 35.

[22] Elwood S. Brown to Pierre de Coubertin, 20 Dec. 1920, 'YMCA, 1909–27', IOC Archives.

[23] Jess T. Hopkins to Pierre de Coubertin, 27 May 1921, 'YMCA, 1909–27', IOC Archives.

[24] See Elwood S. Brown to Jess T. Hopkins, 13 May 1921, 'South American Federation', YMCA Archives; and Procès-Verbaux du 20ème Session du Comité International Olympique, Lausanne, 1921, IOC Archives.

[25] For a brief account of the centennial celebrations see Gregory, 'Rio de Janeiro 1922–23'. See also Jess T. Hopkins to Pierre de Coubertin, 28 Sept. 1921; Elwood S. Brown to Pierre de Coubertin, 18 Nov. 1922, 'South American Federation', YMCA Archives; and Elwood S. Brown to Pierre de Coubertin, 18 Nov. 1921; Elwood S. Brown to Pierre de Coubertin, 13 Jan. 1922, 'YMCA, 1909–27', IOC Archives.

[26] See Jess T. Hopkins to Confederação Brasileira de Desportos, 17 Jan. 1922; Jess T. Hopkins to Pierre de Coubertin, 24 Feb. 1922; and Elwood S. Brown to Pierre de Coubertin, 16 Feb. 1922, '(World Alliance of) Young Men's Christian Associations. (YMCA). 1922–67' (hereafter 'World Alliance of YMCA, 1922–67'), IOC Archives. See also Jess T. Hopkins to Elwood S. Brown, 2 Jan. 1922; Henri J. Sims to Armando Burlamaqui, 30 Jan. 1922; and Arturo Azevedo to Henri J. Sims, 31 Jan. 1922, 'South American Federation', YMCA Archives.

[27] Henri J. Sims to Carlos Sampaio, 16 March 1922, 'South American Federation', YMCA Archives.

[28] Elwood S. Brown to Pierre de Coubertin, 3 May 1922, 'World Alliance of YMCA, 1922–67', IOC Archives.

[29] Ibid; and Elwood S. Brown to Pierre de Coubertin, 2 May 1922, 'World Alliance of YMCA, 1922–67', IOC Archives.

[30] See Procès-Verbaux du 21ème Session du Comité International Olympique, Paris, 1922, IOC Archives.

[31] *El Día* (Montevideo) (hereafter *El Día*), 14 Sept. 1922, 6; *El Mercurio* (Santiago) (hereafter *El Mercurio*), 14 Sept. 1922, 21; *O Estado de São Paulo* (São Paulo), 14 Sept. 1922, 2; and *Jornal do Commercio* (Rio de Janeiro), 14 Sept. 1922, 10. Jess T. Hopkins, First Latin-American Games. Rio de Janeiro – Aug. 27th, to Oct. 15th, 1923 [*sic*]; and Jogos Athleticos Latino-Americanos. Resumo dos Resultados Officiales. Commissão Organizadora dos Festejos Desportivos do Centenario, 'Jeux Régionaux. Correspondance, conférences et documents. 1924–28' (hereafter 'Jeux Régionaux, 1924–28'), IOC Archives. According to the organizing commission's report, the Latin American Games included competition in basketball, boxing, diving, equestrian, fencing, football, rowing, shooting, swimming, tennis, track and field and water polo. This leaves the International Sports Championships empty. Lamartine P. DaCosta has argued that the football competition was not associated with the Latin American Games. This corresponds with *Uruguay Sport*, the official publication of Uruguay's National Commission for Physical Education, which did not include football among the results of the Latin American Games. See DaCosta, 'Olympic Globalization', 96; and *Uruguay Sport* (Montevideo), n.d. (*c.* Oct. 1922), 4017–25.

[32] Jess T. Hopkins, First Latin-American Games. Rio de Janeiro – Aug. 27th, to Oct. 15th, 1923 [*sic*], 'Jeux Régionaux, 1924–28', IOC Archives. For an account of the incidents, see *El Mercurio*, 30 Sept. 1922, 1; *El Gráfico* (Buenos Aires), 30 Sept. 1922, 23, and 14 Oct. 1922, 15; and *La Nación* (Buenos Aires) (hereafter *La Nación*), 2 May 1924, 6.

[33] See *El Universal* (Mexico City) (hereafter *El Universal*), 11 Oct. 1922, Sect. 2, 8.

[34] *El Mercurio*, 21 Sept. 1922, 14.

[35] Ibid; and *El Día*, 19 Sept. 1922, 6; 22 Sept. 1922, 6. See also Rafael Cullen to Henri de Baillet Latour, 11 Aug. 1923, 'Jeux Régionaux, 1924–28', IOC Archives.

[36] See *El Mercurio*, 25 Sept. 1922, 11; *El Día*, 26 Sept. 1922, 8; and *La Nación*, 3 Oct. 1922, n.p.

[37] Jess T. Hopkins to Henri de Baillet-Latour, 5 Jan. 1923, 'Jeux Régionaux, 1924–28', IOC Archives. See also *Excélsior* (Mexico City) (hereafter *Excélsior*), 9 Feb. 1923, Sect. 2, 6; 10 Feb. 1923, Sect. 2, 6; 12 Feb. 1923, 5; 14 Feb. 1923, Sect. 2, 6; *Revista de Revistas* (Mexico City) (hereafter *Revista de Revistas*), 18 Feb. 1923, 93; and *The Havana Post* (Havana), 15 Jan. 1923, 5, 16 Jan. 1923, 5, 21 Jan. 1923, 5 and 22 Jan. 1923, 5. Baillet-Latour's ambassadorial trip finished in the United States but there he was not in an official capacity.

[38] *Excélsior*, 14 Feb. 1923, Sect. 2, 6.

[39] See Jess T. Hopkins to Henri de Baillet-Latour, 27 Nov. 1922; 5 Jan. 1923; and 31 May 1923, 'Jeux Régionaux, 1924–28', IOC Archives. The speech can be found in 'Jeux Régionaux, 1924–28', IOC Archives; and also in *Excélsior*, 14 Feb. 1923, Sect. 2, 6; *El Demócrata* (Mexico City), 4 Feb. 1923, Suplemento Dominical, 2; and *El Universal*, 13 Feb. 1923, 5.

[40] Henri de Baillet-Latour to Godefroy de Blonay, 18 Dec. 1923, 'Blonay, Godefroy de. Correspondance. 1915–31', IOC Archives. Baillet-Latour seemed to have followed the tradition that uses 'América' to designate the whole continent rather than a single country.

[41] Associated Press, 17 March 1923, 21. Baillet-Latour's comments can also be found in the *New York Times*, 18 March 1923, Sect. 1, Part 2, 1; and *El Universal*, 17 March 1923, n.p.

[42] See Procès-Verbaux du 22ème Session du Comité International Olympique, 1923 Rome, IOC Archives; and Rapport Fait par le Comte de Baillet-Latour sur la Mission qu'il a remplie pour le CIO dans l' Amérique du Sud, l'Amérique Centrale et l'Amérique du Nord, '22 E Session Rome 1923. Rapports. Rap. De mission en Amérique, 1923. 1923–23' (hereafter '22 E Session'), IOC Archives.

[43] Elwood S. Brown to Henri de Baillet-Latour, 23 Oct. 1923, 'Baillet-Latour, Henri de. Correspondance. 1915–25' (hereafter 'Baillet-Latour'), IOC Archives.

[44] The following references to Argentina and Uruguay are based on Torres, 'Tribulations and Achievements' and '"If We Had Had Our Argentine Team Here!"'

[45] See Miguel de Beistegui to Pierre de Coubertin, 10 Nov. 1921, 'Beistegui, Miguel de. Correspondance. 1901–31', IOC Archives; and Frantz Reichel to Pierre de Coubertin, 3 Oct. 1923, 'Baillet-Latour', IOC Archives. Apparently, the rival association was also known as *Comité Nacional Olímpico Mexicano* (Mexican National Olympic Committee): see *Revista de Revistas*, 9 Sept. 1923, 50.

[46] Elwood S. Brown to Henri de Baillet-Latour, 21 Nov. 1923, 'Baillet-Latour', IOC Archives. 'Insurrecto' means rebel or insurgent in Spanish. This effort at 'Spanglish' by the YMCA captures very well its attitude towards the dissidents.

[47] See Enrique C. Aguirre to Henri de Baillet-Latour, 6 Oct. 1923, 'Jeux Régionaux, 1924–28', IOC Archives; and Pedro Mier, '¿Cómo estuvo eso de la Olimpiada?' *El Mundo* (Mexico City), 21 Dec. 1923, n.p.

[48] Enrique C. Aguirre to Henri de Baillet-Latour, 1 March 1924; Alfonso Rojo de la Vega to Henri de Baillet-Latour, c. March 1924; and Anon. to Enrique C. Aguirre, 24 March 1924, 'Jeux Régionaux, 1924–28', IOC Archives. Some reports mentioned the institution as *Confederación Deportiva Nacional* (National Sporting Confederation). This period of Mexican Olympic history has been explored by the *Academia Olímpica Mexicana* (Mexican Olympic Academy) in an unpublished 2003 manuscript entitled 'Inicios del Movimiento Olímpico en México'.

[49] *El Mercurio*, 16 Nov. 1922, 7, 6 Dec. 1922, 9, 10 Dec. 1922, 13, 25 Dec. 1922, 14, 28 Dec. 1922, 9 and 31 Dec. 1922, 15; and *La Nación*, 5 June 1924, 2.

[50] *O Estado de São Paulo*, 13 Sept. 1922, 5, 2 Oct. 1922, 3, 5 Oct. 1922, 7, 14 Oct. 1922, 6 and 20 Oct. 1922, 7.

[51] *O Estado de São Paulo*, 12 Nov. 1922, 6.

[52] See de Franceschi Neto, 'A Participação no Brasil', 35–7; and de Castro Filho, *Jogos Olímpicos*, 56–7. For an account of the Brazilian *Comité Olympico Nacional* see the former, 25–30.

[53] *La Prensa* (Havana), 27 May 1923, Deportes, 6, and Suplemento de Sports, n.p. See also Comité Olympique Français, *Les Jeux de la VIII Olympiade*.

[54] Jess T. Hopkins to Henri de Baillet-Latour, 11 Oct. 1923, 'Baillet-Latour', IOC Archives.

[55] Anon. to Pierre de Coubertin, 26 Dec. 1924, 'Amateurisme/General. 1924–26', IOC Archives.

[56] Minutes of the Latin American Congress, 3 July 1924, 'Jeux Régionaux, 1924–28', IOC Archives. See also *La Vanguardia* (Buenos Aires) (hereafter *La Vanguardia*), 5 July 1924, 8. A handful of Ecuadorian and Haitian athletes also competed in Paris. See Comité Olympique Français, *Les Jeux de la VIII Olympiade*.

[57] Minutes of the Second Session of the Central American Congress, 4 July 1924, 'Jeux Régionaux, 1924–28', IOC Archives. See also *La Vanguardia*, 5 July 1924, 8. The remaining information in this paragraph comes from these documents.

[58] Enrique C. Aguirre to Henri de Baillet-Latour, 4 Aug. 1925, 'Jeux Régionaux, 1924–28', IOC Archives; José Martínez Ceballos and Jesús E. Monjaráz to Henri de Baillet-Latour, 12 Aug. 1925; and Enrique C. Aguirre, Report of the First Central American Games Held in Mexico City from Oct. 12 to Nov. 2, 1926, 'Jeux de l'Amerique Centrale' (hereafter 'Amerique Centrale'), IOC Archives.

[59] Arbena, 'Sport, Development, and Mexican Nationalism', 354. See also McGehee, 'The Origins of Olympism in Mexico' and 'Sports and Recreational Activities'.

[60] Enrique C. Aguirre to Henri de Baillet-Latour, 7 Jan. 1927, 'Amerique Centrale', IOC Archives.

[61] Luis Harnecker to Henri de Baillet-Latour, 8 June 1926; Alfredo Benavides to Henri de Baillet-Latour, 20 May 1928, 'Jeux Régionaux, 1924–28', IOC Archives; and Torres, '"If We Had Had

Our Argentine Team Here!'", 15 and 23. Some authors cite economic or technical reasons for Brazil's absence from Amsterdam (see de Castro Filho, *Jogos Olímpicos*, 58; and Brazilian Olympic Committee, *Dream and Conquest*, 48); however, that does not seem to have been the case (see Arnaldo Guinle to Henri de Baillet-Latour, 27 July 1924; Raul do Rio Branco to Henri de Baillet-Latour, 25 Jan. 1926, 'Jeux Régionaux, 1924–28', IOC Archives; and Arnaldo Guinle to Henri de Baillet-Latour, 22 Jan. 1926, 'Guinle, Arnaldo. Correspondance. 1925–61', IOC Archives). A couple of Haitian and Panamanian athletes also competed in Amsterdam. See Van Rossem, *The Ninth Olympiad.*

[62] Conference des Jeux Sud-Americains; and Conference Amerique Centrale, 'Jeux Régionaux, 1924–28', IOC Archives. See also *Official Bulletin of the International Olympic Committee* 3, 11 (Oct. 1928); and Alberto Barreras to Henri de Baillet-Latour, 28 Sept. 1928, 'Amerique Centrale', IOC Archives.
[63] Elwood S. Brown, Report, 1 Jan. 1921, 'World Alliance', YMCA Archives.
[64] Henry J. Sims to Jess T. Hopkins, 27 April 1922, 'South American Federation', YMCA Archives.
[65] Jess T. Hopkins to Pierre de Coubertin, 4 June 1923, 'YMCA, 1909–27', IOC Archives. For the 'big stick methods' quotation see Jess T. Hopkins to Elwood S. Brown, 9 July 1921, 'World Alliance', YMCA Archives.
[66] See Henri de Baillet-Latour, Rapport sur la Mission qu'il a remplie pour le CIO dans l'Amérique du Sud, l'Amérique Centrale et l'Amérique du Nord, '22 E Session', IOC Archives.
[67] De Coubertin, *Olympic Memoirs*, 171, 203.

References

Arbena, Joseph L. 'Sport, Development, and Mexican Nationalism, 1920–70'. *Journal of Sport History* 18, no. 3 (1991): 350–64.
——. 'Sports'. In Vol. 1 of *Encyclopedia of Latin American History and Culture.* 5 vols., edited by Barbara A. Tenenbaum. New York: C. Scribner's Sons, 1996.
Ascoli, Nestor. *Projeto de Commemoração do Primeiro Centenario da Independencia do Brasil.* Rio de Janeiro: Revista de Lingua Portuguesa, 1924.
Boulongne, Yves-Pierre. 'Pierre de Coubertin (1896–1925)'. In Vol. 1 of *The International Olympic Committee – One Hundred Years 1894–1994. The International Olympic Committee – One Hundred Years. The Idea, The Presidents, The Achievement.* 3 vols., supervised by Raymond Gafner. Lausanne: International Olympic Committee, 1995.
Brazilian Olympic Committee. *Dream and Conquest: Brazil's Participation in the 20th Century Olympic Games.* Rio de Janeiro: Ouro sobre Azul, 2004.
Comité Olympique Français. *Les Jeux de la VIII Olympiade, Paris 1924: Rapport Officiel.* Paris: Librairie de France, 1924.
Coubertin, Pierre de. *Olympic Memoirs.* Lausanne: International Olympic Committee, 1997.
DaCosta, Lamartine P. 'Olympic Globalization: Sport Geopolitics or IOC Power Politics?' In *Olympic Studies*, edited by Lamartine P. DaCosta. Rio de Janeiro: Editora Gama Filho, 2002.
de Castro Filho, Antonio Pires. *Jogos Olímpicos. Histórico e participação do Brasil. Dados e documentação.* N.p., 1977.
de Franceschi Neto, Marcia. 'A Participação no Brasil no Movimento Olímpico Internacional no Período de 1896 a 1925'. Ph.D. diss., Universidade Gama Filho, 1999.
Federación Sudamericana de Asociaciones Cristianas de Jóvenes. *Quince Años de Educación Física en las Asociaciones de América del Sur.* Montevideo and Buenos Aires: Editorial Mundo Nuevo, 1927.

Gregory, Michael L. 'Rio de Janeiro 1922–23. Exposição Internacional do Centenario do Brasil'. In *Historical Dictionary of World's Fairs and Expositions, 1851–1988.* edited by John E. Findling and Kimberly D. Pelle. New York: Greenwood, 1990.

Guttmann, Allen. *Games and Empires. Modern Sport and Cultural Imperialism.* New York: Columbia University Press, 1994.

——. *The Olympics. A History of the Modern Games,* 2nd edn. Urbana, IL: University of Illinois Press, 2002.

——. *Sports. The First Five Millennia.* Amherst and Boston, MA: University of Massachusetts Press, 2004.

Kraemer-Mandeau, Wolf. 'National and International Olympic Movements in Latin America'. In *Contemporary Studies in the National Olympic Games Movement,* edited by Roland Naul. Frankfurt am Main: Peter Lang, 1997.

Latourette, Kenneth S. *World Service. A History of the Foreign Service of the Young Men's Christian Associations of the United States and Canada.* New York: Association Press, 1957.

Lyberg, Wolf. *Fabulous 100 Years.* Lausanne: International Olympic Committee, 1996.

McGehee, Richard V. 'The Origins of Olympism in Mexico: The Central American Games of 1926'. *The International Journal of the History of Sport* 10, no. 3 (1993): 313–32.

——. 'Sports and Recreational Activities in Guatemala and Mexico, Late 1800s to 1926'. *Studies in Latin American Popular Culture* 13 (1994): 7–32.

Mallon, Bill. *The Olympic Record Book.* New York: Garland, 1988.

Mayer, Otto. *A Travers les Anneaux Olympiques.* Geneva: Pierre Cailler, 1960.

Müller, Norbert and Tuttas, Ralf. 'The Role of the YMCA: Especially that of Elwood S. Brown, Secretary of Physical Education of the YMCA, in the World-Wide Expansion of the Olympic Movement during Pierre de Coubertin's Presidency'. In *Bridging Three Centuries: Intellectual Crossroads and the Modern Olympic Movement.* edited by Kevin B. Wamsley, Scott G. Martyn, Gordon H. MacDonald and Robert K. Barney. London, Ontario: University of Western Ontario Press, 2002.

Pope, S.W. *Patriotic Games: Sporting Traditions in the American Imagination, 1876–1926.* New York: Oxford University Press, 1997.

Torres, Cesar R. 'Mass Sport Through Education or Elite Olympic Sport? José Benjamín Zubiaur's Dilemma and Argentina's Olympic Sports Legacy'. *Olympika: The International Journal of Olympic Studies* 7 (1998): 61–88.

——. "If We Had Had Our Argentine Team Here!' Football and the 1924 Argentine Olympic Team'. *Journal of Sport History* 30, no. 1 (2003): 1–24.

——. 'Tribulations and Achievements: The Early History of Olympism in Argentina'. *The International Journal of the History of Sport* 18, no. 3 (2001): 59–92.

——. 'Ideas encontradas: la educación física y el deporte en el debate parlamentario sobre la participación argentina en los Juegos Olímpicos de 1908'. *Olympika: The International Journal of Olympic Studies* 11 (2002): 117–42.

——. 'Like Father, Like Son: The Tale of Francisco Carmelo and Carmelo Félix Camet at the Olympic Games'. *The International Journal of the History of Sport* 19, no. 4 (2002): 179–91.

Van Rossem, G., ed. *The Ninth Olympiad: Being the Official Report of the Olympic Games of 1928 Celebrated at Amsterdam,* trans. Sydney W. Fleming. Amsterdam: J.H. De Bussy, 1928.

Wakefield, Wanda E. *Playing to Win: Sports and the American Military, 1898–1945.* Albany, NY: State University of New York Press, 1997.

Wallechinsky, David. *The Complete Book of the Summer Olympics.* New York: Overlook, 2000.

The Modern Olympic Movement, Women's Sport and the Social Order During the Inter-war Period

Florence Carpentier and Jean-Pierre Lefèvre

Since the inter-war period, women have been demanding the right to fully participate in the Olympic Games, the most prestigious of all international sports competitions. Yet the International Olympic Committee (IOC) has only recently adopted a policy of true equality for men and women. [1] In the Athens Games of 2004, women's overall participation surpassed 40 per cent for the first time and the number of women's events had risen appreciably. [2] Today, at the Olympic Games, only baseball (dropped recently from the 2012 programme) and boxing remain exclusively masculine sports. Despite progress in the status and representation of women in our societies, it is interesting to note that the IOC has never capitulated to outside pressures; it opened the Games to women essentially as the result of internal factors. [3] The constitution and internal functioning of the committee has remained virtually unchanged since 1925, the date when its founder, Pierre de Coubertin, resigned. It confers on its members absolute control over the future of the committee itself and that of the Olympic Games. This article explores how the IOC under Henri de Baillet-Latour, [4] the founder's successor, protected itself from and reacted to women's first demands for access to the Games. [5]

At the same time that the International Olympic Committee and the modern Olympic Games were founded in 1894 the first IOC members were also recruited by Coubertin from amongst a small group of mainly aristocratic men. In a European society that has traditionally separated the rich from the poor and men from women, it was normal and convenient that these first IOC members would all come from the same social class and be of the same sex. One might even say that the Olympic Movement was conceived as a tool to promote and spread European aristocratic values and masculine values. [6] Pierre de Coubertin did not express himself very often on the subject of women's sport, but the few opinions that he did express were particularly harsh on women athletes. His criticisms were essentially based on the biological differences between the sexes and comprised two main arguments. First, and most important, he argued that women were not physically made for athletic activity, which he considered too violent for them. Women, to his mind, were like other 'weak' members of society – children, the elderly, and the sick – and were best suited for physical education and the pursuit of public and personal health-oriented goals. [7] Moreover, Coubertin believed that women's athletic 'exhibitions' were a distinct threat to the spectators' morals. Noting that athletic clothing was lighter than ordinary dress, he was concerned that the sight of women's nearly nude bodies would arouse the primordial passions of the male spectators. A clear danger was thus that the spectacle of the lightly clothed female body would become more attractive than the athletic performance itself. [8] For these reasons, the Olympic Games created in 1894 were off limits to women athletes. It is thus interesting to note that as of 1900 the sports programmes show that women's events were held (see Table 1). [9]

Sheila Mitchell has explained this remarkable inclusion of women as follows: up to the Stockholm Games of 1912, the actual organization of athletic competition was completely outside the control of the IOC and Coubertin:

> Although the IOC purported to have control over the program, in fact, the responsibility of actually formulating the program was in the hands of the organizing committees.... It was under these conditions that women were first admitted to the Games without the official consent or comment from the IOC. [10]

After the First World War, the IOC thus decided to create an organizing committee that would be structured and controlled by its own members, but this move did not bring about the withdrawal of the women's events. To avoid disavowing

Table 1 Women's participation in the Olympic Games under the Presidency of Pierre de Coubertin (1896–1925)

	Women's participation	Men's participation	Women's sports
Olympic Games of 1900, Paris	22	975	Golf Equestrian sports (mixed) Tennis (mixed) Sailing (mixed)
Olympic Games of 1904, St Louis	6	645	Archery
Olympic Games of 1908, London	37	1,971	Figure skating (mixed) Tennis Archery Sailing (mixed)
Olympic Games of 1912, Stockholm	48	2,359	Swimming Diving Equestrian sports (mixed) Tennis Sailing (mixed)
Olympic Games of 1920, Antwerp	65	2,561	Swimming Figure skating Diving Equestrian sports Tennis Sailing (mixed)
Olympic Games of 1924, Paris	135	2,954	Fencing Swimming Diving Equestrian sports Tennis Sailing (mixed)

Note: The number of men and women, as well as the details on the women's sports, can be found on the official IOC site on the specific Games related page for each of these editions of the Olympic celebration. The data differ slightly depending on the bibliographic source.

the preceding organizations, Coubertin's IOC found that it could not just dismiss the women's sports competitions that had already been included. Nevertheless, Coubertin was determined not to allow women open access to the competitive programme. In 1919, just as women's sport was blossoming in France, the future President of the Fédération Sportive Féminine Internationale (FSFI), the Frenchwoman Alice Milliat [11], requested that the IOC include women in the track and field programme. As she recounted it, she 'came up against a solid wall of refusal, which led directly to the creation of the Women's Olympic Games'. [12] Thus, in the Olympic Games of 1920 and 1924 that were organized during the presidency of Coubertin, women, despite a few participants, were not yet largely integrated into the Olympic sports programme. [13] For some historians of the modern Olympic Movement, the first notable instance of women's participation is that of the Games of the Olympiad which were held in Amsterdam in 1928. They were the first Summer

Games to be organized during the term of the new IOC President, Henri de Baillet-Latour. Nonetheless, Coubertin's resignation and the introduction of a new IOC President did not automatically translate into an increased inclusion of women in the Olympic Games. [14] Coubertin's successors held the same values as he, and the relative participation of women in the Amsterdam Games must, in fact, be attributed to the intervention of the International Amateur Athletic Federation and its Swedish President, Sigfried Edström. [15] Athletics dominated women's sport between the two wars, and thus it is not surprising that the IAAF would play a role in this history. The IAAF President had been an influential member of the IOC Executive Board since its creation in 1921 and had been acting as an intermediary between the Olympic governing body, the IAAF and the FSFI since 1926. We will see that the overtures made to women in 1928 were, more than anything, a means for male institutions to better control women in a changing social context that seemed favourable to granting them more freedom.

In the period between the two world wars, a women's movement towards greater liberty was just beginning to gather steam, continuing a phenomenon that had begun prior to the First World War with the appearance of many national feminist movements. [16] Against this background, a women's sports movement was also emerging, not only in the United States and Europe but also in Asia, to the point that a federation was formed in 1921 to organize regular 'Women's Games'. Given that the reigning social model imposed a separation of the sexes in most spheres of life (in the workplace, at school and in leisure activities), it should not be surprising that an explicitly 'feminine' sports movement would eventually develop in parallel to the implicitly 'masculine' world of sports. This type of organization was in fact a logical response to the established social order, though it may not have been chosen willingly. And once the women's emancipation movement was perceived as a threat to institutional domination by men, thereby throwing into question the social order, significant reactions on the part of sports leaders in general and Olympic leaders in particular were not long to follow. This article focuses on the reactions of Olympic leaders to the challenges registered by the women's emancipation movement to Olympic sport. Specifically, it seeks to concentrate on several key questions: What debates ensued within the IOC regarding the rise of women's sport and women's demands for equality? What arguments did these conservative aristocrats offer to justify rejecting or including women in the Olympic Games? What elements were believed by them to be at stake when they granted women athletes partial inclusion in the 1928 Olympics? What solutions were adopted by the leaders in the hope of returning to a more satisfactory social order?

The goal of this article is to show that the presidency of Henri de Baillet-Latour marked a turning-point in the history of women's participation in the Olympic Games, by presenting previously unstudied materials from the archives of the IOC [17], the FSFI [18], and from an earlier study of the IAAF. [19] The male hegemony of the Olympic institution was increasingly being called into question – in its social context and particularly its sports context. This challenge to the status quo led to women's admission in Olympic competition but, paradoxically, the power of the Olympic leadership over women being strengthened. This was accomplished through a delicate strategy making use of the complementary powers of the IOC, the IAAF and their respective Presidents; it eventually led to the demise of the FSFI and consigned Alice Milliat to the past.

This work is divided into two sections. In the first, we explain how the development of women's sport between 1921 and 1926 incited the IAAF to take steps to control its growth by encouraging women's participation in the Olympic Games. We then examine the debates concerning the integration of women from 1926 onwards, as well as the different negotiations between the FSFI, the IAAF and the IOC regarding the rights of women athletes at the Games. This period of negotiation ended with the total absorption of the FSFI by the two other institutions in 1936.

The Birth of the FSFI and the Worries of the IAAF

The first French women's track and field championships were organized in 1917 towards the end of the First World War. The most important outcome of these championships was the creation of the first French federation of women's athletics: the *Fédération des Sociétés Féminines Sportives de France* (FSFSF). The treasurer, Alice Milliat, thus began her career at the national level as a committed leader of women's sport. In June 1918, she became the general secretary and then was unanimously elected President of the Federation in March 1919. Her first act was to ask the IOC President – Pierre de Coubertin – to allow for women's participation in the 1920 Olympic Games in Antwerp, Belgium. After a blunt refusal, the FSFSF leaders decided to organize a women's athletics competition that would be open to all countries. In March 1921, the first international women's athletics competition was held in Monte Carlo (Monaco) and brought together women from France, England, Italy, Norway and Sweden, countries in which women's sport had begun to show signs of progress. This international initiative was a frank success not only for the athletes, but also for the public [20] and the specialized press. Thus encouraged, the diverse women's federations soon united into an international federation, the Fédération Sportive Féminine Internationale, at an inaugural congress on 31 October 1921 in Paris in the presence of French, American, English Czechoslovakian, Spanish, Austrian, Scandinavian and German representatives. The minutes of this meeting indicate that Alice Milliat played a key role in the debates and the initiatives undertaken. During the second congress on 18 August 1922, before the opening of the first 'Women's Olympic Games' in Paris, the skills and dedication of this Frenchwoman were recognized by all and she was named as the FSFI President:

> Monsieur Anthoine thanked the international delegates for their work in furthering the cause of the FSFI, but declared that the flourishing health of the FSFI was in great part due to the activity of Madame Milliat. This pronouncement was met by applause from the congress attendees…. On proposal from the United States, Madame Alice Milliat was named president by acclamation. [21]

The federation members then made the decision to perpetuate the Women's Olympic Games by holding them every four years. This major decision displayed the federation's readiness to expand. Like all international organizations, it needed a regular world championship not only to justify its existence, but also to bring it into the public's eye. This decision also proved that the federation had attained a certain prominence. In fact, 38 countries representing five continents were already affiliated in 1922, and several nations still aspired to join. At this point, the women's federation had as many affiliated countries as the IAAF. Not least, the willingness to host the Women's Olympic Games every four years showed that women were seeking to position themselves in relation to the men's organization. According to the federation's minutes, it was not a question of 'doing the same as' but rather of taking a model that worked and adapting and improving it for the specifications of women. However, it may very well be that this decision was also a deliberate provocation to the IOC and its disdainful President, Coubertin.

Although the federation was deemed a success by women athletes the world over [22], it faced financial difficulties that were underlined during the third congress on 31 July 1924. The President noted that 'According to our statutes, a Congress should be held every year' but that 'because of our financial problems, we have decided that the Congress will be held every two years and, in the intervening years, the international committee will meet'. [23] Two years later, the financial question had become a major problem on the agenda for the federation's fourth congress:

> Financial report – On July 31, 1926, the FSFI had 1,308 francs in its account; a bit more money remains to be collected but only prodigious efforts of economy have allowed the Federation to survive to date with such meagre resources. The Congress members agree that an increase in financial resources is needed and they are looking for ways to accomplish this. [24]

The subsequent minutes unfortunately cast no light on the solutions to this major problem. It is interesting to note, however, that this is the exact year that the IAAF entered into contact with the FSFI. Was this purely by chance? At this point, the FSFI had the human means, but not the financial means, to hold regular international competitions. [25] Moreover, track and field events were the major events in women's competitions. These are quite likely some of the reasons that the federation attracted the attention of the men's track and field federation. Before 1921, women's track and field interested very few of the IAAF leaders. But when the FSFI was created and then quickly developed to the point of having as many affiliated countries as the IAAF in 1926, this anomaly came to the attention of the IAAF leadership and was seen by certain sections as a symbolic threat calling the social order into question. [26]

The financial argument seems to be an important key to understanding the relationships between men and women in the world of sport. In any case, money provided a supplementary means for men to control women's sport by the withholding or granting of subsidies. In fact, the financial problems of the FSFI precipitated the meeting of the three institutions. Materially weakened, the women leaders finally had little choice but to become subject to the male order, despite their valiant efforts to maintain autonomy.

Women's Inclusion in the Olympic Games: A Cleverly Laid Trap

The Women's Olympic Games were among the first matters that Henri de Baillet-Latour had to deal with when he became IOC President in the autumn of 1925. From the first meeting of the IOC Executive Board on 3 to 6 November 1925, the Women's Olympic Games were an item on the agenda. However, the stated goal was not to hinder these Games or gain control of them. Only the name was a point of contention:

> Women's Olympic Games – [the Executive Board] was quite upset to find that the name 'Olympic' has been unrightfully appropriated by the organizers of the Women's Games and it will take the necessary steps to obtain the help of the international federations so that this designation, which is the property of the IOC, is exclusively reserved for the Games organized by the IOC the first year of every Olympiad. [27]

The same statement was issued to the organizers of the 'Student Olympic Games', which seems to prove that the board members' request was independent of any consideration of gender. President Baillet-Latour explained in a memo written to the IOC members on 8 December 1925: 'The IOC, far from being hostile to the development of sport among students and young women, can only regard with favour the efforts being made to stimulate physical education for them. Our only protest is the abusive use of the terms "Olympic Games, Olympiads, and Olympic Committee"'. [28]

Women's sport was thus not specifically targeted; however, the preference for 'physical education' rather than sport should be noted. This distinction was not without significance. Up until the Second World War, physicians in particular commonly recommended physical education for the health of society's 'weakest' members – children and women – instead of sport, which was judged too violent and risky. Baillet-Latour's opinion echoed that of Coubertin and thus seemed to conform to his social position and gender: he wanted no involvement in the development of women's sport but nevertheless reserved for himself the right to orient it – in a direction that was devaluing to women. The record of evidence of attitude of Sigfried Edström that is preserved in the IOC Historic Archives begins with documents dated 1926 and are even more offensive. The record shows that from this date onwards, the President of the IAAF was engaged in a struggle as both federation President and IOC Board member: with the FSFI, but also with the IOC.

Edström's first goal as IAAF President was to convince his colleagues on the IOC Executive Board to accept some women's track and field events in the Olympic Games programme. In fact, to organize the Games, each international sport federation recognized by the IOC had to submit a programme of events to the

Executive Board, then to the membership of the IOC. The archives show that throughout Baillet-Latour's presidency, all decisions taken by the Executive Board were systematically endorsed by the rest of the committee. [29] This effectively concentrated great decision-making power in the hands of a small number of men. In March 1926, Edström expressed his federation's opinion that four women's track and field events should be authorized for the 1928 Olympic Games. Remarkably, this request was made without any preliminary consultation with the FSFI. Here, the leaders of men's athletics made no attempt to hide their meddling in the organization of women's athletics, despite the fact that the women wanted to be independent of male control. The motives of Edström and his federation are clear: to gain control of women's track and field sports and, by extension, of any and all sports linked with athletics.

Despite the small number of events requested, the Swede's proposal was hesitantly greeted by his Executive Board colleagues, who postponed their decision to the next IOC plenary meeting. During the Olympic session in Lisbon in May 1926, the decision was finally made that the 'committee will admit a limited number of women to athletics competition in the Olympic Games'. [30] A narrow breach thus appeared in the hitherto entirely male programme of the Olympic Games, without the women leaders even being informed in advance. However, Reginald John Kentish, a British IOC member, lucidly and prophetically announced that 'the women's federations will [not] be satisfied by the IAAF's proposal to admit women to four events'. [31]

The FSFI and Alice Milliat were contacted by Edström shortly after the Executive Board meeting of March 1926. The principal objective of the international committee of the FSFI, which met on 28 April 1926, was to prepare for the next day's meeting with the IAAF members. Alice Milliat clarified that the discussions recently and unofficially started with the men's federation were at the initiative of Edström: 'Mr. Edström's proposal consists simply of the dissolution of the FSFI and the creation of a commission to oversee women's athletics, the members of which would be appointed by the IAAF'. [32] Nothing was said about the steps undertaken with the IOC. Even though the IAAF had deftly suggested the inclusion of certain 'leading members of the FSFI' in this commission, the proposal aroused a sentiment of revolt in the women's federation: 'All the federations are unanimous in wishing to maintain the autonomy of the FSFI. In particular, Great Britain, Switzerland, Italy, and Czechoslovakia vehemently and at length protested against the demands of the IAAF'. [33]

It was thus decided that

> the FSFI does not want to be dissolved, given the degree of success it has achieved. As a last resort, the creation of a technical commission composed of members from both federations [FSFI and IAAF] will be proposed to the IAAF, as well as the acceptance of a delegation of powers to the FSFI.

It was also planned that 'if we come to an understanding with the IAAF, the committee will drop the title of "Olympic Games" and replace it with "Women's Games"'. [34]

Despite the initial protests of the federation's women members, it is surprising to note that the leaders were ready to give up a part of their autonomy to the male federation. The argument advanced was that they were willing to 'do anything to avoid conflict with the IAAF'. [35] One can also imagine that the FSFI was seeking credibility. A male 'protectorate' would encourage the political and institutional powers of different countries to better subsidize the women's federations, for example. Once they had united into a single federation, the FSFI leaders were always careful to ensure that women had the majority vote in any decision-making body, but they also kept men aboard to facilitate their relations with the exterior. Keenly aware of the importance of doing this in a society where men held all the power, the FSFI leadership may also have used this logic in planning their proposal for the technical commission.

This critical meeting with the representatives of the IAAF was held the following day [36] and yielded the agreement expected by the FSFI leaders:

> The FSFI will direct the women's track and field sports in compliance with an advisory delegation of the IAAF. It will conform to the technical rules decreed by the IAAF, who will appoint a special commission for this, as well as for all decisions of a general order concerning this sport. [37]

The concrete value of this text was technical: it allowed women's athletics competition to be based on established sports regulations, which made it possible, for example, to ratify new world records. Satisfied with the agreement, the women leaders were ready to abandon the title 'Women's Olympic Games'. From then on, unaware of having opened wide the door to male control, Alice Milliat and her FSFI colleagues were locked into a process that would bring about their end.

The leaders discovered the IAAF's intentions only in August 1926, [38] during their fourth Congress: 'The President reported on the conversation that she had yesterday afternoon, August 28, with Mr Edström and Professor Kjellmann regarding this subject [incorporating women's competition into the Olympic Games of Amsterdam]. She declared that the FSFI had never made such a request'. [39]

The news provoked wide debate among federation members. The signatories of the IAAF agreement confirmed that participation in the Olympic Games had never been implied during the negotiations. Alice Milliat added that

> in her opinion, women's participation in the Olympic Games can only make sense if it is total, since women's athletics has proved itself and does not want to serve as an experiment for the Olympic Committee. If women's participation is so limited, it will not serve the cause of making women's athletics better known. [40]

The English representative, Sophie Eliott-Lynn, equally and energetically defended the autonomy of the women's athletics movement. [41] Certain FSFI members (men) were not opposed to women's participation in the Olympiads. To curtail debate, decisions were postponed until the next meeting of the federation's international committee. While waiting, Alice Milliat entered into contact with Baillet-Latour.

Instead of negotiating with the IAAF members to try and convince them to go back on their decision to include women's competition in the track and field programme, Milliat chose to address the IOC directly to defend the interests of the women athletes. Instead of arguing for the removal of women from the Olympic Games, she asked that they participate fully (that is, in as many competitions as at the Women's Games). This particular decision by Alice Milliat reveals her unwillingness to enter into conflict with the IAAF, as well as her hope perhaps that, should the IOC accept her request, the FSFI would be able to resolve its financial problems. Unfortunately, on both counts the FSFI President would be disappointed.

Between 20 November 1926 and 27 April 1927, 11 letters were exchanged by Alice Milliat and the IOC. The FSFI President had two demands: she wanted the promise of full and regular participation of women in Olympic track and field events and a total recognition of the FSFI at the same level as all the other international federations affiliated with the IOC. Specifically, she argued that two full days be devoted to women athletes during the 1928 Games and that all 12 women's track and field events from the Women's Games be integrated into the Olympic Games by 1932. Lastly, the President sought to have the FSFI members serve on the national Olympic committees (NOCS).

Faced with these fervent demands, Baillet-Latour tried to stall by postponing the study of these questions to the annual Olympic session of April 1927 where, finally, the IOC members ably entrenched themselves behind the Olympic regulations. Their response was that the decision to increase the size of the women's Olympic programme could only be made by the international federations. Since the IOC only recognized one federation per sport, this meant that the FSFI had to turn to the IAAF. A further argument was that only the NOCs decided on their membership and that the IOC could thus not intervene at this level. Given these replies, one might think that the IOC had only a limited decision-making capacity, which was obviously not the case. Its members could indeed choose the number of women's events, and each, as a member of his country's NOC, could intervene to help FSFI leaders to serve on the NOCs. But Alice Milliat once again ran into the brick wall of a closed system whose regulations perfectly protected it from outsiders. The IOC knew how to protect its Executive Board, which itself exercised power over the international federations and NOCs, which in turn reinforced and protected the power of the Executive Board. This strategy of protection was the expression of a hegemonic masculine conservatism. Women's sport was never once openly disapproved of in the course of the IOC's meetings with the FSFI. However, at other moments, the opinions of the IOC President, Henri de Baillet-Latour, and Executive Board member Sigfried Edström were made clear. Women could participate in the Olympic Games only on condition that they in no way cast a shadow over the men. The Executive Board was, for example, very attentive to the ratio of men to women in each sports discipline. In 1927 and 1933, the international federations of gymnastics and swimming were called to order because their ratios were deemed too favourable to the women. [42] For the Olympic leaders, women athletes were welcome, but only on condition that the men remain dominant and that the women respect the existing social order.

Women's participation further declined when the IOC was faced with the problem of 'gigantism' in the Games. Sigfried Edström did not hesitate to propose the total removal of women, revealing himself to be, along with Baillet-Latour, one of the leaders most resistant to women's sport. This radical view was underlined by Adams in her citation of a letter from the IAAF President: 'I suppose you know that Mme Milliat's Federation has caused us so much trouble that we certainly have no interest at all to support it. We should like the whole thing to disappear from the surface of the earth'. [43] Baillet-Latour, however, was well aware of the difficulty of imposing his point of view:

> I can only hope for one thing: to soon see the day when women are completely freed from the tutelage of men so that they can organize their own worldwide Women's Games, because this would allow us to exclude them completely from the Olympic Games. I would have made the proposal in Berlin last year if I hadn't been absolutely sure of having no chance of seeing it passed. [44]

As he could not totally remove the women, the IOC President proposed a limited number of socially acceptable sports for them: swimming, gymnastics, tennis and figure skating, and rejected all activities that were judged too energetic or not aesthetic. [45] But in this period between the two world wars, the men's leaders were actually divided on the issue of participation of women in the Olympics. Certain leaders seemed to recognize their demands as legitimate, while others, such as the IAAF, only wanted to better control them. Whatever the case, this division prevented the disappearance of women from the Olympic Games in the inter-war period.

In 1928, the Olympic Games of Amsterdam had 277 women participating, more than three times as many as at the previous Women's Games in Göteborg (Sweden) in 1926, and this was despite the more restricted number of events and a boycott by the British women's federation. [46] The first official participation of women was thus a success, but to the future detriment of the FSFI. At the next Olympic Games, in 1932 in Los Angeles, and then in 1936 in Berlin, the number of events barely increased, but the rise in the number of women continued: 126 women travelled to the United States despite the distance and 331 women went to Germany. The introduction of competition at the Olympic Games thus sounded the eventual death knell for the FSFI. Meanwhile, as its leadership continued the struggle to survive financially and organize the Women's Games, the tutelage of the men's federations allowed these to control the numbers and practices of women in the Olympic Games and to respond to the athletes' financial needs, which Alice Milliat's federation could no longer do. In 1928, the French government reduced its subsidies to the FSFI by two-thirds. The Women's Games were held in Prague in 1930 and then again in London in 1934, but the battle-weary Alice Milliat soon quit the federation, and on 6 August 1936 the FSFI vanished with her while the Berlin Games were in full swing.

Conclusion

The brief existence of the FSFI (from 1921 to 1936) was enough to create the momentum and international unity needed for the growth of women's sport between the two world wars. The repeated, regular and successful organization of the Women's Games was a source of worry for the men's sports movement: the domination and power of men in organized sport were threatened in the face of the women's demands. The IAAF leaders, seeing the opportunity to benefit from the federation's financial weakness, provoked the entrance of women athletes into the Olympic Games with the sole goal of better controlling its development. This manoeuvre was against the will of the women's leaders. It brought about the death throes of the Women's Games and eventually of the FSFI, despite the constant and active opposition of its President, Alice Milliat, and the particularly vocal British members. The tragic destiny of this federation was the work of the men's sports movement, in particular through the combined forces of the IAAF and the IOC. This shared history of three international sports institutions highlights the major role of the Swede Sigfried Edström, who used his dual membership in the IAAF and the IOC to subjugate women in Olympic sport. It also reveals the profound disdain of this leader for women athletes, who were perceived to be threats to the established social order. The members of the IOC, even when divided on the issue of women's sport, all ultimately supported the social principle of women's domination by men. Whether they wanted to see a complete separation between the women's and men's sports movements, like IOC President Henri de Baillet-Latour, or preferred to integrate the women in order to better control them, like the majority of members, one principle was common to them all: sport is the affair best led by men. After the Second World War and the death of Henri de Baillet-Latour, Sigfried Edström became President of the IOC and remained so until 1952. He was then succeeded by his good friend Avery Brundage, who would carry forward the Olympic tradition of stringent control over women that had occurred during the period between the two wars into his presidency, much to the detriment of women athletes.

As a final note, it should be added that this shared history emphasizes the asymmetry at the heart of the men's and women's sports movements. Although this period between the two World Wars is an important time in the history of worldwide women's sport, it is but an anecdote in the IOC's overall history, threatened at the time by the growing power of international federations, the incessant debates about amateurism versus professionalism and the thorny problem of preparing for the Berlin Olympic Games in 1936. [47]

Acknowledgements

This study was made possible through a grant from the Postgraduate Research Grant Programme of the IOC Olympic Studies Centre, located in the Olympic Museum in Lausanne, Switzerland. All translations are our own.

Notes

[1] Since 1991, all new sports included in the Olympic programme must have women's events. In 1995, the first 'women and sport' working group was created among the IOC members to promote women's admission to the Olympic Games, as well as to the general sport movement, but only in 2004 under the presidency of Jacques Rogge did it become a permanent commission of the IOC.

[2] According to the IOC, on its website in 2006, www.olympic.org/uk/organisation/missions/women/activities/women_uk.asp

[3] 'The Games organization enabled its members to make decisions regardless of external influences': Mitchell, 'Women's Participation', 209.

[4] Count Henri de Baillet-Latour became President of the IOC in 1925, after the resignation of Pierre de Coubertin, and remained so until his death in 1942. He was born in Brussels in 1876. King Leopold of Belgium offered him the opportunity to organize and direct sport in Belgium. He presided over the National Committee on Physical Education, which oversaw all Belgian sports federations. In 1903, he joined the IOC and the following year he founded the Belgian Olympic Committee. The count organized the Third Olympic Congress in Brussels in 1905. Through his influence and personal competence, he was able to organize the 1920 Olympic Games in Antwerp, despite the difficult post-war context. The result of this success was that Baillet-Latour became an increasingly influential member of the IOC. He became a member of the new IOC Executive Board that was created in 1921, and he was 49 years old when he was elected by a wide majority to succeed Coubertin as IOC President in 1925.

[5] Henri de Baillet-Latour was President of the IOC until 1942. Because of the Second World War, however, the Committee's work was substantially curtailed from 1939 through to 1946.

[6] For this topic, see Carpentier, *Le Comité International Olympique en Crises*.

[7] Maternity was the principal concern behind this argument. The strength of a nation was greatly dependent on the health of its childbearing women, and this was a major preoccupation of the Third French Republic (1870–1936).

[8] 'Whereas for men's sport, the vast majority is there to watch the sport so that the lowest of the low in the crowd can be ignored, it will always be different for women's sport.... There is nothing to learn by watching them; also, those who assemble in this goal do so for reasons having little to do with sport': Coubertin, *Pédagogie sportive*, 114.

[9] Traditionally, the sports on the Olympic programme posed no problem for women's participation as they were deemed 'socially' acceptable. Tennis, golf, sailing, archery and equitation were aristocratic sports. For the aristocrats of the end of the nineteenth century, it was normal for women to join men in their leisure activities. The playing field thus became a place for meeting and socializing among individuals of the same social origins. Artistic skating, swimming and diving were also within the norms established for women in the period between the two world wars. Skating and diving had a strong aesthetic component that was closely associated with femininity. Swimming, on the other hand, was perceived as an essentially health-oriented practice at the beginning of the twentieth century and was thus deemed important for women, for the reasons cited above.

[10] Mitchell, 'Women's Participation,' 211–2.

[11] Alice Milliat was born on 5 May 1884, in Nantes, France, to middle-class parents. She studied to become a teacher. Her interest in sport certainly predates the First World War, as during the war she was an active member of the French club Femina Sport. In the years between the two wars, she was a well-known personality in women's sport, active as a leader and very much present for the athletes. She was 38 years old when she became President of the Fédération Sportive Féminine Internationale in 1922. She died in Paris in 1957. For a biography (though quite incomplete), see Leigh and Bonin's 'The Pioneering Role of Madame Alice Milliat' and Drevon's *Alice Milliat*.

[12] Minutes of the fourth Congress of the FSFI, 27–29 Aug. 1926, Göteborg, Archives du Musée National du Sport, Paris, France (hereafter AMNS).

[13] Pierre de Coubertin remained hostile to the participation of women athletes throughout his life. This was displayed in 1935, two years before his death, in his radio speech of 4 August in Berlin: 'To my eyes, the true Olympic hero is the *individual male adult*'. (Coubertin, 'The Philosophic Foundation of Modern Olympism', 13).

[14] Despite the claim, for example, of Uriel Simri ('The Development of Female Participation').

[15] Sigfried Edström was born on 21 November 1870, in Göteborg, Sweden. He studied engineering in Sweden and Switzerland before going on to become in 1903 the President of the largest electrical company in Sweden. As a committed athlete, he also became involved in developing and organizing sport in his country as President of the Swedish Gymnastics and Sports Association and the Swedish Amateur Athletic Association. Most importantly, he was the founder-President of the IAAF (1913–46). His Olympic career began in 1920 with simple membership, when he was 50 years old. In 1921, he was elected to the new Executive Board of the IOC. He became its vice-President in 1937 and then served as its President after the Second World War until 1952.

[16] The English and American feminist movements appeared at their most virulent just before 1914, at which point they seemed to lose steam and remained disorganized through the 1920s and 1930s. In contrast, the French feminists made greater demands in the post-First World War years. For an overview of the different feminist movements in America and Western Europe, see Thébaud, *Histoire des Femmes en Occident, Le XXe Siècle*; Evans, *Born for Liberty*; Cott, *The Grounding of Modern Feminism*; or Katzenstein and McClurg Muller, *The Women's Movements of the United States and Western Europe*.

[17] In addition to the minutes of the diverse committee meetings, this concerns essentially all the active and passive correspondence of the President, Henri de Baillet-Latour, and the members of the IOC Executive Board between 1925 and 1940.

[18] The FSFI archives are conserved at the Musée National du Sport, Paris, France. They comprise all the minutes from meetings and congresses between 1921 and 1936, the period of its existence.

[19] See the references.

[20] Twenty thousand spectators attended the first Games, according to Leigh and Bonin, 'The Pioneering Role of Madame Alice Millliat'.

[21] Minutes of the second Congress of the FSFI, Paris, 18 Aug. 1922 (AMNS).

[22] For financial and material reasons, the 1926 Göteborg Games had fewer participants than the 1922 Paris Games – 81 as against 101. In contrast, from 1922 onwards the number of participating countries and athletic events continued to grow and the duration of the Games was extended (from a single day in 1921 and 1922 to three days in 1926).

[23] Minutes of the third congress of the FSFI, Paris, 31 July 1924 (AMNS).

[24] Minutes of the fourth congress of the FSFI, Göteborg, Sweden, 27–29 Aug. 1926 (AMNS).

[25] The organization of the 1926 Göteborg Games was made possible by private funding. The French women's delegation, which was overlooked by the male sport authorities, also had to raise private funds to send the athletes to Sweden. For this reason, only eight French women were in the delegation, although there were 50 in 1921.

[26] 'The success of the Games [of 1921] increased the awareness and fears of both the IOC and the IAAF', according to Adams, 'Fighting for Acceptance', 144.

[27] Minutes of the IOC Executive Board, Paris, 5 Nov. 1925 (IOC Archives, Lausanne, Switzerland, hereafter AIOC).

[28] Memo from Henri de Baillet-Latour, 8 Dec. 1925, Baillet-Latour/Blonay, correspondence, 1915–37 (AIOC).

[29] See Carpentier, *Le Comite International Olympique en crises*.

[30] Minutes of the Olympic session of the IOC, Lisbon, 6 May 1926, 25th session of Lisbon, 1926 (AIOC).

[31] Reginald John Kentish, IOC Executive Board minutes, Paris, 7 March 1926 (AIOC).

[32] Minutes of FSFI international committee meeting, Paris, 28 April 1926 (AMNS).

[33] Ibid.

[34] Ibid.

[35] Ibid.

[36] The IAFF was represented by its President, Sigfried Edström; a Frenchman, Joseph Genet; and a Belgian, Wydemans. The FSFI was represented by its President, Alice Milliat; a British member, Major Marchand; and a Czechoslovakian, V. Valousek. The only woman present to defend the women's cause, Alice Milliat, also served as the 'secretary' of the meeting. Minutes of the IAAF-FSFI commission, Paris, 29 April 1926 (AMNS).

[37] Ibid.

[38] Despite the fact that the decision to systematically distribute the minutes of the IOC meetings was made in November, 1925, in 1926 they were not always widely distributed. Those who wanted access to them had to pay a fee of ten Swiss francs per year. Not surprisingly, Alice Milliat and the FSFI leaders found it difficult to stay abreast of all decisions concerning them.

[39] Minutes of the fourth FSFI congress, Göteborg, 29 Aug. 1926 (AMNS).

[40] Ibid.

[41] See Duval, 'The Development of Women's Track and Field'.

[42] The International Gymnastics Federation authorized the participation of 16 to 18 women and seven or eight men at the 1928 Olympic Games. The swimming programme of the 1936 Olympic Games comprised nine events for men and seven for women. Minutes of the IOC Executive Board meetings, Lausanne, 31 Oct. 1927, and Vienna, 5 June 1933 (AIOC).

[43] Letter from Sigfried Edström to Avery Brundage, 3 Jan. 1935, ABC Box 42, reel 24 (Archives of the International Centre for Olympic Studies, University of Western Ontario, Canada), cited by Adams, 'Fighting for Acceptance', 144.

[44] Letter from Henri de Baillet-Latour to Godefroy de Blonay, 31 Aug. 1931, Baillet-Latour, correspondence, 1931–38 (AIOC).

[45] Minutes of IOC Executive Board meeting, Lausanne, 11 June 1932 (AIOC).

[46] See Wamsley and Schultz, 'Rogues and Bedfellows', 115.

[47] See Carpentier, *Le Comité International Olympique en Crises*.

References

Adams, Carly. 'Fighting for Acceptance: Sigfrid Edström and Avery Brundage: Their Efforts to Shape and Control Women's Participation in the Olympic Games'. Paper presented at the Sixth International Symposium for Olympic Research, 2002: 143–8.

Carpentier, Florence. *Le Comité International Olympique en Crises* [The International Olympic Commitee through its Crises]. Paris: L'Harmattan, 2004.

Cott, N.F. *The Grounding of Modern Feminism*. New Haven, CT: Yale University Press, 1987.

Coubertin, Pierre de. *Pédagogie Sportive*. Paris: G. Crès, 1922.

——. 'The Philosophic Foundation of Modern Olympism'. *Revue Olympique* 14 (1949).

Drevon, André. *Alice Milliat, la* Pasionaria *du Sport Féminin* [Alice Milliat, the *Pasionaria* of Women's Sport]. Paris: Vuibert, 2005.

Duval, Lynne. 'The Development of Women's Track and Field in England: The Role of the Athletic Club, 1920s–50s'. *The Sports Historian* 1 (2001): 1–34.

Evans, S. *Born for Liberty: A History of Women in America*. New York: Free Press, 1989.

Katzenstein, M.F. and C. McClurg Muller, eds. *The Women's Movements of the United States and Western Europe: Consciousness, Political Opportunity and Public Policy*. Amherst, MA: University of Massachusetts, 1986.

Leigh, Mary H. and Thérèse M. Bonin. 'The Pioneering Role of Madame Alice Milliat and the FSFI in Establishing International Trade and Field Competition for Women'. *Journal of Sport History* 1 (1977): 72–83.

Mitchell, Sheila. 'Women's Participation in the Olympic Games 1900–26'. *Journal of Sport History* 2 (1977): 208–28.

Simri, Uriel. 'The Development of Female Participation in the Modern Olympic Games'. *Stadion* 4 (1980): 187–216.

Thébaud, F., ed. *Histoire des Femmes en Occident, Le XXe Siècle* [Women's History in the West; Twentieth Century]. Paris: Plon, 2002.

Wamsley, Kevin B. and Guy Schultz. 'Rogues and Bedfellows: The IOC and the Incorporation of the FSFI'. Paper presented at the Fifth International Symposium for Olympic Research, 2000: 113–8.

Conflicts of 1930s Japanese Olympic Diplomacy in Universalizing the Olympic Movement

Sandra Collins

Promoting 'Exquisite' Japan at the Annual IOC Sessions

No one expected Tokyo to win the host city bid race for the 1940 Olympic Games in the early 1930s, least of all the Japanese national government. Rome had been the favoured candidate, given both its proximity to the other European nations that dominated the Olympic community and its inability to host the 1908 Olympic Games due to the unfortunate 1906 volcanic eruption of Mount Vesuvius. [1] Most members of the International Olympic Committee (IOC) were convinced that 1940 was for Rome. Many believed that nothing short of a miracle could save the Tokyo campaign. Also, before convincing the IOC of the value of the Tokyo Olympic Games, Tokyo campaigners had to first persuade Japanese nationals. The chaotic state of 1930s Japanese domestic politics had serious consequences for the Tokyo campaign. Constant cabinet changes, unstable political alliances, deepening friction between the House of Peers and representatives in the Diet, and the expanded role of the military in the national government prevented the emergence of an influential national leader to champion the Tokyo campaign. [2] In 1933, the Tokyo City Bid Committee began two simultaneous movements: a domestic campaign to convince the government officials of the nationalistic merits of the Tokyo Olympics and an effort to promote Tokyo internationally as a venue that would truly universalize the Olympics. It may be suggested here that the 1932 IOC Session does mention an interest shown by Tokyo to host the 1940 Games. However, it was from 1933 that this effort had assumed far more serious proportions. [3]

At the 1933 IOC Session held in Vienna, the Tokyo campaign relied upon time-tested measures in promoting the city of Tokyo. The Japanese IOC delegate, Kanô Jigôrô, networked with members of the IOC through formally organized lectures, including one on judo, and officially hosted a sumptuous IOC banquet that facilitated private conversations with fellow IOC colleagues. [4] With the help of the IOC delegate in Austria, Theodor Schmidt, the Tokyo campaigners 'improved the impression of Japan a great deal before each IOC member'. [5] Soon after the Vienna IOC Session ended, however, Rome announced its campaign for the 1940 Games as a national priority. The competition from Rome forced the Tokyo bid campaigners to acknowledge that a more nationally unified Japanese movement was required to compete against Rome. [6] IOC member Kanô Jigôrô supported a more nationally based campaign: 'Just as Mussolini is leading the campaign for Italy, it is imperative that our plan to bring the Olympics to Tokyo must be supported by the entire nation and not just by the city of Tokyo'. [7] The City Bid Committee decided to draft a plan to expand its membership to include the desired cabinet ministers and other government officials. [8] Until this new invitational committee was formally adopted by the national government, the City of Tokyo and the JAAA decided to be jointly responsible for the Tokyo bid. [9] In order to help promote the Tokyo candidature internationally, the Tokyo Assembly approved a three-year, 200,000 yen ($100,000) budget for the campaign.

In the new year of 1934, the campaign employed more radical means to promote Tokyo which came into direct conflict with the established protocols of the IOC. First, advocates of the Tokyo bid elicited the advice of diplomats and ambassadors, who were not IOC members and therefore considered outsiders to the Olympic community. It was common practice to focus on select IOC members, and the move by Tokyo to campaign directly to nationally appointed ambassadors, outside the framework of the IOC, was extremely novel. [10] Tokyo campaigners met with Belgian Ambassador Passonpierre, who advised the Bid Committee on how to make the Tokyo bid attractive to Europeans, saying that 'Tokyo should also stress that the Olympic Games have not been held in the East'. [11]

At the 1934 IOC Session at Athens, Tokyo inaugurated its new campaign by accentuating the attractiveness of its candidacy, in part by characterizing Japan as unique in the world system. A close reading of the representational strategies used by the proposal reveals how the Tokyo Olympiad became tied to the larger issues facing

1930s Japan. To each of the members of the IOC present at the Session, Kanô presented a small tan-coloured booklet with the title 'Tokyo: Sports Center of the Orient' embossed in gold on the upper right hand corner. [12] The proposal outlined specific features of the Japanese bid, but the majority of the booklet consisted of black-and-white photographs of various scenes throughout Japan, with an emphasis on Tokyo. The proposal's rhetoric and the semiotic imagery of the photographs highlighted the unique ability of Japan to blend the distinct culture and heritage of the 'East' in what was characterized as Western forms of modernization and industrialization. Tokyo, Japan was presented as a visual puzzle of the old within the new and the West within the East.

The booklet played a critical role in stimulating the emerging discourse on the nationalistic importance of the 1940 Tokyo Olympiad. For the first time, the 1940 Tokyo Olympic Games were placed in a direct relation to nationalistic concepts that were gaining currency in the 1930s: the spirit (*seishin*) of Japan, *bushidô* (way of the warrior) and the commemoration of the 2,600th year of *Kigen*. The Tokyo proposal stressed the ability of Japan to successfully adapt and modernize while simultaneously retaining her unique cultural and imperial dynasty: 'To set the Twelfth Olympiad against the background of a civilization thousands of years old, against the national celebration of the Empire's 2,600th anniversary under a single Imperial Dynasty, would be to lend to the competitions an added interest, a *complementary* attraction'. [13] As an *unique* nation state that embodies both the East/West and the old/new, Japan was presented as the perfect candidate to host the Games, for only Japan among many nations realized a *rare* montage of the old within the new. Bid officials coded the unseen traditional values and forms of old Japan as visible in the speed and shock of Tokyo's modernity: '[I]t is only with difficulty that the foreign visitors to these cities recover from the shock of Tokyo's modernity ... as concomitant of a strictly Western stature. It [Tokyo] is a city which had made immense progress, while still advancing at an almost unbelievable rate'. [14] The proposal reflected the growing sentiment of many Japanese ideologues, that Japan alone of all industrialized world powers could preserve its indigenous and irreducible cultural elements with its technical achievements. Similar to the readings by H.D. Harootunian and Tetsuo Najita that analyse the pre-war discourses on Japanese modernity as a revolt against the West and as a form of cultural exceptionalism, the proposal also similarly appropriated these discourses to show Japan as a distinctive empire among all world powers. [15]

The Japanese Diplomatic Scandal at the 1935 Oslo IOC Session

After the success of the 'Athens' booklet in defining the significance of a Tokyo Olympiad both domestically and internationally, the Tokyo Bid Committee escalated its international campaign with more aggressive and unprecedented diplomatic tactics. In order to ensure the success of Tokyo at the upcoming vote for the 1940 Games at the 1935 Oslo IOC Session, proponents of the bid sought to increase the attractiveness of the Tokyo candidature through several measures. First, in order to alleviate the economic hardship of dispatching Olympic delegates from Europe to Asia, the Tokyo City Assembly heeded the advice of the Belgian Ambassador and ratified a measure to secure one million yen to subsidize foreign travel to Tokyo. [16] Secondly, Tokyo Bid Committee members promoted the Tokyo Olympics to the national government as a venue for promoting people's diplomacy (*kokumin gaikô*) that would enable the world to understand the real Japan. The Tokyo Olympics became important to the nation state of Japan as it faced increasing international isolation. A Tokyo official identified this fact:

> If you ask why we must make great sacrifices and efforts in order to compete against other nations for the Olympic Games, it is...the thinking that given today's international situation, it is of the utmost importance that we attract numerous foreigners to our nation in order to promote a correct understanding and appreciation of our nation. [17]

One year after Japan left the League of Nations, the Olympic Games were transformed into a forum for Japanese diplomacy. But the national government, however eloquent the bid rhetoric, remained partially uncommitted, although the mayor continued to press for a meeting with the Prime Minister. Tokyo Mayor Ushizuka succeeded in meeting with the Minister of Foreign Affairs, Hirota Kôki, to discuss the role of the Foreign Ministry in the bid. [18] The mayor emphasized the diplomatic merits of the Tokyo bid for the Japanese nation: 'Is it not a sincere and appropriate desire to want to host the Games in the Far East, especially in our nation, so that our world rank will be seen by all the people of the world who support the Olympic Games?' [19]

According to the Tokyo campaign, the 1940 Olympic Games would satisfy several goals for Japan. The 1940 Olympiad would commemorate the founding of the Empire within an international context, which would provide Japan with the distinguished acknowledgement by the international community as being the first Asian host of the Olympic Games, which could then in turn help promote positive international relations for Japan. During an era in which Japan was growing increasingly isolated from the outside world, hosting an Olympiad could be invaluable to Japan. The continued international isolation, however, began to fuel Japanese suspicions that the world did not understand the true nature of Japan. As Lyn Spillman has described in another analytical context: 'Relations to the rest of the world defined national identity in two ways.... The world's gaze confirmed the distinct national identity and an identification with other powerful nations also strengthened it'. [20] The Tokyo City Bid Committee also believed that the Tokyo Olympiad could positively influence Japan's international standing. However, the foreign affairs minister declined to provide his support for unspecified reasons.

With the continued failure to receive support from the national government, the Tokyo campaign resorted to more aggressive measures to ensure the international appeal of the Tokyo candidacy. IOC delegate Kanô challenged the IOC President on the claims made by the IOC concerning the universality of the Olympic Movement: 'Since the inauguration of the International Olympic Games, they have been held only in Europe and America, but, to our great regret, never in Asia, which has nearly one half of the world's inhabitants'. [21] Kanô then argued that the Olympics must belong to all of the world, and that Japan with its amazing athletic accomplishments should be the first Olympic host outside the West: 'I believe that athletic interest is now world-wide and that Japan has shown sufficient loyalty to the Olympic Spirit and athletic ability since her participation to the Games to command the confidence of the IOC'. [22] Cognizant that the biggest weakness of the Tokyo candidature was the distance from Europe, Kanô gave the IOC President two critical pieces of information. Firstly, 1940 would draw far more tourists to Japan than any other time because of the imperial jubilee, 'because we can expect millions of visitors to Tokyo from both in and outside of the country at that time'. [23] Secondly, Tokyo would help subsidize the travel costs for the European teams to the Far East. Kanô detailed the travel subsidy that the Tokyo Municipal Assembly had approved. [24] With his letter he enclosed an English translation of the letter written by Tokyo Mayor Ushizuka Tôratarô. In it, the mayor mirrors the plea of Kanô and beseeches the President to 'please ask every member of the IOC to vote for Tokyo as the Olympic City of 1940, and thus help us to realize the true spirit of the Olympiad, because in spite of Japan's loyalty to the Olympic Spirit, the Games have not yet been held in the Orient'. [25] Tokyo Mayor Ushizuka also contacted each IOC delegate individually by cablegram: 'The Mayor of Tokyo asks you to please vote for Japan as host to the 1940 Olympic Games'. [26]

The watershed event that guaranteed the success of the Tokyo campaign was also the most controversial for any host city in the history of the IOC bidding process. The City of Tokyo commissioned the Japanese IOC delegates, Sugimura Yôtarô and Count Soyeshima Michimasa, to meet with Italian Prime Minister Benito Mussolini before the start of the Oslo IOC Session. [27] It was highly controversial for any member of the IOC to actively campaign to any politician, let alone the head of state outside the Olympic community. Nevertheless, the Japanese IOC delegate Soyeshima was sent to Rome in January 1935 to join Sugimura in imploring Mussolini to withdraw the candidature of Rome for the 1940 Games in favour of Tokyo. [28] On 8 February, Soyeshima explained to Mussolini why Rome should rescind her claim in favour of Japan: '1940 is the 2,600th anniversary of the Japanese empire. The ardent desire of all the citizens of Japan is to host the 1940 Olympic Games to celebrate this national holiday'. [29] Soyeshima pleaded with Mussolini that 'if the Olympics were held in Tokyo it would help to bind together in close bounds of amity the East and West, thus contributing to the peace of the world'. [30] The Duce Mussolini surprisingly agreed: 'We will waive our claim for 1940 in favour of Japan if Japan will support Italy's effort to get the XIIIth Olympiad for Rome in 1944'. [31] While some speculated that using the 1940 Tokyo Olympics to commemorate the 2,600th year of *Kigen* appealed to the dynastic pretensions of Mussolini, others believed the escalation of the 'incident' between Italy and Ethiopia was the true reason behind the unexpected support by Mussolini for the Tokyo bid. [32]

The withdrawal of Rome on behalf of Tokyo by Mussolini became an instant media sensation in Japan. Sugimura forwarded a telegram to Hirota Kôki, the minister of foreign affairs, reporting: 'We should thank Mussolini for his goodwill. We [Soyeshima and Sugimura] ended our meeting with Mussolini in extremely good spirits, promising to enthusiastically support Rome's candidacy for 1944 in exchange for the friendly gesture from Italy'. [33] Armed with the concession of Mussolini, Tokyo Mayor Ushizuka escalated his aggressive domestic and international campaigns in the final weeks before the IOC vote. The endorsement by Mussolini proved influential in securing the support of the Japanese national government. Not only did the mayor succeed in gaining the approval of Prime Minister Okada Keisuke and Foreign Minister Hirota Kôki, he also managed to get a joint resolution passed in both houses of the Diet. Foreign Minister Hirota telegraphed instructions to all consuls and consul-generals residing in Europe and the United States to assist the Tokyo bid. [34] Elite representatives of the Tokyo campaign who were also Diet members encouraged colleagues to transcend factional politics and jointly draft a measure that would pledge the united support of the Japanese national government for the Tokyo Olympiad. [35] The Tokyo bid officials believed that successful passage of the measure would convince the delegates at the Oslo IOC Session that the Tokyo campaign was in fact a national movement. [36] Later, the House of Representatives addressed the measure, debating the Games as important for Japan in 'improving our physical education, increasing international goodwill and advertising Japanese culture abroad'. [37] The proposal was recorded as being unanimously approved. [38] The prestigious House of Peers also supported the 1940 Olympic bid. [39] Hosting the Olympic Games in Japan was a chance to 'advertise the culture of Japan to each nation'. [40] Baron Baba Yoriyasu described in national terms why the Tokyo campaign was so important to Japan: 'If we are chosen to host the Olympics in Tokyo it is not just the acknowledgement that our athletic competitions have progressed but that renascent Japan has advanced in worldly and grand terms'. [41]

Just as the Tokyo campaign was finally becoming a national priority for Japan, it was also becoming the centre of controversy for the IOC. As the organization responsible for the Olympic Games in Italy, CONI made its first public statement clarifying the candidature of Rome. Contrary to the assertions made by Mussolini and the Japanese IOC delegates, CONI stated that it; 'has not abandoned its general policy to campaign for the 1940 Olympics'. However, CONI publicly announced that if Rome was awarded the 1944 Games, it would support Tokyo for the 1940 Games. [42] Not only was the concession made by Mussolini unprecedented in the history of the IOC; the additional stipulation made by CONI regarding Rome for 1944 was also highly unusual. CONI issued a conflicting public statement the following day, intimating to many that the issue was unresolved for Italian Olympic officials. CONI declared: 'Although Italy agreed to waive the right to host the 1940 Olympics in

Rome to Japan, we did not agree to withdraw Rome's candidacy with the stated condition that the XIIIth Olympiad must be in Rome'. [43] The Japanese press also reported that 'whether Rome will remain a candidate or not will actually be decided at the Oslo IOC Session'. [44] Although Benito Mussolini ruled Italy, it was in fact Henri Baillet-Latour who governed the IOC.

At the Oslo IOC Session, the Japan-Italy negotiations over the Tokyo candidature became a controversy that threatened IOC control over the Olympic Games. [45] The state-to-state-organized discussions between Japan and Italy over the 1940 Olympic host city bid was the first of its kind at the time in Olympic history, and the IOC perceived the negotiations as threatening the IOC monopoly over deciding any issue concerning the Olympic Games. [46] At the IOC Session, Japanese IOC delegate Sugimura Yôtarô dutifully informed his IOC colleagues that Mussolini promised to support Japan for the 1940 Games and that Italy would battle against Lausanne and other candidates for the 1944 Games. [47] In response, the IOC President mentioned that only the venue for the 1940 Games was to be decided at the Oslo Session and the venue for the 1944 Games was out of the scope for the Session. [48] Count Alberto Bonacossa, the Italian IOC delegate, further complicated matters by rescinding the verbal promise given by Mussolini to withdraw Rome in favour of Tokyo. [49] Bonacossa demanded that Italy remain a candidate for 1940. [50] Count Bonacossa confided that 'surely what was meant by Prime Minister Mussolini was to give the Italian IOC delegates votes to Japan and not to renounce the candidacy of Rome'. [51] Nothing like the behind-the-scenes negotiations between Italy and Japan had ever occurred before in the history of the bidding process for the Olympic Games. The IOC President was confronted with how to resolve the unprecedented issue during the Oslo Session at which the final vote for the 1940 Olympiad was to take place. The Japanese press reported that the IOC President was to hear from all involved parties and if the situation was not resolved, the vote would be deferred until the 1936 IOC Session in Berlin. [52]

Despite the uncertainty over which cities were candidates for the 1940 Games, the proposals for Tokyo, Rome and Helsinki were detailed on the opening day of the 1935 IOC Session. [53] Sugimura first presented the candidature of Tokyo, outlining the athletic facilities, hotel accommodation and the one-million yen ($500,000) travel subsidy recently made available to help with travelling expenses. [54] He declared: 'Since the Olympic Games have been held in Europe eight times, in the United States twice and not in Asia, the Games should be held in Asia in order to be truly international'. [55] Sugimura continued:

> In order for the Olympic Games to be truly international in reality and not just in name, various nations from the Eastern hemisphere must also contribute to the Olympic Games. Japan would like to host the XIIth Olympic Games not to profit its capital city, but because every Japanese citizen loves sports and wants to celebrate its 2,600th national birthday by hosting the Games. The XIIth Olympics would be a grand opportunity to commemorate this national event, as well as to offer something unique to international sports. [56]

In response to the dispute over the candidature of Rome, Bonacossa claimed 'Mussolini would surely rescind his sacrifice of favouring the Tokyo bid'. [57] Count Bonacossa then detailed the facilities in Rome. Lastly, Ernst Krogius briefly presented the Finnish invitation. The Helsinki proposal reflected the concern of many European IOC delegates of travelling to the Far East so soon after the comparably distant 1932 Los Angeles Games. Finnish officials explained how a Tokyo Olympiad would weaken the Olympic Movement in Europe:

> We on our part can hardly think that the nations of Europe are again prepared to decide that the Games be held outside Europe; expensive voyages – despite all magnificent offers – enormous loss of time for all participants, hardly any participation on the part of the European public and in consequence thereof diminished interest in the Olympic Games in Europe, these would be the consequences of holding these Games outside the Continent to which they of right belong. [58]

Many Europeans believed that the 1940 Olympiad should remain in Europe.

Although Mussolini telegrammed his response instructing the Italian representatives to retract the Rome candidature, the issue was not resolved for the IOC. [59] The Italian Foreign Ministry released an official statement regarding the 1940 Games, declaring that the Italian government rescinded Rome's candidature 'not as a political act, but as a gentleman-like gesture'. [60] Sugimura faithfully informed other IOC members that evening of the telegram from Mussolini and pressed for the candidature of Rome to be withdrawn. [61] The general consensus at the IOC Session, however, was that Mussolini did not have the authority to make any concessions regarding the Olympic Games, and that the political intervention must be denounced as restricting the progress of the IOC. [62]

The IOC formally discussed the different candidates on 1 March 1935 and tried to resolve whether the final vote for the 1940 venue should take place as planned during the IOC Session. Some IOC delegates expressed the opinion that since only a minority of IOC delegates were present at Oslo and given that the votes were mailed without knowledge of the negotiations that took place between Japan and Italy, the decision to vote should be postponed until the following year. [63] IOC chairman Baillet-Latour stated that 'The vote for the 1940 Olympic Games will be postponed until next year in light of the fact that recent outside political interference created this impossible situation which ignored the rules and tradition of the IOC that it is the IOC that disposes of the Olympic Games'. [64] The unprecedented decision to postpone the vote astounded many concerned with the Olympic Movement. The remaining candidates, Helsinki and Tokyo, welcomed the deferral as an opportunity to escalate their promotional campaigns. In Finland, many believed that the postponement greatly improved the chances of Helsinki. Drawing attention to this sentiment, the *New York Times* reported Finnish sport leaders 'asserted that Japan's impetuous attempt to secure the Games spoiled Finland's chances and created rather unpleasant feelings'. [65] In Japan, it was stated that the baffling postponement was an opportunity to 'foment Olympic fever in our nation'. [66]

Not all members of the Olympic community responded positively to the state-to-state pact negotiated between Japan and Mussolini that led to the postponement of the 1940 Olympic venue vote. The President of the IOC, Count Baillet-Latour, publicly condemned the Japan-Italy pact because it was 'outrageous that any IOC member would try to exert any political influence' over any Olympic concern. [67] Count Bonacossa also criticized the Japanese negotiations with Mussolini for '[t]he IOC should be independent, sincere and unfettered by external (political) intervention'. [68] In response, Sugimura took great offence to the remarks made by counts Baillet-Latour and Bonacossa. Sugimura attacked the belief held by the IOC that it alone had the authority to determine matters concerning the Olympic Games:

> This issue of 'outside political interference' is nothing other than the IOC members of Japan conveying to Rome that Japan hopes to host the 1940 Olympic Games. Consequently, the members of Our Imperial Government and the Italian Government who have supported the Rome and Tokyo bid for the 1940 Games have been involved in numerous negotiations which do not violate [*shingai*] the independence or freedom of the IOC. [69]

But for the IOC, what was at stake with the Japan-Italy pact was its control of the Olympic Games. The IOC President believed that the IOC alone had the authority to determine any matter concerning the Olympic Games. Any agreements reached between members outside of the Olympic community were viewed as actions that encroached upon the authority of the IOC to decide an Olympic issue. As the role of national governments increased in the 1930s, the political dimension of the Games also intensified. The Japan-Mussolini negotiations were viewed by Japan as a logical extension of the national policy that did not interfere with the jurisdiction of the IOC over the Olympic Games.

Although the IOC President gave the Japanese delegates some latitude for being 'newcomers' who 'knew nothing of the rules and tradition of the IOC', the President nevertheless condemned the negotiations. He implored the Japanese delegates:

> Under the impression that you were doing the right thing you got in touch with authorities outside the committee, which was bound to create an impossible situation, the IOC being determined to retain alone the right and the privilege of disposing free of any influence of the Olympic Games which are its own property. [70]

Finally, the IOC President earnestly requested that the Japanese delegates stop all 'outside work'. [71] Other representatives of the Tokyo campaign were also urged by the IOC President to use less aggressive promotional tactics in the Tokyo bid effort. The IOC President cautioned Tokyo campaigners, stating; 'There are many political decisions to make when allocating the site for the Olympic Games. I think that Japan should wait patiently, quietly for the right opportunity to address these issues, rather than attack them too aggressively'. [72] Thus he was clearly advising Japan to abstain from any further political negotiations about the Tokyo bid in order to avoid any more conflicts. The politeness that the President reserved for the Japanese delegates was absent in the frank letter Baillet-Latour wrote to his predecessor, Pierre de Coubertin:

> The [Oslo] Session went well, very Olympic, for it was unanimously agreed to show with no uncertainty that we were not going to let governments force our hand and have the assignment of the Games depend on political reasons.... Postponing the decision to next year was wise. No one will come back any more with secret arrangements and we will be able to vote in complete independence. [73]

The conflict over the Japan-Italy pact on the 1940 Games was the first instance of many disagreements between Japan and the IOC President about the assumed tradition of behaviour and ethics governing the institution of the IOC.

The international publicity from the controversy over the Japan-Mussolini pact and the postponement of the vote escalated the Tokyo campaign as a national concern in Japan. After five years of discussion, the Education Ministry finally agreed to provide national leadership for the bid effort. [74] The Education Minister, Matsuda Genji, adopted the outline for an official national Bid Committee that was drafted earlier by the JAAA and the City of Tokyo. [75] Matsuda explained why the Olympic Games were critical to Japan:

> [The] Olympics is an opportunity for our nation to host one of the world's grandest ceremonies for the first time in Asia, which is truly significant. It is also an extremely opportunistic chance to impress on a wider group of foreign spectators the civilization and humanity of our nation and to recognize the actual situation of our nation. [76]

A new 'Invitation Committee' was formed in December 1935 to include 68 members from several prominent official positions, such as Japanese International Olympic Committee representatives, the Mayor of Tokyo and vice-ministers from the cabinet. [77] The formation of this more national Invitation Committee, coupled with the support of the National Diet, signalled that the 1940 Tokyo Olympic Movement had finally shifted from being a municipal to being a national concern. [78]

The IOC President Goes to Japan

The Oslo IOC Session proceedings revealed the degree to which the IOC President was ambivalent towards the Tokyo candidacy, and Tokyo bid officials vowed to change his opinion by inviting him to Japan. Japanese sport officials described the IOC President as being 'sympathetic towards Japan only as a curious object of exoticism, like one would love a cute pet. In his innermost thoughts, he does not think that Japan could be called a strong Olympic host candidate despite the fact that Japan is a top-ranked sports nation'. [79] Accordingly, the Bid Committee decided upon yet another unprecedented move: to have the City of Tokyo invite the IOC President to inspect Tokyo and Japan. [80] In fact, it was the IOC President who coached the Bid Committee on how to invite him to tour Japan and how to present his trip to Japan to the international media so as to not appear partial to Finland. [81] Baillet-Latour agreed to visit Japan on the condition that the city of Tokyo pay his expenses and publicize his tour as a 'private trip'. [82] He encouraged the Japanese Foreign Ministry to work with the City of Tokyo to label the tour a 'private trip' (*kojinteki ryokô*) which was unprecedented in the history of IOC protocols. [83] The highly controversial nature of the inspection tour required the exercise of utmost discretion from the Japanese government and also the IOC President. [84]

As planned, the Japanese media helped promote the trip as a 'personal, pleasure trip'. The Tokyo *Asahi* reported that this was the second visit for the IOC President to Japan. [85] Despite the 26 February military coup, Baillet-Latour arrived in Yokohama as planned on 19 March and was greeted by a large group of elementary schoolchildren waving the Olympic flag. [86] The Invitation Committee promoted Tokyo with ceremonial fanfare and kept Baillet-Latour busy with various conferences, inspections and receptions, including a rare audience with the Emperor. 'Even the Emperor', Baillet-Latour later told the international press, 'who is very interested in the topic granted me a 30-minute talk during which we discussed all aspects of the Tokyo bid'. [87]

The IOC President was soon converted into a strong supporter of the Tokyo candidacy, making the trip worthwhile, but only under specific conditions that he stipulated to the bid officials. He soon outlined conditions under which he would publicly support Tokyo hosting the Olympic Games at a conference organized by the JAAA during his tour of Japan. [88] He stated:

> Present economic conditions in many of the European countries are such that this would prevent many from coming. Now, they may really like Japan, and they may really dislike Finland, but as in all matters where the pocket-book makes the decision, they may be obliged to vote for the latter because of the relative costs involved. It is therefore quite necessary to find the best possible means to bringing the athletes here in such a way as to minimize this handicap. [89]

Next, the IOC President stated that he believed that Tokyo would emerge as a formidable candidate if the Invitational Committee could guarantee the following conditions:

1. Increasing the previous unprecedented travel subsidy of one million yen by 500,000 yen;
2. Hiring a technical adviser appointed by the IOC;
3. Appointing a capable staff of translators;
4. Guaranteeing that the cost of board and lodging expenses would not exceed two gold dollars per day;

5. Guaranteeing the sum of five gold dollars per day for each official, not to exceed 200 officials (or 1,000 gold dollars per day);
6. Holding the Games around the last week of August and first week of September. [90]

Finally, he declared that in his personal opinion, Tokyo was capable of hosting the Olympic Games. To members of the foreign press, the IOC President confided: 'I will vote for Tokio [sic]...Japan might very well see the XII Olympiad take place in Tokio'.

In order to remain neutral in the eyes of the IOC, the President also planned another 'personal' trip to Finland in June. [91] In a private letter to Pierre de Coubertin, he mentioned traveling to Finland 'in order to not be accused of partiality' to Japan. Baillet-Latour was most impressed with Japan and stated:

> I came back from Japan, enthusiastic about the very Olympic sportsmanship of the Japanese. They deserve the Games; besides it would be an excellent thing to give the so-called sportsmen of Europe and America the opportunity to see what a nation can do, a nation that has not been contaminated by our evils [of professional sport]. [92]

Baillet-Latour and fellow IOC delegate Theodor Lewald arrived in Finland on 3 June 1936, and stayed for only five days. [93] The Finnish Bid Committee brought the count to the new stadium that was being erected in Helsinki for the 1940 Games. While the IOC President's tour was enthusiastically received by the Finnish people and exhaustively covered by the Finnish press, the IOC President left Finland still an ardent supporter of Tokyo.

The Unexpected London Bid for the 1940 Games

The international publicity surrounding the development of the favourable opinion of the IOC President towards the Tokyo candidature seemed to secure the success of the Tokyo bid. However, news of the positive visit to Japan by the President may also have spurred British Olympic officials to bid for the 1940 Games in order to prevent the Games from being held so far from Europe. The unexpected London bid forced yet another round of aggressive campaign manoeuvres from not just those representatives of the Tokyo bid but also the IOC President himself. Although Baillet-Latour had previously denounced the Japanese negotiations with Mussolini, this time around the IOC President was uncommonly silent regarding the Japanese negotiations with various British politicians and Olympic officials. In fact, the strong unprecedented support given to Tokyo by Count Baillet-Latour indicated the extent to which the hospitality of the visit to Japan improved the stature of Tokyo in his eyes.

Prior to the last-minute bid by London, only Helsinki remained a viable competitor for Tokyo; in fact no one expected London to vie for the 1940 Games.

The Lord Mayor of London, Sir Percy Vincent, was circumspect enough to inform the British government foreign secretary before submitting the official invitation to the IOC. [94] In response, the office of the foreign secretary replied that 'from the point of view of foreign policy...we should be quite glad to see the next Olympic Games held in London, and that we can therefore safely tell the Lord Mayor that we see no objection'. [95] On receiving sanction, the Lord Mayor of London sent the official invitation to Count Baillet-Latour formally applying for the 1940 Games. [96] The British Olympic Association (BOA) soon informed each IOC delegate that London was officially applying for the 1940 Games.

In response to the unexpected candidacy of London, members of the Tokyo Bid Committee vowed to negotiate with influential British politicians, Olympic officials and businessmen in order to persuade London to withdraw in favour of Tokyo. Tokyo Mayor Ushizuka sent an urgent cablegram on 30 June to the Lord Mayor of London stating that the XIIth Olympic Games had been the ardent desire of Japan for years and requested the Lord Mayor to rescind London's candidacy. [97] The mayor responded by saying 'he is deeply sorry that he cannot support the entreaty to rescind the invitation'. [98] After sailing on the Queen Mary, Count Soyeshima arrived in London ready to initiate another series of behind-the-scenes negotiations, but this time with the British. Soyeshima believed that the London bid was based on the failure of the English to realize that 'the Japan proposal for the Olympics is unusual in that the year falls on the 2,600th national anniversary, and that all Japanese – from the emperor to the people – are completely united in their desire for the Games'. Through thoughtful diplomacy, Soyeshima was certain that London would come round to withdrawing its candidacy. [99]

Count Soyeshima continued his meetings with British officials and finally emerged victorious because the British government decided not to complicate British foreign policy with Japan. Also, the London candidature caught the attention of Sir Robert Vansittart, the permanent under secretary, who pushed for the BOA to withdraw the bid. Vansittart communicated to the British Cabinet:

> It is quite true that in principle it is better for Governments not to intervene, but I feel that it is a matter for serious consideration whether in view of Japanese sensitiveness, their very great desire to have the Games held in Tokyo in 1940 and the difficulties that we are having and are likely to have with Japan in the Far East, His Majesty's Government should not on this occasion intervene and suggest to the British Committee that they should make a graceful gesture and withdraw in favour of Japan. [100]

The Cabinet decided to take appropriate steps to 'give the British [Olympic] Committee a hint not to put forward the proposal'. [101] Soon after, Soyeshima met with IOC President Baillet-Latour in London to discuss the recent turn of events, including the press release from British authorities that the British government supported the Tokyo bid. [102] The IOC President told Soyeshima that he personally hoped that the Tokyo bid would be successful and confided: 'The Olympic Games have been held in the United States twice and in Europe nine times. I believe that the time is most opportune for the first Olympic Games to be held in the Far East. [103] In an unprecedented move, Baillet-Latour dispatched letters to each IOC delegate expressing his support for the Tokyo bid. [104] Soyeshima also met with Lord Aberdare of Duffryn, the IOC member for Great Britain, to plead on behalf of the Tokyo campaign. [105] Lord Aberdare informed Count Soyeshima that London would be withdrawing the bid for the 1940 Games. [106] Rather than reprimand Japan for another series of behind-the-scenes negotiations that interfered with the Olympic Movement, the IOC now championed the cause of Japan for Tokyo to host the 1940 Games. [107]

The 1936 Berlin IOC Session

The fate of the 1940 Olympiad was to be determined by a vote of IOC delegates scheduled to take place during the 1936 Berlin IOC Session. The working meetings of the Session began on 30 July 1936, days before the historic Berlin Olympic Games were slated to start. [108] The campaigners for Tokyo had succeeded in their aggressive and unprecedented diplomacy in promoting Tokyo's candidacy: not only did the President of the IOC now publicly support Tokyo, but also the cities of Rome and London withdrew their candidacies after the diplomacy exacted by Japan. After explaining the reasons that led to postponing the allotment of the Games during the 1935 IOC Session in Oslo, the President announced that since then Rome had withdrawn her candidature and another city, London, had extended hers. When he was called to present the candidature of London, Lord Aberdare explained:

> My British colleagues and I have during this last twenty-four hours realized that members of the International Olympic Committee have considered that London has put in her entry rather late in the day – although perfectly legitimately – and that in consequence in the best interests of the Olympic Ideal, I am empowered not to press its application but to put in its formal application for the Games of 1944. [109]

Thus, living up to his promised to Count Soyeshima, Lord Aberdare duly withdrew the London candidature for the 1940 Games.

The candidature of Tokyo was then presented using a variety of promotional strategies. At the IOC Session, the rhetoric of the bid began to incorporate the dimension of internationalism in the Olympics Games. Kanô appealed to the ideology of Olympism, by arguing that 'Since the revival of the Games, they have been celebrated in Europe and the United States exclusively. Asia wishes to have them in her turn'. [110] Fellow IOC delegate Count Soyeshima detailed different aspects of the Tokyo candidature: travel subsidy, the total budget of 15 million yen, and Tokyo's athletic facilities. Soyeshima concluded: 'The Japanese people hope to greet the athletes of the world. The Olympic ideals would be strengthened throughout the Orient through the assignment of the twelfth Olympic Games to Tokyo'. [111]

Japanese bid officials viewed Japan as uniquely positioned to disseminate Olympic ideals throughout the world, for they saw Tokyo as the new centre of the world and a formidable imperial power. Tokyo was presented as the most logical entry point for popularizing the Olympic Movement in Asia. In addition, the bid rhetoric of 1936 encouraged the IOC to assume the difference between the East and West, while the definition of what constituted a harmonious blending was left unanswered. Count Soyeshima described the importance of the Tokyo Olympiad as blending the different cultural heritages of the East and West:

> The true aspects of Japanese culture, old and new, would be open to the eyes of the world. Therefore, the organizers are advised to be well aware of the fact that the most careful attentions should be given in the preparations in order to convey the true spirit of the East and West and to aim at the harmonious blending of the two great cultures. [112]

Furthermore, the financial package emphasized that Japan had not only gained enough surplus capital to invest in the construction and planning required to host the modern Olympics, but also to finance the travel and living expenses of foreign athletes. [113] The financial package was unprecedented in Olympic history; no other host nation had ever resorted to subsidizing the participation of other nations. [114]

Additionally, Count Baillet-Latour used his influence as IOC President to ensure the success of the Tokyo bid by declaring that he felt 'justified in recommending Tokyo as the choice for his colleagues, a choice which would mean the extension of the Olympic ideals to this part of the world'. [115] After the presentation of the Tokyo and Helsinki candidatures, IOC members discussed the candidates before they voted. The IOC minutes reported:

> Certain members dwell upon the universal character of the Olympic ideals which demand that the Games be held in all parts of the world. Others, speaking for the smaller nations, point out that their financial resources make it difficult for them to participate in distant lands, and that if there is not a return to simplicity the increasing grandeur accompanying the celebration of the Games will render their participation in future Olympiads impossible. [116]

Many IOC delegates perceived that voting for Tokyo was symbolically linked to universalizing the Olympic Games while voting for Helsinki was tied to increasing the participation of both small and large European nations.

The final vote between Tokyo and Helsinki was expected to be close. [117] After several hours, with a final vote of 36 to 27, the Games of the Twelfth Olympiad were allotted to the City of Tokyo. After seven long years of aggressive campaigning and politicking, Japan won the right to host the 1940 Olympiad. The careful diplomacy of the Japanese, the forceful rhetoric of universalizing the Olympic Games and the generous financial package (perhaps the first documented 'Olympic' bribe) supporting travel to the Far East all undoubtedly added to the attractiveness of the Tokyo bid. Despite the fact that Japanese Olympic diplomacy was interpreted as conflicting with existing Olympic protocols, Tokyo was successful in its attempt to win the right to host the Games. By exerting careful and calculated political influence, the Japanese received IOC support for Tokyo. From 1936, when Tokyo won the 1940 Games, until 1938, when Tokyo rescinded the Games, the Japanese were involved in the national project of how best to showcase inter-war Japan to the Olympic fraternity. [118] Many debates erupted within Japan – over planning the Olympic flame relay, the location of the main stadium, the degree to which Japanese nationalism would be showcased and so on – that were never resolved when the Games were finally cancelled. [119] Afterwards, Helsinki would be awarded the Games until the outbreak of the Second World War led to the cancellation of the Olympic Games until 1948 in London. The first campaign to bring the Olympic Games to Asia would only be fully realized in 1964 with the staging of the Tokyo Games.

Acknowledgements

I would like to thank the very helpful research staff of the IOC Olympic Studies Centre, located in the Olympic Museum in Lausanne, for their assistance while I was a postgraduate research fellow. I would also like to thank the staff at Sports Library of Finland, the Sports Archives of Finland, the City of Helsinki archives and the Carl Diem Archive at the National Sports Library in Cologne, Germany.

Notes

[1] Rome was awarded the Games on 22 June 1904, and after Rome rescinded in 1906, London hosted the 1908 Olympic Games. See Coates, 'London 1908'. On the eruption itself, see 'Vesuvius', *New York Times* 10 April 1906, 6 and 'Volcano Victims May Number 500', *New York Times*, 10 April 1906, 1.

[2] The standard work on 1930s domestic politics in Japan is Berger, *Parties Out of Power*.

[3] It may be suggested here that the 1932 IOC Session does mention an interest shown by Tokyo to host the 1940 Games. However, it was from 1933 that this effort had assumed far more serious proportions.

[4] Kanô even lectured on judo, putting many IOC members into a deep sleep. Diem, 'Reise nach Wien zum Olympischen Kongress'.

[5] Schmidt traveled to Japan after the Los Angeles Olympic Games. The 32nd Session of the IOC was held from 7 to 9 June 1933, and the number of delegates for Japan was increased to three. The only other nations to have three delegates at the same time were Great Britain, the United States, Germany, France and Brazil. Kanô specifically recommended Sugimura Yôtaro (1884–1939), who held a doctorate in law. At the time of his nomination, Sugimura was the director of the Political Bureau of the League of Nations and later became the Japanese Ambassador to Italy. See Dai-jûnikai Orinpikku Tokyo taikai soshiki iinkai, *Hôkoku*, 6, 8; Kanô Jigoro, 'Orimupikku iinkai yori kaeri', 2–4; *Official Bulletin of the International Olympic Committee* (Sept. 1933), 9; and Kanô Jigôrô, 'Orimuppikuiinkai yori karite', 2.

[6] Tokyo-tô, *Sôchi kara henjô made*, 3; 'Orimuppiku yûchi shijunbiiinkai' ['The Tokyo City Olympic Bid Preparations Committee'], *Asahi* (Tokyo), 19 July 1933; and Tokyo shiyakusho, *Tokyoshi Hôkoku*, 9. It may be mentioned here that many other cities had initially expressed

an interest in hosting the 1940 Games. These include Alexandria, Budapest, Barcelona, Dublin, Buenos Aires, Montreal/Tokyo. London had come into the picture much later and asked to be remembered for 1944.

[7] Kanô discussed this at a reception held in his honor upon his return from Vienna on 22 Nov. 1933. See *Tokyoshi kôhô* [Tokyo City Bulletin] 2347 (12 Dec. 1933), 2341; *Tokyoshi kôhô* 2341 (28 Nov. 1933), 2237; Tokyo shiyakusho, *Tokyoshi Hôkoku*, 4, 10; and Tokyo-tô, *Sôchi kara henjô made*, 3.

[8] The City Bid Committee met on 29 September 1933 and decided to enlist the help of the national government by the setting up of an Invitation Committee. The Invitation Committee membership included: the Tokyo City Bid Committee members, the Tokyo Chamber of Commerce, the Japanese Amateur Athletic association (hereafter JAAA), the Japanese IOC members, ministers from the foreign, home, finance, education, railways and telecommunications ministries, ambassadors to various countries, the police super-intendent, the governor of Tokyo-fû, and the mayors of the largest five cities in Japan. 'Shikai Orimuppikuiinkai' ['Tokyo City Assembly Olympic Bid Committee'], *Asahi*, 30 Sept. 1933.

[9] It would take another two years, until 1935, for the new Invitation Committee to be formally established.

[10] The meeting took place on 15 March 1934. Tokyo-tô, *Sôchi kara henjô made*, 3 and *Tokyoshi kôhô* 2385 (17 March 1934), 2386.

[11] 'Tokyo Orimuppiku undô ni: gaikô no daiippô' ['The First Step in Foreign Diplomacy for the Tokyo Olympic Games'], *Asahi*, 16 March 1934 and Kusayama, 'Tokyoshi to kokusai orimupikku', 38.

[12] The pamphlet, *Tokyo: Sports Center of the Orient*, was the first publicity material created by the Tokyo Municipal Bid Committee (established in May 1933) for the express purpose of documenting Japanese culture and sports for the IOC. A remaining copy of the original pamphlet can be viewed at the Amateur Athletic Foundation of Los Angeles file on the 1940 Olympic Games. The Tokyo Municipal Government, *Japan: Sports Center* (Tokyo: Tokyo Municipal Office, 1933). The pamphlet was widely discussed at the time: Kusayama Shigenobu, *Orimupikku* 12 (Dec. 1934): 38; Terabe, *Orinpikku wo Tokyo he*, 5; and Tokyo shiyakusho, *Tokyoshi hôkoku*, 11. The pamphlet cost about 25 yen in 1934, see Zen-nihon taiiku shinkôkai, *Seika ha higashi he*, 92.

[13] Tokyo Municipal Government, *Japan: Sports Center*, iii.

[14] Ibid.

[15] Japanese philosophers such as Watsuji Tetsuo and Yanagita Kunio have written on representations of Japan as mixed or hybrid. See Harootunian and Tetsuo Najita, 'Japanese Revolt', 711, 762 and 766; Harootunian, *Overcome by Modernity*.

[16] Based on previous advice given by several foreigners to the Bid Committee, the Assembly unanimously voted on 27 December 1934 to provide 1,000,000 yen ($500,000) to subsidize the travel of Olympic athletes and officials in order to increase the attractiveness of the Tokyo candidature. The Tokyo bid campaign had an overall budget of 5,000,000 yen. Tokyo-tô, *Sôchi kara henjô made*, 5.

[17] Kusayama Shigenobu, 'Tokyoshi to kokusai Orimupikku sôchi undô' ['The City of Tokyo and the Campaign for the Olympic Games'], *Orimupikku* 12 (Dec. 1934), 38.

[18] The meeting took place on 10 January 1935. On the same day, letters were sent to each IOC member from the Tokyo Mayor requesting their support for the Tokyo bid. Tokyo shiyakusho, *Tokyoshi hôkoku*, 14.

[19] Ushizuka to Hiroda, 28 Jan. 1935, Tokyo shiyakusho, *Tokyoshi hôkoku*, 15; Tokyo-tô, *Sôchi kara henjô made*, 5.

[20] Spillman, *Nation and Commemoration*, 92.

[21] Jigoro to Baillet-Latour, Tokyo, 10 Jan. 1935, Tokyo, 1940 XIIth Olympic Games Candidature Dossier, IOC Archives.

[22] Ibid.

[23] Ibid.

[24] The Belgian Ambassador Baron de Bassompierre advised the Bid Committee to obtain a travel subsidy during their meeting on 15 March 1934. *Tokyoshi kôhô* 2385 (17 March 1934), 2386.

[25] Ushizuka to Baillet-Latour, Tokyo, 27 Dec. 1934, accompanied by Kano to Baillet-Latour, 10 Jan. 1935, Tokyo, 1940 XIIth Olympic Games Candidature Dossier, IOC Archives.

[26] The letter from the mayor and Kano was dated 10 Jan. 1935. The cost to dispatch telegrams to each IOC delegate was 1,800 yen. Tokyo-tô, *Sôchi kara henjô made*, 5.

[27] On the recommendation of Kano Jigoro, Sugimura Yotaro became the third IOC delegate in Japan in 1934. When Sugimura was a student at the Tokyo Imperial University, he met Kano during judo practice. Sugimura continued to give judo demonstrations during his diplomatic trips to Europe. In 1935, Sugimura was the Japanese Ambassador to Italy and was stationed in Rome. After Sugimura, Soyeshima Michimasa became an IOC member in 1934 upon the death of Kishi Seiichi. Soyeshima was sometimes spelled Soejima in various Olympic materials. IOC, *Olympic Biographies*, 170, 174.

[28] On 16 January 1935, the day Japanese delegates were scheduled to meet with Mussolini, Soyeshima fell ill with high fever, but insisted that he accompany Sugimura to the meeting. While waiting for Mussolini, Soyeshima fainted and was rushed to his hotel room where a doctor was called to examine him. The meeting was later rescheduled. Soyeshima to Baillet-Latour, Rome, 5 Feb. 1935, Soyeshima IOC Member's Correspondence Dossier, IOC Archives.

[29] Soyeshima Michimasa, 'Roma ni tsukaishite' ['The Mission to Rome'], *Orimupikku* 13 (May 1935), 9; Soyeshima to Baillet-Latour, Rome, 5 Feb. 1935.

[30] Soyeshima to Dr Graeff, Yasukuni-maru, 15 March 1935, Soyeshima Letters, His Imperial Highness Prince Chichibu Memorial Sports Library Archive, Tokyo.

[31] Ibid.

[32] Imamura Shichiri, 'Orinpikku Tokyo taikai kittei no shinsô' ['The Truth Behind the Decision for the Tokyo Olympic Games'], *Kaizô* 19 (February 1937), 95–6.

[33] Zen-nihon taiiku shikôkai, *Seika ha higashi he*, 90.

[34] Tokyo Mayor Ushizuka Torataro, Municipal Assembly President Mori Toshinari and Tokyo Bid Committee President Tatsuno Tamotsu met with cabinet ministers on 14 February 1935. Tokyo-tô, *Sôchi kara henjô made*, 6; 'Orimuppiku dandan yûbô' ['The Olympics Gradually Become Hopeful'], *Asahi*, 14 Feb. 1935, 13(G); 'Orimuppiku sôchi' ['The Olympic Bid'], *Asahi*, 15 Feb. 1935, 2(C); 'Orimuppiku Tokyo ni kakuteiseba' ['If Tokyo is Chosen for the Olympics'], *Asahi*, 14 Feb. 1935, 2(C).

[35] The measure, 'Tokyo ni okeru daijûnikai kokusai Orimupikku taikai kaisai no ken' ['The Campaign to Host the XII Olympic Games in Tokyo'] stated that sports and the Olympics must be supported by Japan as a form of cultural enterprise. In the House of Peers, former Tokyo mayor Nagata Hidejiro, along with JAAA vice-President Hiranuma Ryôzô and IOC member, Kanô Jigôrô, submitted the measure that was discussed on 25 February 1935. In the House of Representatives, Hatoyama Ichirô, Noda Junsaku and Sawayo Hiroji were the spokesmen. See *Kanpyô*, 26 Feb. 1935, 112–13; Tokyo *Asahi*, 'Orimpikku dandan yûbô' ['The Olympics Gradually Become Hopeful'], 14 Feb. 1935, 3(G).

[36] Text of 14 Feb. 1935 telegram in Frederick W. Rubien to Brundage, telegram, 15 Feb. 1935, Avery Brundage Collection at the University of Illinois, Urbana-Champaign, Correspondence with IOC Members file (microfiche copy at IOC Archives). See also Tokyo-tô, *Sôchi kara henjô made*, 6; Tokyo shiyakusho, *Tokyoshi hôkoku*, 18; and 'Orimuppiku dandan yûbô' ['The Olympics Gradually Become Hopeful'], *Asahi*, 14 Feb. 1935, 13(G).

[37] The measure was signed by Hatoyama Ichirô, the Education Minister, and introduced by Shimada Shuno, a member of the Tokyo City Bid Committee, during the 23 February 1935 meeting of the House of Representatives. "Daijûnikai kokusai Orimupikku taikai keihihojo kengian" (The Proposal to Financially Assist the XIIth Olympic Games; in Japanese). Shûgiin jimukyoku, *Teikoku gikai shûgiin iinkaigiroku, showahen*, vol. 54, 12–13.

[38] Ibid., 13.

[39] The measure was entitled 'Tokyoni okete dai jûnikai kokusai Orimupikku taikai kaisai no ken ni kansuru kengi' ['The Proposal Concerning the Case of Tokyo hosting the XII Olympic Games']. See *Kanpyô*, 26 Feb. 1935, 112.

[40] Ibid.

[41] Ibid., 113.

[42] This was the first official statement regarding the candidature of Rome after Mussolini promised to concede the 1940 Games to Japan on 13 February 1935. The press release is reprinted in full in both Zen-nihon taiiku shinkôkai, *Seika ha higashi he*, 92 and 'Ikunini jôkenari' ['Italy Has Stipulations'], *Asahi*, 15 Feb. 1935, 2(C).

[43] 'Kyôteki herushinki' ['Helsinki Formidable Enemy'], *Asahi*, 16 Feb. 1935, 3(G); Zen-nihon taiiku Shinkôkai, *Seika ha higashi he*, 92.

[44] 'Rakkan ha dekinai' ['We Cannot Be Optimistic'], *Asahi*, 15 Feb. 1935, 3(G).

[45] The Oslo IOC Session took place from 25 February to 1 March 1935. Sugimura Yôtarô Report 'Dai jûnikai orinpikku kaisaichi ni kansuru Osurô kokusai Orinpikkuiinkai gijikeika hôkoku no ken' ['Report on the Proceedings at the Oslo IOC Session on the Campaign for the XII Olympic Games'] to Hiranuma Ryozo, JAAA President, and Ushizuka Ryotaro, Tokyo Mayor, March 1935, Count Soyeshima Michimasa Letters, His Royal Highness Prince Chichibu Memorial Sports Library Tokyo, Japan (hereafter cited as Sugimura Report). The Sugimura Report was also reprinted in the May 1935 issue of *Orimupikku* magazine. 'Soyeshima taishi osurochaku' ['Ambassador Sugimura Arrives in Oslo'], *Asahi*, 24 Feb. 1935.

[46] Negotiations and candidates standing down in favour of other bid cities was, however, nothing new. Baron Coubertin's original idea to have the first Games in Paris in 1900 (Sorbonne Congress participants enthusiasm meant that Paris instead became the host of the II Olympiad and Athens hosted the I Olympiad in 1896); in the bid race for 1916 both Alexandria and Budapest withdrew before the decision; in the bid race for 1920 both Amsterdam and Lyon stood down before the voting; and the 1924/1928 awarding of the Games to Paris and Amsterdam was made smooth by the fact that before the voting in Lausanne in 1919, Amsterdam had almost received a 'half-promise' that it would get the 1928 Games.

[47] Sugimura Yôtarô, 'Sugimura Report', *Orimupikku* 13 (May 1935), 14.

[48] As for Athens and Paris (1896 and 1900), in June 1921, the IOC announced the selection of two future sites together: Paris (1924) and Stockholm (1928). See Goldstein, 'Amsterdam 1928'.

[49] Sugimura Report, 2; 'Ikuni taido ippenshi' ['Italy's Position Completely Changes'], *Asahi*, 26 Feb. 1935, H(3); 'Italy's Delegate Challenges Japan's Bid for the 1940 Olympics', *New York Times*, 26 Feb. 1935, 23.

[50] 'Italy's Delegate Challenges Japan's Bid for 1940 Olympics; Finland Seen as Choice', *New York Times*, 26 Feb. 1935, 23; Sugimura Yôtarô, Sugimura Report, *Orimupikku* 13 (May 1935), 15.

[51] Sugimura Report, 2.

[52] '"Roma ha hisshô" to Ikuni daiyô yôgen' ['"Italy's Certain to Win" Asserts Italy's IOC Member'], *Asahi*, 27 Feb. 1935, C(2).

[53] Official Bulletin of the International Olympic Committee, August 1935, 7.

[54] Ibid.

[55] Sugimura Yôtarô, Sugimura Report, *Orimupikku* 13 (May 1935), 16.

[56] 'Manba wo shita ensetsu, Sugimurashi no shishiku' ['The Speech that Overpowered the Full Session, the Empassioned Talk of Mr Sugimura'], *Asahi*, 27 Feb. 1935, 13(H).

[57] Sugimura Yôtarô, Sugimura Report, *Orimupikku* 13 (May 1935), 16.

[58] Finnish Olympic Committee, 'Invitation', January 1935, 1935 Dossier, IOC Sessions, IOC Archives.

[59] Kawasaki, 'Osurô kaigi no zengo', 32; Sugimura Yôtarô, Sugimura Report, *Orimupikku* 13 (May 1935), 19; 'Italy Drops Claim for 1940 Olympics', *New York Times*, 28 Feb. 1935, 6.

[60] '44nen taikai ha roma wo kibô' ['Rome Wants the '44 Games'], *Asahi*, 1 March 1935, 1(C).

[61] Sugimura Yôtarô, Sugimura Report, *Orimupikku* 13 (May 1935), 19. Again, there is no mention of this decision in the official minutes of the IOC Session.

[62] 'Tokyo kaisai no unmei?' ['What Is the Destiny of the Tokyo Bid?'], *Asahi*, 1 March 1935, 3(H).

[63] 'Orimuppiku kaisaichi tsuini kettei wo enki' ['The Vote for the Host of the Olympics is Finally Postponed'], *Asahi*, 2 March 1935, 13(H).

[64] Sugimura Yôtarô, Sugimura Report, *Orimupikku* (May 1935), 20; Sugimura Report, 8; 'Wireless to NYT', *New York Times*, 28 Feb. 1935, 26; 'To Decide Next Year on 1940 Olympic Site', *New York Times*, 2 March 1935, 5.

[65] 'Finland Is Optimistic', *New York Times*, 3 March 1935, S(4).

[66] 'Mochikoshi ha saishin' ['The Deferment was First in History'], *Asahi*, 2 March 1935, 13(H).

[67] 'Omoikurushii teinoryû' ['The Heavy Undercurrent'], 2 March 1935, *Asahi*, 13(H).

[68] 'Orimupikku' ['The Olympics'], *Asahi*, 3 March 1935, 2(C).

[69] Sugimura Yôtarô, Sugimura Report, *Orimupikku* (May 1935), 20–1.

[70] Baillet-Latour to Soyeshima, 9 Feb. 1935, Lausanne, Tokyo Candidature, 1940 XIIth Olympic Games Candidature Dossier, IOC Archives; Count Soyeshima Michimasa Letters of His Royal Imperial Highness Prince Chichibu Memorial Sports Library Archive.

[71] Baillet-Latour to Kano, 9 Feb. 1935, Tokyo Candidature, 1940 XIIth Olympic Games Candidature Dossier, IOC Archives.

[72] During the International Student Track and Field Association meeting, Baillet-Latour advised Professor Yamamoto on 9 Aug. 1935; 'Orimuppiku Tokyo kaisai kyôgi' ['The Discussion on the Tokyo Olympic Venue'], *Asahi*, 11 Aug. 1935; 'Tokyo taikai yûbô' ['The Promising Tokyo Games'], *Asahi*, 12 Aug. 1935.

[73] Baillet-Latour to 'Mon cher ami' [Pierre de Coubertin], Lausanne, 27 March 1935, Baillet-Latour, IOC President's Correspondence Dossier, IOC Archives. Translation from French courtesy of Christina Hendelman.

[74] 'Orimuppiku sôchiiinkai' ['The Olympic Bid Committee'], *Asahi*, 5 Sept. 1935.

[75] The meeting was held on 20 September 1936. This new committee would report to the Physical Education Bureau of the Ministry of Education and would serve as the official XIIth Olympic Games Invitation Committee: 'Sôgo soshiki no shimoni, gutaitekina junbi he' ['At the Base of the Comprehensive Committee, Towards Specific Preparations'], *Asahi*, 21 Sept. 1935.

[76] Zen-nihon taiiku shinkôkai-sha, *Seika ha higashi he*, 98.

[77] Tokugawa Iesato was voted. Ibid., 103–5.

[78] Dai-jûnikai Orinpikku Tokyo taikai soshiki iinkai, *Hôkoku*, 6.

[79] Takashima Fumio, 'Raichô wo tsutaherareru- Baie Latouruhaku to Ha-randoshi no fûbô' ['Talking about Their Upcoming Visit to Japan: the Personal Appearances of Count Baillet-Latour and Mr Garland'], *Orimuppiku* 13 (Sept. 1935), 3.

[80] Soyeshima would later reveal that William May Garland, the United States IOC member, suggested in December 1935 that the Tokyo Bid Committee invite Count Baillet-Latour to tour Japan. Soyeshima Michimasa, 'Welcome to a Great Sports Leader', *Orinpikku*, 15 (April 1937), 2–3. The official plan to invite Baillet-Latour and Garland was discussed at the 17 July

1935 directors' meeting of the JAAA. See 'Gijiroku' ['Meeting Notes'], *Orimuppiku* 13 (Aug. 1935), 39.

[81] Although there were no codified Olympic protocols at the time regarding inspection tours, they were seen as out of the ordinary.

[82] The Information Bureau of the Ministry of Foreign Affairs coordinated the efforts to negotiate the visit of Baillet-Latour. See the archives of the Ministry of Foreign Affairs, Tokyo, Japan, Kokusai Orimupikku kyôgitaikai kankei, I-1-12-0-9 (Olympic Games Related Material), Gaimushô gaikô shiryôkan (hereafter cited as GGS) and Zen-nihon taiiku shinkôkai-sha, *Seika ha higashi he*, 110.

[83] Baillet-Latour accepted the invitation on 22 November 1935. The following month, the IOC President discussed his upcoming trip with the Japanese Ambassador in Belgium stating that his trip should not take the form of a formal invitation but should be described as a 'personal trip' (*kojinteki no ryokô*). The IOC President made tentative plans to travel to Japan in March and estimated that his expenses would be around 15,000 yen. The City of Tokyo sent 15,000 yen to the count to cover his expenses on 29 January and the count received the transfer of funds on 31 January 1936. Arita Hachirô to Foreign Affairs Minister Hirota, Telegram, 23 Nov. 1935, GGS; Omori to Hirota, Telegram, 30 Dec. 1935, GGS; Omori to Hirota, Telegram, 31 Dec. 1935, GGS; and Omori to Tashiro, Telegram, 31 Jan. 1936, GGS.

[84] The General Consulate of Japan in Geneva wrote to the former IOC President and founder of the modern Olympic Games, Pierre de Coubertin, discussing the discretion surrounding Baillet-Latour's visit to Japan: 'I make the promise to you that the utmost discretion will be kept around his trip and the newspapers will not be allowed to mention it'. De Coubertin had written a letter to Yokoyama discussing Baillet-Latour's trip to Japan and had apparently informed Yokoyama that he expressed his support for the Tokyo Olympics to Baillet-Latour. Yokoyama sent a cablegram to Foreign Minister Hirota relaying de Coubertin's support. This inspection tour was unprecedented. In September 1934, Avery Brundage visited Germany as President of the AOA to verify that Jewish athletes were being invited to participate in the planned 1936 Berlin Olympic Games before the AOA accepted the invitation to participate in the Berlin Games. See Allen Guttman, *The Games Must Go On*, 68–78. See also correspondence of Yokoyama Masayuki to de Coubertin, Geneva, 10 Jan. 1936, Coubertin, IOC President's Correspondence Dossier, IOC Archives; and Yokoyama to Hirota, Telegram, 14 Jan. 1936, GGS.

[85] The French article 'Les "Installations sportives" que l'on montrera au père des sportes' was also cited by an *Asahi* (Tokyo) article, 9 Jan. 1936. Tokyo, 1940 XIIth Olympic Games Candidature Dossier, IOC Archives.

[86] The 26 February Rising was an attempted coup by young army officers in protest against the trial of Aizawa Saburô. See Shillony, *Revolt in Japan*; Dai-jûnikai Orinpikku Tokyo taikai soshiki iinkai, *Hôkoku*, 12; 'Coup Will Not Affect Award, Says Belgian Nobleman, but Bids of Finland and Italy Are Still to Be Considered', *New York Times*, 28 Feb. 1936.

[87] The IOC President met with the Showa Emperor on 27 March 1936, and the quotation is from 'Tokio ou Helsingfors?' ['Tokyo or Helsinki?'], *XXeuse Siecle*, 12 May 1936, IOC Candidature Files, Tokyo Dossier, IOC Archives. Translation from French courtesy of Christina Hendelman. The schedule for Baillet-Latour was negotiated between the directors of the Tokyo City Bid Committee and the executive committee of the Invitation Committee of the Ministry of Education. R. de Lapomarede, 'Les Belges au Japon', *Independence*, 21 April 1936, in GSS; Suzuki, '*Tokyo tsuni katteri' 1936nen Berurin shikyûden*, 423.

[88] The conference was held on 24 March 1936. Soyeshima Michimasa, 'Welcome to Count Baillet-Latour', *Orimuppiku* 14 (April 1936), 6.

[89] Russell L. Durgin to Count Balliet-Latour [*sic*], 'Draft summary of conversations with Count Baillet-Latour', 24 March 1936. Tokyo Candidature, 1940 XIIth Olympic Games

Candidature Dossier, IOC Archives; Dai-jûnikai Orinpikku Tokyo taikai soshiki iinkai, *Hôkoku*, 12–13.

[90] Durgin, 'Draft summary', 3 and Hiranuma Ryozo to Count de Baillet-Latour, 9 April 1936. Tokyo Candidature, 1940 XIIth Olympic Games Candidature Dossier, IOC Archives.

[91] 'Olympic Head's Visit Stirs Finnish Hopes', *New York Times*, 10 June 1936, 30.

[92] Baillet-Latour to 'Mon cher ami' [Pierre de Coubertin], 22 May 1936, Baillet-Latour, IOC President's Correspondence Dossier, IOC Archives.

[93] Nygrén, *Olympiatuli Joka Sammui Sodan Tuulin*, 14.

[94] Martin Polley has researched the diplomacy surrounding London's 1936 bid for the 1940 Games and then subsequent withdrawal of the bid. My understanding of the London bid draws heavily upon this work. See Polley, 'Olympic Diplomacy'.

[95] Minute, 16 June 1936. PRO FO, L 4049/580/405 as cited by Polley, 'Olympic Diplomacy', 178.

[96] Lord Mayor of London to Baillet-Latour, 10 June 1936, 1940 XIIth Olympic Games Candidature Dossier, IOC Archives.

[97] Tokyo shiyakusho, *Tokyoshi hôkoku*, 48.

[98] Ibid.

[99] 'Eikyô ni hairu, Soye haku' ['Count Soye Enters the English Capital'], *Asahi*, 15 July 1936, 2(C).

[100] Minute, 8 July 1936, PRO FO 370/511, L 4772/580/405 as cited by Polley, 'Olympic Diplomacy', 179.

[101] Cabinet 51(36)4, 9 July 1936. PRO CAB 23/85 as cited by ibid., 179.

[102] 'Rahaku mo seikô ni jinryoku' ['Count Latour Also Assists Success'], *Asahi*, 18 July 1936.

[103] 'Rahaku mo imaya kenmei' ['Count Latour Works Harder than Ever'], *Asahi*, 19 July 1936.

[104] Ibid.

[105] 'Soyeshima haku no katsuyaku sôkô, Niei kankai mo kotensu' ['The Effective Activity of Count Soyeshima: Japanese and English Relations Take a Turn for the Better'], *Asahi*, 20 July 1936.

[106] Sir Edward Crowe to Clifford Norton, 21 July 1936, PRO CAB L 4947/580/405 as cited by Polley, 'Olympic Diplomacy', 182.

[107] 'Orimupikku iinkai kyou hiraku' ['The IOC Session Opens Today'], *Asahi*, 30 July 1936.

[108] At this Session the President welcomed Count Soyeshima, who sat for the first time with his colleagues; announced the resignation of Mr Sugimura and sanctioned the executive committee's recommendation to elect Prince Tokugawa Iyesato as a member of the IOC: *Official Bulletin of the International Olympic Committee*, Nov. 1936, 6.

[109] *Official Bulletin of the International Olympic Committee*, Nov. 1936, 6; '"Tokyo taikai" hotondo kettei' ['The "Tokyo Olympics" Are Pretty Much Decided On'], *Asahi*, 31 July 1936, Tokyo City Edition, 2(H).

[110] *Official Bulletin of the International Olympic Committee*, Nov. 1936, 6; Organizing Committee of the XIIth Olympiad Tokyo, *Official Report*, 7–8. The Organizing Committee Report faithfully reprints the minutes.

[111] Ibid.

[112] Organizing Committee of the XIIth Olympiad Tokyo 1940, *Official Report*, 22.

[113] Ibid., 5.

[114] The IOC meeting notes also stated that Japan was willing to provide a daily stipend of two gold dollars per athlete and five gold dollars per official delegate. This stipend would have amounted to an additional several hundred thousand gold dollars. International Olympic Committee, *The International Olympic Committee: One Hundred Years*, 272.

[115] The IOC President reiterated several details of the Tokyo bid, notably that Japan could be reached in 17 days from Europe, that 1940 was the 2,600th anniversary of the Japanese

dynasty; that a technical adviser would be appointed in consideration of the distance, and how the two towns of Nikko and Sapporo were vying to host the winter Games. *Official Bulletin of the International Olympic Committee*, Nov. 1936, 7.

[116] Ibid.

[117] Japanese Invitational Committee members conducted an informal poll of IOC delegates which revealed that Japan should take around 37 of a total 66 IOC member votes, making Tokyo the clear winner. The IOC members who supported Tokyo were reportedly from the following nations: Germany, France, Belgium, Canada, Italy, Great Britain, the United States, South Africa, India, China, Czechoslovakia, Hungary, Iran, Egypt and New Zealand. The Japanese discourse on the 1940 Tokyo bid often conflated the support of individual IOC members with the supposed support of nations to which they belonged, thus disregarding the original supra-national Olympic ideal. 'Tokyo yûsei no mama, kefu saiketsu ni hairu' ['Tokyo Remains Superior, Going into Today's Vote'], *Asahi*, 1 Aug. 1936; Sugita Masao, 'Ushiwareta Orinpikku' ['The Lost Olympics'], *Bungeishunju*, 27 Aug. 1938, 303.

[118] Nakamura Tetsuo also details the nationalistic bent of the 1940 Games in 'Japan: The Future in the Past'.

[119] See Collins, *The Missing Olympics*.

References

Berger, Gordon. *Parties Out of Power in Japan, 1931–41*. Princeton, NJ: Princeton University Press, 1977.

Coates, James R., Jr. 'London 1908: The Games of the IVth Olympiad'. In *Historical Dictionary of the Modern Olympic Movement*, edited by John E. Findling and Kimberly D. Pelle. Westport, CT: Greenwood Press, 1996.

Collins, Sandra. *The Missing Olympics, the 1940 Tokyo Games: Japan, Asia and the Olympic Movement*. London: Routledge, forthcoming.

Dai-jûnikai Orinpikku Tokyo taikai soshiki iinkai [Organizing Committee for the XIIth Olympiad]. *Hôkokusho* [The Official Report]. Tokyo: Dai-junikai Orinpikku Tokyo Taikai Soshiki Iinkai, 1939.

Diem, Carl. 'Reise nach Wien zum Olympischen Kongress'. *Inhaltsverzeichnis Tagebücher Carl Diem, Kennziffer 0223301*. The Carl Diem Forschungsarchiv, Duetsche Sporthochschule, Cologne, Germany.

Goldstein, Edward S. 'Amsterdam 1928: The Games of the IXth Olympiad'. In *Historical Dictionary of the Modern Olympic Movement*, edited by John E. Findling and Kimberly D. Pelle. Westport, CT: Greenwood Press, 1996: 68–74.

Guttman, Allen. *The Games Must Go On: Avery Brundage and the Olympic Movement*. New York: Columbia University Press, 1984.

Harootunian, H.D. *Overcome by Modernity: History, Culture, and Community in Interwar Japan*. Princeton, NJ, and Oxford: Princeton University Press, 2000.

Harootunian, H.D. and Tetsuo Najita. 'Japanese Revolt Against the West: Political and Cultural Criticism in the Twentieth Century'. In *The Cambridge History of Japan*, edited by Peter Duus, vol. 6. Cambridge: Cambridge University Press, 1988.

International Olympic Committee (IOC). *Olympic Biographies*. Lausanne, Switzerland: IOC, 1987.

——. *The International Olympic Committee: One Hundred Years*. Lausanne: IOC, 1994.

Kanô Jigoro, 'Orimpukku iinkai yori kaeri: Daijûnikai taikai sôchi no shôkô miyu' ['Returning from the IOC Session: A Look at the Prospects for the XII Olympic Games Campaign'], *Orimupikku* 12 (January 1934): 2–4.

Kawasaki Hidejiro. 'Osurô kaigi no zengo: kaisaichi kettei enki made' ['Before and After the Oslo Session: The Postponement of the Allocation of the Games'], *Orimupikku* 13 (April 1935): 29–38.

Kusayama Shigenobu. 'Tokyoshi to kokusai Orimupikku sôchi undô' ['The City of Tokyo and the Campaign for the Olympic Games'], *Orimupikku* 12 (December 1934): 38–39.

Nakamura Tetsuo. 'Japan: The Future in the Past'. In *The Nazi Olympics: Sport, Politics, and Appeasement in the 1930s*, edited by Arnd Krüger and William Murray. Urbana, IL, and Chicago: University of Illinois Press, 2003.

Nygrén, Helge. *Olympiatuli Joka Sammui Sodan Tuulin: XII olympiadin unelmakisat Helsingissä 20.7.- 4.8.1940* (in Finnish). Helsinki: Suomen Urheilumueosäätiö, 1991.

Olympic Organizing Committee of the XIIth Olympiad Tokyo 1940. *Report of the Organizing Committee on its Work for the XIIth Olympic Games of 1940 in Tokyo Until the Relinquishment*. Tokyo: The Committee, 1940.

Polley, Martin. 'Olympic Diplomacy: The British Government and the Projected 1940 Olympic Games'. *The International Journal of the History of Sport* 2 (August 1992): 169–87.

Shillony, B.A. *Revolt in Japan: The Young Officers and the February 26, 1936 Incident*. Princeton, NJ: Princeton University Press, 1973.

Shûgiin jimukyoku. *Teikoku gikai shûgiin iinkaigiroku, showahen* (fukuseikan) ['Meeting Notes of the Imperial Diet (reprint)'], vol. 54. Tokyo: Tokyodaigaku shuppankai, 1990.

Spillman, Lyn. *Nation and Commemoration: Creating National Identities in the United States and Australia*. Cambridge: Cambridge University Press, 1997.

Sugita Masao. 'Ushiwareta Orinpikku' ['The Lost Olympics'], *Bungeishunju* (27 August 1938): 294–307.

Suzuki, Akira. '*Tokyo tsuni katteri*' *1936nen Berurin shikyûden* ['Tokyo Suddenly Wins', the 1936 Berlin Telegram']. Tokyo: Shogakukan raiberari, 1994.

Terabe Raisuke. *Orinpikku wo Tokyo he* ['The Olympics to Tokyo']. Tokyo: Shiseikokyukai, 1934.

Tokyo Municipal Government. *Japan: Sports Center*. Tokyo: Tokyo Municipal Office, 1933.

Tokyo shiyakusho. *Daijûnikai Orinpikku Tokyotaikai Tokyoshi hôkokusho* ['The Official Report of the XIIth Olympic Games Olympic Organizing Committee for Tokyo']. Tokyo: Tokyoshikyakusho, 1939.

Tokyo-tô. *1940nen daijunikai orinpikku Tokyotaikai: Sôchi kara henjô made* ['The 1940 XIIth Olympic Games: From the Bid to the Forfeiture']. Tokyo: Tokyo-tô, 1952.

Zen-nihon taiiku shinkôkai. *Seika ha higashi he: kigen nisen ryoppyakunen no orimupikku taikai ni sonaheta* ['The Olympic Flame Comes East: Preparing for the 2,600th Year of Kigen Olympic Games']. Tokyo: Meguro Shoten, 1937.

'A Debt Was Paid Off in Tears': Science, IOC Politics and the Debate about High Altitude in the 1968 Mexico City Olympics

Alison M. Wrynn

> The IOC points out that to break this rule would be a gross breach of good sportsmanship and it is sure that no-one connected with the Olympic Movement would wish in any way to be guilty of taking an unfair advantage over the other competitors. [1]

Introduction

It is no secret that the connection between good sportsmanship and the Olympic Movement has come under attack in recent years. The revelations about state-sponsored doping on the part of the former East Germany, the site selection bribery scandal surrounding the 2002 Salt Lake City Games, and the ongoing controversies surrounding contemporary drug use at the US and international levels have, according to many, tarnished the past glory of the Olympic Games. [2]

Of course, the past is not always as glorious as our memory would like us to believe. There have been concerns and controversies surrounding the Olympic Games since their inception in the modern form in 1896. Debates about the location of the Games, the addition of various countries to the Olympic fraternity and the inclusion of women in the Olympic frame have haunted the International Olympic Committee (IOC) throughout its history. [3] The 1968 Olympic Games in Mexico City are best remembered for countless significant events including: the student riots that occurred outside the venues, the protests by African-American athletes, drug-testing of athletes for the first time and the sex-testing of female athletes. Prior to the Games, however, the most hotly debated topic surrounding the Games was the impact of high altitude on athletic performance. This study analyses the place of scientific research within athletics and, more specifically, within the Olympic Movement by focusing on influential debate about altitude's impact on athletics before the Mexico City Games.

The selection of Mexico City as the site of the XIXth Olympiad caused much discussion, debate and dissension in the athletic world. Long jumpers, shot putters and sprinters believed that they could possibly gain an advantage by competing at an altitude of nearly 7,500 feet. Distance runners, however, were certain that the 'thinner air' would impair their ability to compete effectively. The greatest concern expressed by distance runners was that their bodies would not be able to overcome what they called the 'oxygen debt' imposed by running at such a high altitude. The term 'oxygen debt' was introduced in 1925 by the distinguished British Nobel Prize-winning physiologist A.V. Hill. The concept of 'oxygen debt' was that with an insufficient supply of oxygen, lactate was produced in contracting muscles during exercise and was converted back to glycogen in the muscle during recovery. [4] As with many scientific and medical terms, 'oxygen debt' has had a long persistence, even as subsequent research has provided more appropriate terms. [5]

Today, scientists believe that high altitude has a definite impact on performance, particularly on events that occur after the return to sea level by altitude-trained athletes. When an athlete lives and trains at high altitude for an extended period of time, the body adapts in a number of ways; most important for the elite athlete is the increased production of red blood cells. This allows the blood to carry oxygen more effectively and it should lead to an improvement in performance. [6] However, four decades ago, in the years immediately preceding the 1968 Games, the scientific understanding of the impact of high altitude on elite athletic performance was still in its nascent stages.

Science has become intimately tied to the Olympic Movement over the past 40 years. Drug testing, for example, is a highly sophisticated technical undertaking. Despite the fact that only a few IOC members were trained in science and medicine, this group played a crucial role in connecting modern science, medicine and elite athletic competition. The approaches that the IOC took to confront these issues during the 1960s reveal that critical policy decisions were made that needed to be based on highly technical scientific and medical knowledge. In the early 1960s, the IOC was faced with a trio of serious technical issues: drug testing, gender verification and altitude physiology. The debate surrounding altitude prior to the 1968 Games was perhaps the first instance when IOC members were compelled to comprehend complex scientific data on human performance. [7]

The 1968 Mexico City Olympics are an ideal vehicle through which the history of scientific, particularly physiological, research in relation to athletic performance can be examined. The 1968 Olympic Games would be the most scientifically studied sports event up to that point in history. They drew the largest contingent of physicians and physiologists ever assembled at a sports event. [8] The six years preceding the Games consisted of a series of research projects at high altitude, using athletes as subjects, and public debate among scientists, coaches and athletes as to the best method of training for competition at high altitude. The IOC, however, did not publicly involve itself in this debate; rather they pronounced regulations as to the duration of training at high altitude that would be allowed prior to the Games.

Altitude Research: A Survey

In his overview on the history of research about high altitude, *High Life: A History of Altitude Physiology and Medicine*, John West provides an outstanding foundation that details the interest on the impact of varying altitudes on the human body. [9] West's work focuses on the entire span of historical research on the topic beginning with the classical world. There is ample discussion of altitude and mountaineering. In addition, there is a thorough examination of work conducted during the Second World War. The adequate analysis of the impact of high altitude on athletic performance is glaringly absent. In his review of *High Life*, applied physiologist R.J. Shepard noted this omission, stating: 'Presumably Dr West would argue that the altitudes confronted by most athletes are a minor concern relative to the challenges of Mount Everest!' [10]

The physiological research that had been conducted on altitude up to 1960 included work on the effects of altitude on: oxygen uptake, the respiratory system, the cardiovascular system, the blood and adaptation to altitude. Nearly all of this work was conducted with small numbers of research subjects (frequently the researchers were the subjects themselves), most of whom were not highly trained athletes. Moreover, up through the 1930s, most of this work was conducted at remote sites located on mountaintops. A unique component of the research that was to be conducted in the years immediately preceding the Mexico City Games was that for the first time there would be a fairly large number of subjects available for the researchers. In addition, and perhaps most importantly, these would be highly trained athletic subjects who were very capable of pushing their body to its limits. Finally, this research would need to be conducted not in remote mountain locations but at the track stadium, preferably in Mexico City.

Physiologist Ernst Jokl wrote extensively about the history of altitude physiology and its impact on athletic performance. [11] In these works, which usually begin with a brief discussion of Lavoisier's 'discovery' of oxygen and the need for increased amounts of oxygen during exercise, Jokl describes the growth in interest in altitude physiology in the latter portion of the nineteenth century – a result, he claims, of the burgeoning interest in mountaineering and emerging forms of aviation. The deaths of two pioneering balloonists, Croce-Spinelli and Sivel (a third passenger – Tissandier – survived) who had in fact worked closely with the physiologist Paul Bert, did not dissuade others who wished to push the envelope and ascend ever higher.

The construction of instruments to quantify the impact of altitude on the human body was another component of this effort. Much of the research that occurred as the nineteenth century ended came from German laboratories, particularly the work of Nathan Zuntz. Most importantly Zuntz and his co-workers developed improved mechanisms for measuring ventilation and oxygen consumption. The Italian physiologist Angelo Mosso built what is claimed to be the first high-altitude research laboratory in order to conduct research utilizing the 'pneumograph' he had invented for measuring respiration. [12]

At the beginning of the twentieth century, a number of American physiologists became interested in the study of altitude; many of these research studies were conducted on Pike's Peak in Colorado (elevation 4,300 meters). [13] Research in the middle decades focused on continued interest in mountaineering, particularly with the growing public interest in the attempts to scale Mount Everest. [14] Technological changes and military needs drove the next phase of research on altitude physiology. In the years leading up to the Second World War, new jet airplanes, capable of soaring to great heights, were emerging. The military needed to know the impact of this radical change in altitude on their pilots. [15] As research into altitude physiology continued following the Second World War, the laboratory became the more common site of this research. [16] The concepts analysed in these studies would soon come to the forefront as elite athletic competitions began to be hosted in cities located at high altitude such as Mexico City.

Mexico City's Candidacy and the Decision to Award the Games

The impact of Mexico City's altitude on performance during athletic competitions was discussed as early as 1926. The year before he became president of the IOC, Count Henri Baillet-Latour chaired the Congress of the Central American Games, supported by the IOC, in Paris in 1924. At this congress it was decided to hold the first Central American Games in Mexico City.

The main focus of one report on these Games was on the great displays of sportsmanship and camaraderie among the athletes and spectators at the event. However, altitude was mentioned twice. The swimming events were spread out over two days, 'so as to not work a hardship on the Cuban swimmers who were accustomed to compete [*sic*] at sea level'. [17] Despite the fact that the Cuban athletes trained in Mexico City for three weeks, Mexico was victorious in all the track events.

In 1955 the second Pan-American Games were hosted by Mexico City. When the site of these Games was selected in 1951, there was virtually no discussion on the issue of altitude in the popular or scientific press. [18] Conflicting accounts of the effect of altitude on the athletes appeared following the Games. [19] One athlete was described as 'exhausted' at the completion of his race, but no mention was made of altitude. However, a second article claimed that altitude would have a detrimental impact on races longer than one-and-a-half miles. Despite this gloomy prediction, Pan-American records were established in 16 of the 22 men's track and field events. [20]

Interest in the 1955 Pan-American Games resurfaced as the time approached to make the decision as to whom to award the XIXth Games of the Olympiad, to be held in 1968. Physiologists Cervantes and Karpovich argued that following competitions in the 1955 Pan-American Games, some athletes collapsed or blacked out. [21] IOC President Avery Brundage was already quite familiar with Mexico City and had in fact attended the second Pan-American Games in Mexico City in 1955. In a letter that year to IOC Chancellor Otto Mayer he wrote; 'Despite the altitude, records are being broken every day'. [22] It is obvious that Brundage knew that altitude impacted performance, but in his opinion, it did not seem to hinder the contests he was viewing.

The cities of Buenos Aires, Argentina, Detroit, USA, Lyon, France and Mexico City were the official contenders for the Games of the XIXth Olympiad. All four cities were asked by the IOC to answer a standard set of questions about their bid. One question that was to prove significant to these Games was question K: 'Please provide general information about your city, its size, population, climate (temperature and rainfall), altitude, and all reasons why it should be considered as a site for the Olympic Games'. [23] The candidate cities responded in a variety of ways. Buenos Aires produced a small book with black-and-white photos and a pamphlet, written in Spanish and English, to answer the questions. Although there was no attempt to criticize Mexico City, Buenos Aires did respond that it was located at sea level. The Argentine city was a serious competitor for these Games as they had hosted the first Pan-American Games in 1951 and had missed out on receiving the 1956 Olympic Games to Melbourne by a vote of 21 to 20. [24] Detroit answered with a pamphlet in French and English and two large-format books with colour photos of the city. In addition, there was a presentation to the IOC that included a visit by US President John F. Kennedy. This was Detroit's sixth attempt to secure an Olympic bid. [25] Mexico City assembled an impressive, rather ornate, *Bid Book* which replied to the questions in French, English and Spanish. [26]

The group representing Mexico City immediately sought to dispel the belief that altitude would be detrimental to athletic performances. Their primary focus was on the scientific research they had compiled that they claimed refuted any possibility of harm to the athletes. In fact, they argued that only three or four days would be needed for athletes to acclimatize to the altitude of Mexico City. Much of the research that was presented did not deal specifically with the ways that altitude might impact athletic performance. The studies, mostly in the area of cardiology, were provided to alleviate fears that serious harm would come to the competitors in Mexico City. The fourth World Cardiology Congress had been held in Mexico City the previous year and a number of the papers presented dealt with the effect of altitude on human respiratory and circulatory systems. According to the Mexico City *Bid Book*, the general conclusion was that Mexico City's altitude would have a 'harmless effect . . . on the athlete's cardiopulmonary capacity, even though they come from lower altitudes'. [27]

Prior to the final vote, representatives from Mexico City were confronted directly by IOC members with the altitude question and the presumed problems of acclimatization for the athletes. In response, the Mexican delegates offered to defray the costs incurred in making physical adaptation possible for the athletes. [28] The conclusion that the Mexico City Organizing Committee reached was 'The altitude of Mexico City permits a rapid adaptation of normal persons and does not impair in any way the capacity to carry out physical work or sporting events. Mexico City's altitude does not cause a pathology of any kind in the human being'. [29]

On 18 October 1963, the 61st general Session of the IOC was held in Baden-Baden, Germany. On the first ballot, Mexico City received 30 of 58 votes and was awarded the XIXth Olympic Games. [30]

Research Leading up to the 1968 Games

Even before the 1968 Games were awarded to Mexico City, some researchers were beginning to investigate the impact of altitude on elite performance. Bruno Balke explained to readers of Johnson's *Science and Medicine of Exercise and Sport* (1960) that the problem with attempting athletic feats at high altitude was that the oxygen supply to the body becomes inadequate as a result of lower pressure of oxygen and the diminished oxygen content of the arterial blood. [31] Acclimatization would take, at a minimum, one week for every 3,000 feet of altitude. Balke argued that performance capacity would advance if an athlete were to train for a long period of time at high altitude between 7,000 and 10,000 feet as compared to training at sea level. He believed that 'an athlete should be able to run the mile in less than 4 minutes if he had come very close to the 4 minute mile by the previous training'. [32]

Per Olaf Astrand is one of the most significant twentieth-century researchers in the area of altitude physiology, so it is not surprising that he would contribute to the investigations conducted prior to the 1968 Games. Astrand conducted a study on Swedish cross-country skiers at the 1959 'Pre-Olympics' and 1960 Olympic Winter Games in Squaw Valley, California. According to Astrand, 'At higher altitudes pathological ECG has been found to occur during heavy muscular work, so also heart failure'. [33] It is interesting to note that relatively little interest was paid to elite athletic competition at high altitude during winter competitions prior to 1960. This is despite the fact that these events are frequently held at higher altitudes to accommodate the alpine skiing events. Brundage did address this concern at one point in a letter to Otto Mayer that explained that some skiers were concerned about the 'langlauf' competitions in the upcoming 1960 Winter Games in Squaw Valley as they were planned for a higher altitude than was customary. However, Marc Hodler, who was president of the Fédération Internationale de Ski (FIS), dismissed this notion and supported the location of the competitions. [34]

Now that the Games had been awarded to Mexico City, who would influence the creation of knowledge about the physiology of elite athletic performance at high altitude? The organizing committee of the Mexico City Games was willing to provide the opportunity for research to be conducted in Mexico City during the designated 'Pre-Olympics' in 1965, 1966 and 1967. [35] Furthermore, individual countries began to organize their own research efforts at home. These included the rapid development of high-altitude training and research sites in their countries. In addition, a variety of international symposia were held, and proceedings published, in the years immediately preceding the 1968 Games which focused on the results of research conducted at the pre-Olympic contests and individual training sites.

In 1965, 1966 and again in 1967 'international sports weeks' (ISWs) were held in Mexico City. The first two were held with the express purpose of allowing scientists and physicians the opportunity to conduct research on athletes in the altitude of Mexico City. The first ISW in 1965 drew more than 200 athletes from 20 countries. One problem that arose was that the testing developed into an all-out competition. [36] The chief complaint by team officials was that conditions were not right for thoroughly controlled scientific tests. Arthur G. Lentz, administrative chairman of the American team and assistant director of the United States Olympic Committee (USOC), claimed that the ideal method of testing altitude effects would be to bring a group of athletes to Mexico City alone and let them work out privately after controlled preliminary tests. [37]

The second event in 1966 drew 788 contestants from 25 countries. Of these 510 were from non-Mexican countries. [38] The final ISW, in 1967 was held for testing the readiness of the Olympic venues and the Mexican hosts unequivocally denied requests to continue physiological testing of athletes during these events. Indeed, in a long article about the contest, there was only a very brief mention of altitude. The head of the organizing committee, Ramirez Vasquez, claimed that the question of altitude was no longer a problem. In his words, in previous Olympiads, athletes frequently had to adapt to conditions different from their homes such as 'the cold in Helsinki, the dampness in London, the heat in Rome'. [39] However, science and medicine continued to be a focus of this event as the preparations for drug testing were evaluated during these contests and 234 tests were conducted with no positive results. [40]

In order to bring together the latest research in the field of altitude physiology, a number of research symposia on this topic were held in the years immediately preceding the 1968 Games. These were held in a variety of locations throughout the world and were attended primarily by European and American scientists, although a few researchers from Central and South America did attend. Reflecting Cold War sensibilities, scientists from the Soviet Union and other Soviet bloc nations were notably absent at nearly all of these meetings.

The USOC, the Lovelace Foundation for Medical Research and the University of New Mexico co-sponsored an 'International Symposium on the Effects of Altitude on Physical Performance' in March 1966. In summarizing the proceedings of the symposium, exercise physiologist Balke stated that scientists and coaches were faced with the responsibility of making definite recommendations to the various Games committees as to how the athletes should be trained in order to secure the greatest advantage from the studies that had been done. Several recommendations were made as a result of this conference. The first was that athletes should train at high altitude. Researchers were not certain as to whether they should train at altitude for prolonged periods of time, or whether an interval programme of going up and down frequently was better. Pre-Olympic training at altitude of only three weeks was the very minimum that was recommended. There was the need to consider expanding the pre-Olympic training period to four or even six weeks, and that was recommended to the IOC. [41]

In September–October of 1966 another symposium on 'exercise at altitude' was held, this one in Milan, Italy. One of the purposes of this meeting, according to organizer Rodolfo Margaria, was the revived interest in high-altitude physiology as a result of the decision to hold the 1968 Games in Mexico City. This was a decision that in his words, '[had] been widely criticized and it has not met the approval of all physiologists'. [42] The papers were organized around the traditional topics of interest in the area of altitude physiology: oxygen uptake, the respiratory system, the cardiovascular system and the blood. A newer area of interest that developed logically as a result of the upcoming Games in Mexico City was on adaptation to altitude. [43]

The *New York Times* reported that the Soviet Union had by early 1965 completed a preliminary conference of scientists and coaches on acclimatization and high-altitude training. A team of Soviet medical and sports specialists prepared comprehensive recommendations for individual athletes and teams to help in their training for the Olympics. [44] According to reports, Tsakhadzor (9,000 feet) within Soviet Armenia was chosen as a 'little Mexico City' by the Soviets. [45] Further reports told of the Soviet training centre at Alma-Ata in the Tien Shan Mountains. Athletes were training at this location accompanied by physiologists, physicians, biochemists and coaches. [46]

Japanese physiologists conducted research during the Mexico City international sports weeks, in their laboratories back home and on Mount Norikura. Sounding a cautious note, the Research Committee for Altitude Training of the Japanese Olympic Committee concluded that more important than the length of time needed for acclimatization was the absolute necessity of cardio-pulmonary examinations of all athletes and officials before they travelled to the 1968 Summer Games. [47]

The French Olympic Committee had established a high-altitude training centre at Font-Romeu. They provided justification for this action based on the establishment of the Soviet training centre in Alma-Ata, and the American centre in Alamosa, Colorado. [48] The centre at Alamosa (7,546 feet) was under the leadership of the Alamosa Olympic Training Project Committee. By the late summer of 1965 they had hosted two different experimental research groups. [49] In addition, a number of international delegations had enquired about training their teams in Alamosa in 1968. The committee cited the work of Ernst Jokl, which claimed that three months of training, at a minimum, were needed prior to competing in the altitude of Mexico City. [50]

The British Olympic Association conducted a medical research project led by L.C. Pugh. Pugh was recognized as 'probably the world's greatest expert in such subjects' [51] and had conducted research on altitude on an Everest expedition. The British study of six 5,000-metre runners indicated that even after four weeks in Mexico City the athletes were unable to return to their original sea-level best times. Asked about the possible health risks, Pugh claimed: 'Nobody has collapsed so far'. [52]

The report compiled by the British team was particularly significant as it was distributed to all members of the IOC by IOC vice-president and International Amateur Athletics Federation (IAAF) president David Burghley (the Marquess of Exeter). In addition, this report was cited frequently by both Burghley and Brundage in their discussion of the length of time needed to adjust to the elevated altitude. One of the main questions that this group examined was how much time was needed by the distance athletes to acclimatize to the altitude in Mexico City. The final conclusion of the British report was:

> All endurance event competitors in the 1968 British Olympic Team should arrive in Mexico City approximately 4 weeks before the Opening Ceremony, with the possible exception of a very occasional individual in some very long continuous endurance events. Competitors in explosive events should arrive in Mexico City a minimum of 3 weeks beforehand. [53]

The problems that female athletes might encounter at high altitude were rarely addressed in the scientific research. Women's distance races in the 1968 Games would include only the 800 metres. The longest swimming distance for women would also be 800 metres. The research that was conducted on the male athletes was assumed to provide an acceptable training standard for the women. Most interest seemed to focus on questions concerning women and menstruation at high altitude. [54]

Questions continued to be forwarded to the IOC by coaches and scientists about the problems of competing at altitude. Brundage declared that the location of the 1968 Games would not be changed under any circumstances (except for the equestrian events, which were moved to a lower altitude). [55]

The Heart of the Matter: Amateurism vs. Altitude

As the scientists conducted research, and attempted to determine the ideal length of time needed by athletes to acclimatize to the altitude of Mexico City; the members of the IOC, particularly those on the executive board, were attempting to decipher the same riddle. How long before the Games should athletes be allowed to travel to Mexico City to acclimatize? How many weeks during the year should athletes be allowed to converge on their countries' newly developed high-altitude training centres to begin training for the Games? For the members of the IOC, however, this was a question that would not be answered by scientific research, despite the massive amount of research that was being produced to answer that specific question. There was one overriding factor in the minds of Avery Brundage and the other decision makers: amateurism.

The IOC leadership, particularly Brundage and IOC vice-president Burghley, spent a considerable amount of time and energy in the 1960s and early 1970s dealing with questions of amateurism. In the Winter Games, problems were emerging as skiers displayed the logos of manufacturing sponsors on their equipment. Eventually, Austrian skier Karl Schranz would be expelled from the 1972 Sapporo Games due to his sponsorships. [56] During the 1964 and 1968 Games and at the IAAF World Championships, the battle between shoe manufacturers Puma and Adidas for supremacy in sponsoring athletes in track and field was beginning to achieve new heights. [57] Although sponsors were not a part of the altitude/amateur debate, the length of time that an athlete could devote full-time to athletic training was. The only amateur recognized by the IOC in the 1960s was a person who had taken no more than four weeks off from work in a single year to train and compete in the Games.

A major battle raged, publicly and privately, within the IOC over the issue of amateurism. Burghley – who was a proponent of the 'old school' belief about amateurism that Coubertin had created – and Brundage, who stood on his beliefs about the sanctity of amateurism more than anyone else in the IOC, were the ones behind the push to keep the Olympics amateur. Brundage, for example, frequently commented that team sports and cycling should be kept out of the Olympics since those were the main opponents of the amateur ideal. After reading the summaries of scientific researches about acclimatization, the two men would eventually agree to extend the time period for training from four to six weeks. Publicly, however, they rarely alluded to the issue of amateurism when they discussed altitude as much as they did privately, as they were frequently criticized in the popular press for their decision to cling to amateur ideals. [58]

In April 1966, during the 65th IOC general Session in Rome, and before most of the research studies had been completed, the IOC decreed that the period of training at high altitude for athletes was not to exceed four weeks during the three months preceding the opening of the Games. [59] Suddenly, as the results of scientific studies began to emerge, Brundage and Burghley began to discuss the possibility of extending the training for an additional period, but during 1968 only. According to Brundage, the results of the research conducted thus far were inconclusive. 'Many [of the scientists and physicians] think that two week periods are just as useful as four week periods, but others differ'. [60]

In August 1966, the IOC reinforced its decision to impose a limit of four weeks on special high-altitude training for the Mexico City Olympics. Nearly every experienced distance runner and coach believed that Olympic officials were completely wrong. Performances by Kenya's distance runners, who did all their training at 6,200 feet or higher, gave them plenty of supporting evidence. John Velzian, Kenya's national coach, claimed that an athlete who was born and raised at high altitude developed a more efficient mechanism for using oxygen. [61] Ron Clarke, the Australian distance runner, who had won all his races at six miles and 10,000 metres since the 1964 Olympics, wanted the IOC to change its four-week limit. He made his case logically. 'If there is no advantage to training at high altitudes, why limit sea level athletes to only four weeks of such training? If there is a definite advantage, then why deny athletes who live at low altitudes a chance to overcome it by longer high-altitude training?' [62]

Other athletes continued to voice their opinions about the selection of Mexico City as the site of the Games. The British track and field team and former track men were most vocal in their opposition to holding the Games in Mexico City. British athletes expressed their displeasure in a letter to the London *Times* in April 1966. The athletes claimed the 7,500-foot altitude would hamper performances in endurance events and give athletes already living in high altitudes or training in them an unfair advantage. The athletes acknowledged that it was probably impossible to remove the Games from Mexico City now, but suggested that at least the endurance events be held at a separate, low-altitude location. [63]

Roger Bannister, the first man to break the four-minute barrier in the mile, was one of the most vocal opponents of holding the Games at high altitude. Bannister, who by 1966 was a physician, wrote a detailed article in the *New York Times Magazine* addressing the issues involving distance running at high altitude. He claimed to be astonished by the choice of Mexico City for the Olympic Games in 1968. Although he did not agree with the remark attributed to the Finnish coach Onin Niakanen that 'there will be those that die' he did feel that altitude could be the critical additional factor leading to the collapse of distance runners. [64]

According to Bannister, an incidental result of the decision to hold the Olympic Games in Mexico City was the introduction of the idea of altitude training in order to improve the performance of athletes running either at high altitudes or sea level. He remarked that it was a strange coincidence that the only athlete who won the marathon with ease in successive Olympic Games was an Ethiopian, Bikile Abebe, who lived and trained at about 7,000 feet above sea level. [65] He felt his point was reinforced when an unknown Kenyan runner, Neftali Temu, who like Kipchoge Keino lived and trained at 6,000 feet, defeated the Australian world-record-holder Ron Clarke in the six-mile race at the Commonwealth Games at sea level in Jamaica. He claimed that several countries had established permanent training camps at high altitudes. This prompted him to ask: 'How far have we come from true sport?' [66] The IOC rule limiting the length of altitude training preceding the Olympic Games was, for Bannister, a tacit admission of the blunder of holding the Games at such an altitude.

The belief that preparation for and competition at altitude were going to alter the results of future competitions at sea level was reinforced following the 1965 and 1966 international sports weeks when a number of athletes returned to sea level and broke world records. This included athletes who always trained at high altitudes, as well as athletes who had previously trained exclusively at sea level. A French swimmer, Alain Mosconi, swam the 400 metres in Mexico City in a time of 4 minutes 23 seconds. A few days later, at sea level in Acapulco, he set a new world record time of 4 minutes 10.5 seconds. [67] Altitude was no longer a 'problem' according to one researcher; the new problem was 'to which altitude has an athlete to go to make the best possible performance when back at sea level'. [68]

The decision on the length of training time at high altitude that would be allowed was essentially a discussion between two men, Brundage and Burghley, who relied in only a limited manner on scientific data. Despite numerous studies conducted by scientists from a variety of nations, the work of the British scientists was held up as the most important. Burghley believed that all athletes would experience the same altitude penalty; thus it was fair to restrict training to a limited number of weeks. [69]

In June 1967, Brundage began to bend and mused that perhaps the IOC should allow an additional four weeks of training (in addition to the four weeks already allowed) for 1968 only. He was, apparently, concerned about public perceptions – for one of the few times during his tenure as IOC president. He informed Johann Westerhoff, who had replaced Otto Mayer as the person in charge of day-to-day operations at IOC headquarters in Lausanne: 'I am not sure in view of the hullabaloo all over the world about the altitude of Mexico City that we should not permit an extra four weeks in the year 1968'. [70]

Westerhoff argued to Burghley that the IOC was bound to honour the comments on acclimatization and altitude training that had been made in the IOC *Bulletin* by IOC Medical Commission member Dirix, who had conducted medical tests on cyclists at the 1965 Tour of Mexico. [71] He was, according to Westerhoff, 'a man with world authority on altitude problems'. [72] Dirix supported the notion that only three weeks at high altitude were needed to fully acclimatize the athlete. Westerhoff interpreted this to mean that 'for 1968 all amateur athletes can interrupt their occupations for special training in a camp for four weeks and that, in addition, they can assemble in Mexico City for another four weeks before the Games'. [73]

Burghley attempted to clarify his position to Westerhoff in his response. Previously, the IOC had only allowed three weeks' training in special camps. However, they had recently extended the time – not due to the Mexico City Games – to four weeks. This, according to Burghley, would force a competitor to be away from his job for a total of six weeks during an Olympic year. He was very much against allowing an additional four weeks as this would force athletes to be in camps or competing for ten weeks. Burghley also argued that it would be an undue financial strain on the smaller national Olympic committees to hold these lengthy training camps. [74] Despite the shifting realities of the amateur/professional world of elite sport, which included American athletes on college scholarships, European club athletes with under-the-table contracts and Soviet athletes who were serving in the military while training full-time for athletic competition, Burghley still remained wedded to the ideals of Olympic amateurism that were in place when he was a competitor in the 1924, 1928 and 1932 Games.

Burghley placed essentially the same arguments in front of Brundage. The main questions to be answered were how to be fair to all of the athletes and how to uphold the traditional code of amateurism while still allaying the fears and concerns of athletes about competition at altitude. [75] A year later, in August 1967, the National Olympic Committees were given the final decree on the length of time that would be allowed to train at high altitude. Notably, the proclamation tied the notion of training at altitude with the ideals of amateurism. However, a concession was made on the part of the IOC for a limited amount of extra training in 1968 only:

> In the first place we want to make it plain that, although it is not prohibited, the general operation of special training camps is not in accordance with the spirit of amateur sport. In our eligibility code, it is provided that participation for special training in a camp for more than four weeks in any one calendar year is not permitted. There has been so much misinformation circulated on the effect on performance of high altitude such as that of Mexico City we have decided to make a special allowance for the year 1968 only of two weeks. This means that six weeks in special training camps during the year 1968 will be permitted but no more than four of these weeks shall be during the three months preceding the opening of the Games in October 1968. [76]

The Games Will Go On

The Games of the XIXth Olympiad opened in Mexico City's Estadio Olympico on 12 October 1968. They opened in a world amidst a sea of cultural and political change. They opened on a beautiful day despite the lingering smell of gunpowder from the military's slaying of scores, perhaps hundreds, of student protestors on the eve of the opening ceremonies in the Plaza of Three Cultures. They opened amid suggestions of rampant drug use on the part of the athletes that had led to inception of drug-testing at these Games. They opened with the gender verification of female athletes – an artifact of drug use and fear of change as women became larger, stronger, faster and increasingly more competitive. This was the first time a female athlete, Mexico's Norma Enriqueta Basilio de Sotelo, had lit the flame at an Olympic Games opening ceremony. It was also the first time an American female athlete, Janice Lee York Romary, carried the nation's flag in the parade of nations. [77]

The Games opened despite the political protests of African and African-American athletes over the debate about the inclusion of South Africa in the Olympic family and the racial discrimination that many of the African-American athletes faced at home. They opened in the middle of an escalating battle over the ideals of amateurism. Adidas and Puma freely distributed equipment to athletes, even in the Olympic Village itself. [78] With all of these events, it is easy to see how the problem of competing at high altitude has faded in the historical memory. But it was an important issue that can be closely tied to the debate about amateurism.

Brundage reflected on virtually none of these controversies as he addressed those present at the opening of the IOC Session. There was no mention of drug-testing, gender verification or the murder of the student protestors just prior to the opening of the Games. The political problem of South Africa was completely ignored. Altitude was the focus of his speech, and the fact that despite the dire predictions when the Games were first awarded to Mexico City, which echoed complaints about the 'southern hemisphere' Melbourne Games, it was important to note that the Games belonged to the whole world, 'hot and cold, dry and humid, high and low, East and West, North and South'. [79] Amateurism also found its way into the talk as athletes and coaches were reminded that the purpose of the Games was not to train in order to optimize the chances that records would be broken. Finally, in the conclusion to his speech, Brundage summarized his belief in the transcendent nature of sport as a panacea to the ills of the modern world by claiming: 'Mexico has discovered that the more sport grounds and swimming pools provided for its young people, the fewer hospitals, the fewer jails, and the fewer asylums required. You don't find hippies, yippies or beatniks on sport grounds'. [80]

The first distance race of the Games was the 10,000 metres, held on the day after the opening ceremonies. The results were as Roger Bannister, Ron Clarke and others had predicted. Neftali Temu of Kenya won the gold, followed by Mamo Wolde of Ethiopia and Mahamed Gammoudi of Tunisia, all runners who lived and trained at high altitude. Temu's winning time was one minute and 48 seconds slower than Australian Ron Clarke's world record time in the race. Clarke collapsed at the end of the race and was unconscious for ten minutes. [81] Kenyan Kipchoge Keino won the 1500 metres and his countrymen Amos Biwott and Benjamin Kogo finished first and second in the steeplechase. The 5,000-metre race was swept by high-altitude-trained runners Mohamed Gammoudi, Kipchoge Keino and Naftali Temu. Ethiopian Mamo Wolde captured the gold medal in the marathon. [82]

What were the results of the other events, the anaerobic events that were supposedly unaffected, or potentially improved, by high altitude? Certainly Bob Beamon's incredible 29-foot 2½-inch long jump was a combination of amazing skill, technique, luck and perhaps altitude. World records were established in all of the men's athletics events shorter than 400 metres, including the relays and the triple jump. An additional factor in this rash of record breaking could have been the fact that this was also the first time that a 'tartan' track surface was utilized in the Olympics. [83] Testing for anabolic steroids was still four years away; thus it is impossible to conclude that altitude alone led to improvements in performance in events such as these. Women set only two world records in athletics, in the 400 metres and the 4 × 100-metre relay. Their longest race was only 800 metres in length. In the field events, women set world records in the long jump and the shot put, where the victor, East Germany's Margitta Gummel, far exceeded her previous best throw, which was also the world record, by 29 inches. [84]

Conclusion

The Mexico City Games demonstrated that four weeks immediately preceding the Olympics was not enough training for sea-level athletes to compete at high altitude in distance races against runners who lived and trained at high altitude. Although several studies were conducted in the three years preceding the Games, researchers were not able to definitively tell coaches and athletes how long they would need to train at altitude in order to prepare for the distance races. The IOC ignored suggestions by some coaches and athletes that four to five months of training at altitude might be needed. Western nations attempted to find the best method of training in the time period imposed by the IOC, going to great expense to provide the athletes with training centres at an altitude similar to Mexico City's in the months preceding the Games.

This period was a crucial time for the IOC with regard to the enormous amount of scientific information that became critical to the conduct of elite sport in the 1960s. Today, there are still debates about the effect of altitude on performance. There is a belief that the athletes who 'by an accident of geography' are born, grow up and train at a high altitude are predisposed to success in distance events in track and field. Increasingly, sea-level athletes believe that the success of these 'altitude' athletes can by replicated either by moving to altitude or by living in a specially designed facility that mimics the environmental factors of life at high altitude. Perhaps one of the factors that spelled the end of amateurism was the understanding that living and training at altitude could potentially improve performance in certain events. Thus, athletes needed the freedom to live and train where it would best improve their performance.

The USOC moved its headquarters to Colorado Springs, Colorado in 1978. With an altitude of 6,000 feet it provided a welcoming central location for many of the national governing bodies of sports that now wanted to train elite athletes at altitude. It is also located close to Pike's Peak, where early twentieth-century altitude studies introduced research on the impact of living at high altitude. There is no apology on the part of the city for the fact that they are located at high altitude and that is the reason athletes want to live and train there. [85] By 1968, most elite athletes had already made the ideological shift, based on real-world priorities, from amateurism to professionalism. However, those who were still in charge of sport organizations such as the IAAF and the IOC still clung to the beliefs they held when they were young men and competitive athletes. In a world that was rapidly changing, they clung to the vestiges of the past in the realm where they still exerted the most control: athletics.

Acknowledgements

Research for this project was funded, in part, by the 1999 Postgraduate Research Grant Programme of the IOC Olympic Studies Centre, located in the Olympic Museum in Lausanne.

Notes

[1] 'Acclimatization at the Mexico Altitude'. Circulaires 1965 a 1966 [circular letters], n.d., (between 20 and 28 June 1966), unsigned, Mexico 1968 General 1966–93. Archives of the International Olympic Committee, Olympic Studies Centre, Lausanne, Switzerland (hereafter cited as OSC Archives).

[2] See for example Ungerleider, *Faust's Gold*; M. Gorrell, 'End of Scandal Missing Media Blitz of Start', *Salt Lake Tribune*, 7 Dec. 2003, available online at http://www.sltrib.com/2003/Dec/12072003/utah/117830.asp, accessed 12 March 2004; D. Mackay, 'New Drug Scandal Shakes Sport', *The Guardian*, 18 Oct. 2003, available online at http://sport.guardian.co.uk/news/story/0,10488,1065865,00.html, accessed 12 March 2004.

[3] For more details on the general historical context of the Olympic Games see Findling and Pelle, *Historical Dictionary of the Modern Olympic Movement*.

[4] Jokl and Simon, *International Research in Sport and Physical Education*, 361–2. It is now known, however, that the post-exercise fate of lactate is mainly to oxidation, and that a variety of factors explain the recovery oxygen consumption seen in excess of a resting baseline. In the 1920s and 1930s, the appearance of lactate during exercise was taken to represent insufficient oxygen supply, a situation that was compensated for in recovery. See Stainsby and Brooks, 'Control of Lactic Acid Metabolism'.

[5] Anshel, *Dictionary of the Sport and Exercise Sciences*, 107, 55. The *Dictionary of the Sport and Exercise Sciences* has a listing for oxygen debt that refers the reader to 'excess post-exercise oxygen consumption'.

[6] Technological sophistication entered the equation many years ago with the practice of blood doping and the production of drugs such as erythropoietin that increase the red blood cell count. In addition, as the latest theories now argue that the athlete should perhaps 'live high and train low' there have been a number of products developed that allow competitors to simulate different altitudes via breathing apparatus or in specially constructed tents and chambers. See A. Baker and W.G. Hopkins, 'Altitude Training for Sea-level Competitions', *Sportscience Training & Technology*, 20 July 1998 (available online at http://www.sportsci.org/traintech/altitude/wgh.html, accessed 17 March 2004) for an example of the technology of altitude simulation. See Hypoxico's website (http://www.hypoxico.com) that claims 'following the 1968 Olympic Games in Mexico City (altitude 7,200ft/2,200m) the world of athletic science virtually exploded with exploration of the effects of altitude on athletic performance. More than thirty years later it's no longer a secret that altitude can have a major effect on an athlete's competitive results'.

[7] Wrynn, 'The Human Factor'.

[8] Rusk, 'Olympic Game Health: Mexico City Events to Be Watched by Scientists for Many Unusual Aspects', *New York Times*, 13 Oct. 1968.

[9] West, *High Life*.

[10] Shepard, *High Life* [Review].

[11] See for example: Jokl, 'The Effect of Altitude on Athletic Performance'; Jokl, 'Exercise at Altitude – Historical Remarks'.

[12] Jokl, 'Exercise at Altitude', 203–4.

[13] Schneider, 'Physiological Observations'; Sundstroem, 'Studies on Adaptations of Man to High Altitudes: I'; Sundstroem, 'Studies on Adaptation of Man to High Altitudes: VI'; Sundstroem, 'Studies on Adaptation of Man to High Altitudes: VII'; Keys *et al.*, 'Individual Variations in Ability'. See Buskirk, 'From Harvard to Minnesota', for a complete analysis of Keys's work. Also see Dill, 'Effects of Physical Strain and High Altitudes', for a more detailed discussion of this study.

[14] Henderson, 'The Last Thousand Feet on Everest'.

[15] Henry, 'The Role of Exercise in Altitude Pain'.

[16] Michael and Cureton, 'Effects of Physical Training on Cardiac Output'.

[17] Aguirre, 'Report of the First Central American Games', 546.

[18] US Stars Take Four Pan-American Track Titles', *New York Times*, 7 March 1951, 44.

[19] 'Jones of US Lowers World Mark in the 400 Meter Run at Mexico City', *New York Times*, 19 March 1955, 19.

[20] 'US First as Meet in Mexico Closes', *New York Times*, 27 March 1955, 3(S).

[21] Cervantes and Karpovich, 'Effect of Altitude on Athletic Performance'.

[22] Brundage to Mayer, 17 March 1955, OSC Archives. Otto Mayer was the chancellor of the IOC and ran the day-to-day operations of the organization in Lausanne when Brundage was not there. The 1960s, in addition to all the other issues going on, are a time of upheaval at the IOC administratively. When Otto Mayer retired, Eric Jonas came in on 1 July 1964 and was officially discharged on 13 April 1965. Johann Westerhoff was then hired for a short time and was later discharged. Next, Artur Takac was hired for a short time, and finally Monique Berlioux came on board.

[23] 'Demande-Requests-Solicita', XIX Jeux Olympiques-Olympic Games-Juegos Olimpicos 1963', *Mexico*, OSC Archives.

[24] 'Replies to the Questionnaire to be Answered in Presenting Buenos Aires as site for the XIX Olympic Games 1968' [pamphlet]. *Buenos Aires Aspira a Los Juegos Olimpicos De 1968*, OSC Archives.

[25] 'An Invitation to the International Olympic Committee to Celebrate the XIX Olympiad at Detroit, Michigan, USA', *Detroit, 1968*, OSC Archives. Detroit had already made bids to host the Games of 1944, 1952, 1956, 1960, and 1964.

[26] 'Demande-Requests-Solicita', *Mexico*, OSC Archives. Lyon's 'bid book' has not been located by the author.

[27] Organizing Committee of the Games of the XIX Olympiad, *The Organization*, 31, 99.

[28] Minutes of the 61st Session of the International Olympic Committee', OSC Archives.

[29] Organizing Committee of the Games of the XIX Olympiad, *The Organization*, 100.

[30] Minutes of the 61st Session of the International Olympic Committee, OSC Archives. The results of the vote were Mexico City 30, Buenos Aires 2, Detroit 14, Lyon 12. A majority of 29 votes were needed, so Mexico City won. Avery Brundage voted for Detroit, although he did not believe that 'they would get the Games'. See Brundage to Mayer, 22 Nov. 1963, OSC Archives.

[31] Balke, 'Work Capacity at Altitude'.

[32] Ibid., 346.

[33] Astrand, 'Physiological Aspects on Cross Country Skiing at the High Altitudes', 51.

[34] Brundage to Mayer, 29 Oct. 1956, OSC Archives.

[35] The IOC was upset that these contests were being referred to as 'pre-Olympics'. 'It was brought to everybody's attention that the International Sports Weeks, preceding the Olympic Games, should not be called Pre-Olympics as they are normal international competitions'. Minutes of the 66th Session of the International Olympic Committee', OSC Archives.

[36] 'Officials at Mexico City Games Object to "All-Out" Competition', *New York Times*, 17 Oct. 1965, S3. During the trials at the 'little Olympics' in 1965 the infield of the University of Mexico's huge stadium was a bizarre sight. Attendants raced over the infield with huge balloon-like plastic bags of oxygen and nose attachments to clamp on athletes who had just finished their events. These 'Douglas Bags' were used to collect expired air from the athletes. The athletes were then taken to examination rooms set up by each team and were given heart, breathing and blood tests. See also Underwood, 'Way Up High and Out of Breath', 30.

[37] 'Officials at Mexico City Games Object'.

[38] Mulder and Westerneg, *Olympic Games Mexico*. The countries that were represented included Cuba, France, England, Italy, Japan, USA, USSR, Spain, Jugoslavia [*sic*], Hungary and Holland.

[39] 'Mexico Ready to Host 17,000', *Daily Mirror* 28 Dec. 1967, 15 (clipping), Grenoble '68/ Coupures de Presse 1966–78, OSC Archives.

[40] 'Sever Controle pour Eviter', Comite Organisateur de Jeux de la XIX Olympiade Departement de Services de Presse, 24 Sept. 68, Mexico 1968/Service de Presse 1968, OSC Archives.

[41] Balke, 'Summary of Proceedings', 167, 173, 177. For additional results from American research see also Shepard, 'Physical Performance of Unacclimatized Men'; Balke, '4. Altitude [B] Inanimate Environmental Factors'.

[42] Margaria, *Exercise at Altitude*, 5.

[43] Ibid.

[44] 'Soviet Olympic Body in Study', *New York Times*, 13 March 1965, 21.

[45] J.L. Manning, 'Will There be Action to Prevent Olympic Cheating?' *Daily Mail* (Australia), 3 Jan. 1967, 10, Mexico 1968 General 1966–93, OSC Archives.

[46] R. Huntford, 'Olympic Training: Inside Russia's Non-Existent Camp', *Observer* 9 April 1967, Mexico 1968 General 1966–93, OSC Archives.

[47] Kuroda, 'Clinical Observation on Altitude Training'.

[48] R. Debaye, 'Font-Romeu Cite Pre-Olmpique', undated clipping, Mexico 1968 General 1966–93, OSC Archives.

[49] Cotton to Brundage, New York, 2 Aug. 1965, OSC Archives.

[50] 'Altitude is Important: Aim High for Your Pre Olympic Training' [pamphlet] (Alamosa, CO: Alamosa Olympic Training Committee, 1965), Mexico 1968 General 1966–93, OSC Archives.

[51] David (Marquess of Exeter) to Johann (Westerhoff), 30 June 1967, OSC Archives. Written on the letter is a note that says 'discussed with Mr AB and replied' – probably written by Westerhoff.

[52] 'Altitude Proves Barrier', *New York Times*, 13 Nov. 1965, 21.

[53] British Olympic Association, *Report of Medical Research*, 13.

[54] Hannon, 'High Altitude Acclimatization in Women', 37, 43.

[55] Brundage to Jonas, 13 Jan. 1965, OSC Archives; Mulder and Westerneg, *Olympic Games Mexico*, 17. 'The International Equestrian Federation has decided to hold the three day equestrian event of the 1968 Mexico Olympics outside of Mexico City because of the possible effects of the factor of high altitude on horses.... The three-day programme was too gruelling for horses and horsemen to be held in cities as high as Mexico City.... The International Federation decided that the horse jumping event, which usually closes the Olympic Games, would be held at the Mexico City Olympic Stadium as scheduled'.

[56] '1972 Olympics – Sapporo', *Infoplease Online*, 2000–01, available online at http:// www.infoplease.com/ipsa/A0300768.html, accessed 27 Feb. 2004.

[57] Simson and Jennings, *Dishonored Games*.

[58] With the retirement of Brundage from the IOC in 1972, the standards of amateurism were among the first changes implemented by new IOC president Lord Killanin. For example, athletes would now be provided with financial support during their training period of 60 days prior to the Games. In addition, athletes could now receive shoes and workout gear through their national Olympic committees. Killanin continued to relax the attitude of the IOC towards professionalism in the Olympic Movement throughout his tenure. See for example, Henry and Yeomans, *An Approved History of the Olympic Games*; Killanin, *My Olympic Years*. Another factor in the decision to hold the Games in Mexico City was a part of Brundage's belief in sharing the Olympic Movement with the world. He felt that one of the best ways to do that was to have the Games hosted in locations other than Europe or North America. He was certainly one of the strongest supporters of the decision to award the 1964 Games to Tokyo. Brundage did vote for Detroit as the site of the 1968 Games, but perhaps he already sensed that Mexico City would win convincingly, and

he felt that he could 'support' the American city. Brundage to Mayer, 22 Nov. 1963, OSC Archives.

[59] Westerhoff to National Olympic Committees, 27 May 1966, OSC Archives.

[60] Brundage to (David) Marquess of Exeter [Burghley], 22 June 1967, OSC Archives. Both Brundage and Burghley were concerned that they would get into a battle of semantics with athletes and officials over the length of time allowed for training at high altitude prior to the Games. Burghley, for example, claimed some athletes would go to altitude in August 1968 and argue that it was the end of their training year. They would then stay in September at the higher altitude with the argument that they were commencing a new training year. Finally they would travel to the Games in October with two months of high-altitude training. What was worse, at least for Burghley and his ideological sympathizers, was that they had spent two full months away from their professions, thus harming their amateur standing. Burghley argued that athletes must be instructed that they may only train at high altitude for one month 'in the 12 months before the Olympic Games'. The Marquess of Exeter to Brundage, 7 March 1967, OSC Archives.

[61] 'Distance Runners Troubled by Effects of High Altitudes', *New York Times*, 14 Aug. 1966, 4.

[62] Ibid.

[63] 'Olympic Official Defends High-Altitude Training Limit', *New York Times*, 26 Nov. 1966, 47.

[64] R. Bannister, 'The Punishment of a Long Distance Runner', *New York Times Magazine*, 18 Sept. 1966, 78, 87.

[65] Ibid.

[66] Ibid. Surprisingly, within IOC correspondence and publications, Burghley does not appear to ever address his countryman Bannister's complaints directly.

[67] Mulder and Westerneg, *Olympic Games Mexico*, OSC Archives.

[68] Ibid.

[69] Ibid.

[70] Brundage to Westerhoff, 22 June 1967, OSC Archives.

[71] Dirix and Sturbois, *The First Thirty Years*.

[72] Westerhoff to Marquess of Exeter, 28 June 1967, OSC Archives.

[73] Ibid.

[74] David (Marquess of Exeter) to Johann (Westerhoff), 30 June 1967, OSC Archives.

[75] Ibid.

[76] 'Training Camps', Circular Letter to the National Olympic Committees, 11 Aug. 1967 Ref. No C/373, Circulaires No. 341–401 1967, OSC Archives.

[77] Arbena, 'Mexico City, 1968', 139–47.

[78] Ibid.

[79] 'Address by Avery Brundage', OSC Archives.

[80] Ibid.

[81] R. Bannister, 'Debt Was Paid Off In Tears: Effects of Altitude on Distance Runners in Mexico', *Sports Illustrated*, 11 Nov. 1968, 22–3.

[82] 'Medal Winners at the Olympics, 1968', *Sports Illustrated*, 6 Nov. 1968, 92–6.

[83] Arbena, 'Mexico City, 1968', 143.

[84] Wallechinsky, *The Complete Book of the Olympics*.

[85] Meri-Jo Borzilleri, 'Rumors of USOC Move Spark Debate', *Mercury News*, 28 June 2003, available online at http://www.mercurynews.com/mld/mercurynews/sports/6193830. html, accessed 17 March 2004; 'Colorado Springs Local History', *Colorado Springs Page on Web*, n.d., available online at http://www.cospgs.com/history.html, accessed 17 March 2004.

References

Aguirre, E.C. 'Report of the First Central American Games held in Mexico City, from October 12 to November 2, 1926'. *American Physical Education Review* 32 (1927): 542–8.

Anshel, M.H., ed. *Dictionary of the Sport and Exercise Sciences*. Champaign, IL: Human Kinetics Publishers, 1991.

Arbena, J.L. 'Mexico City, 1968'. In *Historical Dictionary of the Modern Olympic Movement*, edited by J.E. Findling and Kimberly D. Pelle. Westport, CT: Greenwood Press, 1996.

Astrand, P.-O. 'Physiological Aspects on Cross Country Skiing at the High Altitudes'. *The Journal of Sports Medicine and Physical Fitness* 3 (1963): 51.

Balke, B. 'Work Capacity at Altitude'. In *Science and Medicine of Exercise and Sports*, edited by Warren R. Johnson. New York: Harper, 1960: ch. 18.

——. 'Summary of Proceedings'. In *The International Symposium on the Effects of Altitude on Physical Performance*, edited by R.F. Goddard. Chicago: The Athletic Institute, 1966.

——. '4. Altitude [B] Inanimate Environmental Factors Influencing Activity Area I: Physical Activity: General'. In *Encyclopedia of Sport Sciences and Medicine*, edited by Leonard Larson. New York: The Macmillan Company, 1971.

British Olympic Association. *Report of Medical Research Project into Effects of Altitude in Mexico City in 1965*, Middlesex: The Magnet Press, 1966.

Buskirk, E. 'From Harvard to Minnesota: Keys to our History'. *Exercise and Sport Sciences Review* 20 (1992): 1–26.

Cervantes, J. and Peter V. Karpovich. 'Effect of Altitude on Athletic Performance'. *Research Quarterly* 35 (1964): 446.

Dill, D.B. 'Effects of Physical Strain and High Altitudes on the Heart and Circulation'. *American Heart Journal* 23 (1942): 441–54.

Dirix, A. 'The Problems of Altitude and Doping in Mexico'. *Olympic Review 1967 Bulletin du Comitee International Olympique* 97 (Feb. 1967): 43–6.

Dirix, A. and Xavier Sturbois. *The First Thirty Years of the International Olympic Committee Medical Commission*, 3rd edn, Lausanne: International Olympic Committee, 1998.

Findling, J.E. and Kimberly D. Pelle, eds. *Historical Dictionary of the Modern Olympic Movement*. Westport, CT: Greenwood Press, 1996.

Hannon, J.P. 'High Altitude Acclimatization in Women'. In *The Effects of Altitude on Physical Performance, A Collection of Papers Presented at the International Symposium on the Effects of Altitude on Physical Performance*, edited by Roy F. Goddard. Chicago: The Athletic Institute, 1967.

Henderson, Y. 'The Last Thousand Feet on Everest'. *Nature* 143 (1939): 921–3.

Henry, B. and Patricia Henry Yeomans. *An Approved History of the Olympic Games*, Los Angeles, CA: Southern California Committee for the Olympic Games, 1984.

Henry, F. 'The Role of Exercise in Altitude Pain'. *American Journal of Physiology* 145, no. 3 (1946): 279–84.

Jokl, E. 'The Effect of Altitude on Athletic Performance'. In *International Research in Sport and Physical Education*, Springfield, IL: Charles Thomas Publishers, 1964: 361–71.

——. 'Exercise at Altitude – Historical Remarks'. In *Exercise at Altitude*, edited by R. Margaria. Amsterdam: Excerpta Medica Foundation, 1967.

Jokl, E. and E. Simon, eds. *International Research in Sport and Physical Education*. Springfield, IL: Charles C. Thomas, 1964.

Keys, A., B.H.C. Matthews, W.H. Forbes and R.A. McFarland. 'Individual Variations in Ability to Acclimatize to High Altitude'. *Proceedings of the Royal Society*, B 126 (1938–39): 1–29.

Killanin, Lord (Michael). *My Olympic Years*, New York: Morrow, 1983.

Kuroda, Y. 'Clinical Observation on Altitude Training'. In *Proceedings of the International Seminar for the Study of University Sports*, edited by Renji Kiode. Tokyo: The Organizing Committee for the 1967 Universiade in Tokyo, 1967.

Margaria, R., ed. *Exercise at Altitude*. Amsterdam: Excerpta Medica Foundation, 1967.

Michael, E. and Thomas K. Cureton. 'Effects of Physical Training on Cardiac Output at Ground Level and at 15,000 Feet Simulated Altitude'. *Research Quarterly* 24 (1953): 446.

Mulder, E. and Cor Westerneg, eds. *Olympic Games Mexico 12–27 October 1968*. Schiphol, The Netherlands: Sport Department, KLM – Royal Dutch Airlines, 1968 [Booklet produced by KLM]. Folder: Mexico 1968 Reglement Sports Petites Brochures, OSC Archives.

Organizing Committee of the Games of the XIX Olympiad. *The Organization, Book 2 of Mexico City – Official Report of the Games 1968*, Mexico City: Organizing Committee of the Games of the XIX Olympiad, 1969.

Schneider, E. 'Physiological Observations Following Descent from Pike's Peak to Colorado Springs'. *American Journal of Physiology* 32 (1913): 295–308.

Shepard, R.J. 'Physical Performance of Unacclimatized Men in Mexico City'. *Research Quarterly* 37 (1966).

——. '*High Life: A History of High Altitude Physiology and Medicine*' [review]. *Canadian Journal of Applied Physiology* 25 (2000): 79–80.

Simson, V. and Andrew Jennings. *Dishonored Games: Corruption, Money and Greed at the Olympics*, New York: SPI Books, 1992.

Stainsby, W.N. and George A. Brooks. 'Control of Lactic Acid Metabolism in Contracting Muscles and during Exercise'. *Exercise and Sport Science Reviews* 18 (1990): 29–63.

Sundstroem, E.S. 'Studies on Adaptations of Man to High Altitudes: I. Effect of High Altitude on Pulse, Body Temperature, Blood Pressure, Respiration Rate, Output of Urine and Loss of Energy in Feces'. *University of California Publications in Physiology* 5 (1919): 71–86.

——. 'Studies on Adaptation of Man to High Altitudes: VI. Effect of High Altitudes on the Number of Erythrocytes'. *University of California Publications in Physiology* 5 (1919): 133–48.

——. 'Studies on Adaptation of Man to High Altitudes: VII. Effect of High Altitudes on the Size of Erythrocytes'. *University of California Publications in Physiology* 5 (1919): 149–57.

Ungerleider, S. *Faust's Gold: Inside the East German Doping Machine*, New York: Thomas Dunne Books, 2001.

Wallechinsky, D. *The Complete Book of the Olympics*, New York: Penguin Books, 1984.

West, J. *High Life: A History of High Altitude Physiology and Medicine*, New York: Oxford University Press, 1998.

Wrynn, A. 'The Human Factor: Science, Medicine and the International Olympic Committee, 1900–70'. *Sport in Society* 7, 2 (2004): 211–32.

'If You Want to Cry, Cry on the Green Mats of Kôdôkan': Expressions of Japanese Cultural and National Identity in the Movement to Include Judo into the Olympic Programme

Andreas Niehaus

Road to Hosting the Games in 1964

John MacAloon writes in his article 'The Turn of Two Centuries: Sport and the Politics of Intercultural Relations': 'To be a nation recognized by others and realistic to themselves, a people must march in the Olympic Games Opening Ceremonies procession'. [1] Taking part in the Games is therefore not only a question of being recognized, that is, presenting the nation to the outside, but is also a question of cultural and national identity. Attesting to the validity of these observations, the Olympic Games played a vital role in Japan's international rehabilitation as well as restoring Japanese national identity following the nation's defeat in the Second World War.

The IOC denied Japan the right to 'march' in the first post-war Games of 1948 when the Japanese Olympic Committee was re-established. [2] In the Minutes of the April 1949 IOC Executive Board Session that took place in Rome, however, evidence can be found of the discussions concerning the re-entry of Japan into the Olympic Movement. Japan's rehabilitation as member of the world community followed shortly thereafter in 1951, when Japan signed the peace treaty. One year later in 1952, Japan would regain her national sovereignty. [3] The reintegration of Japan into the world community was strongly supported by Douglas MacArthur, the Supreme Commander for the Allied Forces in Japan. In a letter addressed to J.J. Garland, the US IOC member, MacArthur wrote:

> It is my personal hope that conditions will make it possible for Japan to be a competitor with the other nations of the world in 1952. Performances in swimming during the Occupation indicate that, in this sport particularly, the Japanese may be expected to make outstanding records. Participation in the Games at Helsinki should contribute greatly to a deeply felt and desirable goal of the Japanese people to join again with other nations in peaceful and cultural pursuits. [4]

1950 was a key year for Japan. On 25 June 1950, the Korean War had started and marked a shift in the politics of the occupational authorities which considered Japan an important factor in the fight against Communism. Although Article 9 of the new post-war Japanese Constitution denied Japan the right to have an army, a 'Police Reserve Force' was established in 1950. Furthermore, with the support of the US, former wartime leaders (including convicted war criminals) were able to occupy influential positions in government, bureaucracy and industry once again. By endorsing the participation of Japanese athletes in the Olympics, MacArthur, whose attitude towards Japan had always been a paternalistic one, wanted to show that the 'bad child' was allowed to play with the others again. [5] And Japan 'played' considerably well in the 1952 Olympics in Helsinki: 69 athletes participated, winning one gold (freestyle wrestling), six silver, and two bronze medals.

The Tokyo parliament was aware of the symbolic meaning that hosting an Olympic Games could have for Japan's way towards rehabilitation (besides the expected influence on national and local economical growth) and decided in 1952 to apply to host the 1960 Games. When the IOC in 1955 chose Rome to host the 1960 Games, Tokyo immediately decided to apply for the 1964 Games and Japanese state organizations took the leading role at all levels of decision-making. [6] Important meetings of the commission to prepare the Games were held in the residence of prime minister Kishi Nobusuke (formerly imprisoned but not tried for war crimes) and the organizational efforts were organized under the Ministry of Education (*Monbushô*). [7]

Under the guidance of the Ministry of Education, the Games were programmatically used to resocialize Japan into the world community as well as to promote and strengthen the post-war Japanese identity, which centred around the terms *hitozukuri* (forming people) and *konjôzukuri* (building spirit, building perseverance). Seki Harunami, in his book *Sengo Nihon no supôtsu seisaku* ('Sport politics in Postwar Japan'), shows that Japanese sport politics in Japan under the guidance of the occupational forces after the Second World War went through a short process of democratization only to find an objective that better suited their goals in the 1950s: medals. After all, in the end it is not enough only to march in the Games; the Japanese realistically understood that to be truly recognized among the competing nations, it is the number of medals you win that counts. In order to enhance the chances of medals, sport education and governmental sport sponsorships focused on the development of athletes capable of winning international competitions. [8]

Although the selection of the host city for the 1964 Games did not actually take place until a year after the 55th IOC Session was held in Tokyo in 1958, the members of the IOC were able to get a first-hand impression of the sport situation in Japan. Because the third Asian Games opened on 24 May, immediately after the IOC meeting, the members of the IOC were able to witness the organizational skills of the Japanese. Significantly, both events were opened by the Japanese emperor. An account in the *Bulletin du Comité International Olympique* summarizes: 'They [the members of the IOC] were pondering, while witnessing the Games, whether Japan is likely to be a worthy successor to Rome in the matter of organizing the next Olympic Games. One can almost guess that they left Tokyo most favourably impressed'. [9]

The question of which city would host the 1964 Games of the XVIIIth Olympiad was finally decided in Munich 1959 and the JOC, especially its president Azuma Ryôtarô, tried to find allies for the Japanese bid. It was Avery Brundage who became the most important supporter and actor behind the scenes. During the Munich Session, the Tokyo delegation of Hirasawa Kazushige and Yasui Seiichirô presented their bid and answered questions on 25 May, starting at 4:55 p.m. Tokyo was elected with 34 votes during the next day's Session (Detroit received ten, Vienna had nine, and Brussels had five). [10]

The decision in favour of Tokyo meant that the organizing committee had considerable influence on the selection of sports to be included in the Games, and the Japanese organizers were able to have judo included into the programme for the first time. Judo's inclusion into the Olympic programme was, as Allen Guttmann writes, 'clearly a favour done to the Japanese hosts'. [11] This statement, however, ignores the fact that not only Japanese politicians and sport administrators but also sportsmen from Japan, Europe and the United States pressed for Olympic judo. The inclusion of judo into the Games was thus not a mere generous gesture.

Finally Olympic Judo

Kanô Risei, son of the judo founder Kanô Jigorô, head of the Kôdôkan and president of the International Judo Federation (IJF), had asked in 1952 that judo be included into the Olympic programme for the first time. [12] The IJF had been recognized by the IOC a year earlier on 15 September 1951 as the international body representing the non-Olympic sport of judo. The question of judo was put on the agenda of the 1953 IOC Session in Mexico. However, during this Session the IOC decided to postpone the discussion whether judo should be included until 1954 in Athens. Ironically enough, the question was then placed in the agenda under 'Reducing the Games Program' and the odds were firmly against judo in 1954. [13] The Executive Committee of the IOC decided during its meeting with delegates of the National Olympic Committees (NOCs) in Athens in May of 1954 'that no new sport shall be introduced at the Melbourne Games of 1956'. [14] During the 50th Session of the IOC, convened following the meeting between the IOC Executive Committee and the NOCs, the final decision was postponed for a second time after the French representative Armand Massard, the 1920 Olympic gold medalist in fencing, argued that volleyball, roller skating and judo could 'well be entered on the list of optional sports'. [15]

The question of including judo (as well as volleyball, archery and roller skating) in the Olympic programme was discussed again during the 51st IOC Session in Paris in 1955. However, none of these four sports reached the necessary quorum of two-thirds (in this case 34 votes). Judo even ended last with only three votes (volleyball had 26; archery 19; roller skating seven). [16] It was certainly too early for a Japanese sport to enter the Olympics. It should also not be forgotten that the Japanese Olympic Committee had only been recognized in 1951 at the Vienna meeting of the IOC, whose members still had reservations towards the Japanese.

But when in 1960 the IJF asked again to include judo into the programme of the Olympic Games, Tokyo had already been chosen to host the 1964 summer Games and Kanô Risei could rely on political support in Japan. [17] Besides the strong support of then Tokyo governor, Azuma Ryôtarô, the motion was also supported by the Judo Federation of Japanese Diet Members that was formed in 1961. The president of the federation, Shoriki Matsutarô, described the group's aims as 'to make the whole nation raise the Olympic Movement, to make complete arrangements for the enforcement of judo event at the XVIII Olympic Games to be held in Tokyo'. [18]

When the IJF motion to list judo as an optional Olympic sport was discussed during the 58th IOC Session in Rome in 1960, it was connected to the question of whether judo should be included in the Tokyo Games: 'This federation [IJF] asks to be recognized as an Olympic sport, and that JÛDÔ [*sic*] be included in the programme of the Tokyo Games'. [19] The Japanese IOC representative, Azuma Ryôtarô, strongly supported the candidature of judo during this Session and expressed hope that judo might be included in the Tokyo Games. The assembly, after hearing their members Francois Piétri, Josef Gruss and Ferenc Mezö, decided to accept the judo candidature by 39 votes to two. [20] Despite this decision, it was still unclear as to whether or not judo would be on the final programme for Tokyo.

The decision to accept the candidature left IOC members as well as the organizing committee with the question of how to reduce the overall programme for the Games. The plan to limit the number of sport events had been on the IOC agenda for a while and a commission was expected to propose a change of Rule 30, which stipulated the number of sports for the Games. When the question of judo was discussed, Brundage made clear that 'the mere fact of including Judo in the Tokyo Games inevitably calls for an adjunction to the list of sports prescribed in Rule 30'. [21] During the Session in Rome, K. Andrianov and A. Romanov proposed a change of the first sentence of Rule 30, which allows for only 18 sports, and the following change was decided: 'The official programme shall include minimum 18 and maximum 21 of the following sports . . .'. [22] However, in the end, Rule 30 read as follows: 'A minimum of 15 and a maximum of 18 of the events enumerated above must figure in the programme'. [23]

Already during the JOC congress in December 1960, the organizing committee of the Tokyo Games, which had been set up in September 1959, decided to put judo on the list of sports to be practised during the Games. Following Rule 30, the Tokyo Committee first limited the events of the Tokyo Games to 18: 'The Tokyo Committee suggests the elimination of the Modern Pentathlon (owing to lack of horses in Japan) and the rowing events. On the other hand, it asks for including judo and finally proposes a maximum of 18 sports to figure on the programme of the 1964 Games'. [24] However, the next day (21 June) a heated debate on the number of sport events for 1964 arose. One day earlier, Brundage had already mentioned that the number of sports did not matter as long as they were in accordance with the Olympic rules. After further discussion, the final vote decided on 20 events, eliminating handball and archery. [25] But judo was only an optional sport, and the officials of the IJF already knew in 1963 that judo would not be part of the Games in 1968. [26]

Much of the success of the bid to host the Games of 1964 can be ascribed to the support of Avery Brundage, whereas the success of the IJF candidature certainly owed thanks to the support of IOC chancellor Otto Mayer. In a 28 May 1960 letter to Kanô Risei, Mayer wrote: 'You may be assured that I shall do all what is in my power to help you'. To make sure that the members of the IOC were 'acquainted with this sport', he advised his friend Eric Jonas, who was at that moment vice-president of the European Judo Federation, how to proceed:

> I helped him a lot and told him how to act. He is now organizing an action so that every member of the IOC here in Europe will be visited by a Jûdô man in view of having his vote! In our next Bulletin he will give me a text for an article which I shall publish. [27]

Thus it came as no surprise that Kanô thanked Mayer as early as 23 August for his support. [28]

The Japanese organizers – who were in fact linked to the state, like the members of the Ministry of Education – were politically pushing for judo as an Olympic sport because it could represent Japanese tradition to the world and serve as reference for an as-yet-undefined Japanese self-identity. However, to clearly understand the importance of the inclusion of judo in the Olympics and what it meant for Japan and the Japanese, we have to understand the significance of judo in the construction of Japan's cultural and national identity and the formation of 'Japaneseness' in modern Japan.

Judo and Japanese National Identity

Judo was developed by the physical educator Kanô Jigorô in 1882 as a modernization of traditional Japanese *jûjutsu* styles. For Kanô Jigorô, judo was not merely a form of martial fighting but a form of physical education. In the late nineteenth century, under the guidance of Minister of Education Mori Arinori, Japanese education was moral education oriented in an attempt to serve the needs of the state (*kokka no tame no kyôiku*). In this period, physical education was expected to provide the state with the healthy and patriotic young men required to build a strong economy and military for the nation (*fukoku kyôhei*). Through judo, Kanô was reacting to this nation-centred educational philosophy. In 1889 he explained:

> Jûdô is not morality but moral education in the broad sense. If we include jûdô as subject into the curriculum of our schools throughout the country, it can certainly compensate for the weak points of our present educational system, support the character formation of our pupils and strengthen their patriotism. Should we ever have international conflicts, and should we ever be attacked by enemies from all sides, by following the teachings of jûdô, we not feel fear and will not surrender. And in peaceful times the foreigners will admire the modern development in our country as well as our customs and habits. If we follow the teachings of jûdô ... the time when our country will be one of the strongest civilized countries will be close. [29]

Kanô thus implemented the idea of creating patriots through judo and presented this new martial sport to governmental institutions as a tool to help revive Japan's national identity, which Japan desperately needed to overcome the feeling of inferiority towards the West.

Thus judo was predestined to serve as a metaphor for the Japanese self-image and nation of the Meiji period because it was seen as a martial art in which physically weaker men could overcome physically stronger men by means of technique and spirit. In Kanô's autobiographical writings as well as in his biographies, his 'confrontation' with the West plays a prominent role. Kanô is represented as a protector of the nation, who, through the training of judo, is able to demonstrate the Japanese spirit to the world. Kanô's story was popular in turn-of-the-century Japan for it united an individual's personal history with the nation's imagined future.

Yet in the early nineteenth century, judo was far from being a fixed system. It underwent a series of technical, organizational and theoretical modifications. When Kanô came into contact with the Olympic Movement and the Olympic idea after he was elected to become the first Olympic Committee member to an Asian country in

1909, his ideas shifted towards a more internationally orientated perspective. Kanô incorporated de Coubertin's sport philosophy into judo and hoped to include Japanese martial arts, especially kendo and judo, into the Olympic programme: 'I hope that martial arts and athleticism will develop hand in hand. Even though they are different, their goal is still the same: the strengthening of body and mind. It is therefore wise to include kendo and judo and the attitude of bushido into the Olympic Games'. [30]

In the 1930s and early 1940s, however, judo became more and more intertwined with Japanese ultranationalism. It had been part of the curriculum in middle schools as early as 1911. In the early nineteenth century, however, no clear distinction was drawn between the tradtional *jûjutsu* styles and judo, which was merely seen as a form of traditional wrestling. Only in 1926 had judo reached a hegemonic status in education, superseding the traditional *jûjutsu* styles. In 1931, judo together with kendo finally became compulsory in the schools. During the 1930s and 1940s, judo was increasingly seen as part of a pre-military education and nationwide mobilization and reinvented as 'a counter to Western values to infuse Japan's modern sports culture with Japanese spirit'. [31] As part of the war machinery, judo was held as an accessory to the Japanese participation in the war, and subsequently, the Supreme Commander for the Allied Forces forbade the training of judo, like that of all other martial arts with the exception of sumo. Only in 1949 was judo allowed to be officially taught again. The same year the *Zen Nihon Jûdô Renmei* was founded and Kanô Jigorô's son, Kanô Risei, was elected as president. By this move, the Kôdôkan was able to control the development of judo in Japan.

In the Japanese discourses of the post-war period – in movies, literature and songs – judo can be seen as a metaphor for Japan as well as a means of transmitting post-war values. In the 1942 *enka* (popular) song of *Sugata Sanshiro*, Kôdôkan and judo are described:

> Keep in your heart the saying
> 'It is not important to win against others,
> but to win against yourself'.
> Train hard without complaining.
> The moon laughs, Sugata Sanshirô
> More than the flowering grass
> I love the spirit of the grass that has been trampled down
> but is still alive.
> What I love is the love that is forbidden.
> When I cry it rains,
> Kôdôkan. [32]

Sugata Sanshirô is the title of the first movie directed by Kurosawa Akira, which was released in 1943. It tells the story of the young Sanshirô, who puts all his efforts into his dream to become a famous judo master. After *Sugata Sanshirô* was a success, Kurosawa filmed the follow-up *Zoku Sugata Sanshirô* (*Sugata Sanshirô II*) in 1945. In contrast to the first part, however, *Zoku Sugata Sanshirô* is characterized by national propaganda claiming the superiority of Japanese culture, by matching judo with Western boxing. Since the early years of the Shôwa period, judo was seen more and more as a uniquely Japanese practice embodying the Japanese soul. This image was productively used in the post-war years to channel the nation's struggle to recover. 'Train hard' became one of the major maxims of sport politics in the late 1950s and 1960s and mirrors the spirit of post-war Japan, when the nation's efforts were bundled together with the task of rebuilding the country (*kunizukuri*) and putting Japan on the road to economic growth and prosperity. In yet another *enka* song, entitled *Jûdô ichidai* ('A Life for jûdô'), we read: 'A life for jûdô / I throw a light into the darkness of the world'. [33] Rebuilding the country demanded stamina as well as personal sacrifice from all Japanese nationals, and this 'patriotic' spirit became connected to Kôdôkan judo. In the metaphorical framework of these popular songs, judo and the Kôdôkan serve as the homeland (*furusato*) of an imagined community.

It should not be forgotten that judo training had been part of the education of most Japanese men in their 30s, and they had incorporated and memorized not only the moves but also the atmosphere of the training halls and the training spirit. Judo thus became a space of shared nostalgia for these men, a place were the past was connected not only to the present but to the (shining) future as well.

Maguire has observed that male sport 'appears to play a crucial role in the construction and representation of national identity' [34] and Roche has linked male sport cultures to the shaping of personal and group identities. [35] Despite the fact that women were already trained in judo in Japan around the 1910s (the first accounts date from before 1900) and the Kôdôkan had established a department for women in 1926, judo remained a male sport (especially the tournaments) possessing the means to construct a masculine identity and embodying the idea of defending the nation.

Throughout Japanese history, the wrestler had been seen as the representative of his home. During the Heian period (784–1185) at the imperial court and during the Edo period (1600–1868), wrestlers were granted a special status in society. When Commodore Perry came to Japan in 1853 and 1854, sumo wrestlers were present and the Americans were invited to throw a punch at their impressive bellies. In the years following the forced opening of Japanese harbours, woodblock prints went on sale in which sumo wrestlers were depicted defeating Western soldiers and sailors; these woodblock prints cathartically digested and healed the nation's cultural shock. Sumo wrestlers during that time were certainly 'symbols of Japan's might in the face of the invaders from the West'. [36]

Wrestling fights in the past were thought to show the well-being of a province and the matches between foreigners and Japanese were supposed to show that the nation was up to the foreign 'threat'. The significance of these matches can be seen in what is called *Santeru jiken* (the Santel Incident). In 1914, Itô Tokugorô, a fifth *dan* (level) in judo, was defeated by the American wrestler Ad Santel. In 1917, Santel also beat the judomen Miyake Tarô and Sakai Daisuke in Seattle. Santel went to Japan in 1921 to challenge the Kôdôkan. The fights took place at a highly symbolical location:

Yasukuni Shrine, where the souls of soldiers who died fighting for the Japanese emperor are located and worshipped from the beginning of the Restoration War (1868) to present-day Japan. Santel won his fight against Nagata Reijirô and managed a draw against Shoji Hikô. [37] Another prominent example is the wrestler Rikidôzan, who was able to drew huge masses into stadiums during the 1950s. His specialty was fighting against 'huge' and dirty-fighting foreigners whom he usually defeated following a well-structured choreography.

These victories against foreigners certainly helped to soothe the memories of Japan's military defeat. [38] The anticipated victories in the judo competitions at the Tokyo Olympics were meant to achieve even more. Tagsold has shown that through the Olympics, the symbols of Japan's imperialistic and nationalistic past, such as the *tennô* (the Emperor) as well as the military, were positively reconstructed and included into the new post-war Japanese national identity. [39] By including judo in the Olympic programme, Japan was thus able to rehabilitate another of its wartime tools and to showcase the value of its tradition, which was denied in the early post-war years not only to the world but also to Japanese nationals. In this sense, 1964 marks an important year during which tradition became once again a reference of and source for a cultural and national self-identity. But how traditional was judo in 1964? And what did the inclusion of judo mean for the Olympic Movement and its internationalization?

Internationalization of Judo

Japanese *jûjutsu* began to spread to the Western world during the early twentieth century as 'ju-jitsu'. In Seattle, a training hall was opened in 1903 and in England ju-jitsu spread with the arrival of Tani Yukio in 1900 and Koizumi Gunji in 1906. In Germany it was Ono Agitarô who taught ju-jitsu as early as 1906 to the military in Berlin. These early figures taught traditional Japanese *jûjutsu* styles and not the newly developed judo. However, it was the Kôdôkan judo style of Japanese wrestling that became dominant not only in Japan but also in the US and Europe. The success of Kôdôkan judo can be ascribed to Kanô Jigorô's influence as a sports administrator and politician as well as his far-sighted decision to send teachers abroad to award *dan*-graduations to key figures in the already established European ju-jitsu community, thus binding these sportsmen to the Kôdôkan. This form of friendly takeover can be seen in England, where Tani Yukio and Koizumi Gunji were awarded second *dan* after they joined the Kôdôkan, but it was also applied in Germany, France and Austria. Another important factor is that Kôdôkan judo was highly organized and centralized. As Frühstück and Manzenreiter state: 'With numerous schools, ideologies, and masters striving hard to coexist, jûjutsu could never establish the strong following that judo did'. [40]

Although the early teachers were mostly Japanese, European judo went through a process of acculturation and developed along Western sporting traditions; however, it should not be forgotten that the creation of judo itself was based on Western sport concepts and Western sport education. The acculturation of European judo was also partially due to the fact that judo teachers in Europe included their own experiences gained in the circus fights that were very popular at the time. During this period, fighting rules such as weight classes were also newly introduced. The system of multicoloured belts spread most likely from Paris, where it was introduced by Kawaishi Mikonosuke in the second half of the 1930s.

The European development of judo after the war took shape with the foundation of the European Judo Union (EJU) in London on 28 July 1948, only a day after the formation of the British Judo Association. The EJU was founded under the initiative of the London-based Budokwai and representatives from Italy, Holland and Switzerland participated under the eyes of one French observer. The first European Championships were held in 1951 – a time by which judo in Japan had only started to recover.

The field of judo in the beginning of the post-war years was dominated by Western sport administrators and sportsmen. The need for an international body became increasingly evident and in 1951 the fourth meeting of the EJU was first dissolved and then automatically replaced by the International Judo Federation (IJF). However, the written proposal put forward by the Kôdôkan to place the headquarters in Tokyo was declined and only at its second meeting in 1952 was the position of president offered to the head of the Kôdôkan, Kanô Risei. [41]

Power and dominance are reflected spatially; during the 1960s as well as early 1970s not only were the IJF headquarters situated in Tokyo and its president Japanese, but the first championships in 1956 and 1958 were also held in Japan. In both years Japanese fighters placed first and second. [42] The world returned to the birthplace of judo only to be shown that the Japanese were still superior in their fighting skills. In contrast to the European weight classes, the first three world championships knew only one weight category: the open. This meant that the Japanese fighters who were comparably smaller had to face physically larger and stronger European and American fighters. Fighting in only one weight category complemented the idea that 'a weaker person can overcome a stronger through technique and spirit' and Japanese technique and spirit certainly seemed better in the 1950s.

But already in 1961, when the championships were held outside Japan for the first time, Anton Geesink won the title of world champion, and the Japanese became aware that although technique and spirit continued to be their forte, it was better to initiate weight classes. [43] The decision to have different weight classes during the Olympics in Tokyo certainly helped Japan to win three gold medals and one silver medal in the four weight categories. [44] But 1961 also foreshadowed Geesink's victory at the Olympics and the end of the dominance of the Kôdôkan in terms of administration, rules and fighting skills.

When judo administrators in the IJF and EJU hoped to turn judo Olympic, a paragraph concerning amateurism was added to the statutes of the IJF in 1961 – 'Only judokas who are amateurs strictly in respect of the rules defined by the

International Olympic Committee can take part in the Olympic Games' [45] – thus adopting judo even more to the modes of Western sports. Guttmann states that 'the Olympic program remains essentially Western' [46] despite the inclusion of judo. It is certainly true, as we have seen, that judo developed along the path of modern sport and according to Olympic rules. However, it is not the 'reality' that we find in the changed rules that governs our perception of cultural phenomena but the reality of our own cultural history of perception. Almost no one cared about European weight classes, coloured belts and the 'amateur rule' while on the screen Westerners in white 'kimonos' bowed to each other to apply 'mysterious techniques' that the Japanese developed 'hundreds of years' ago. In other words, in order to understand what the inclusion of judo meant for the Olympic Movement, we must understand the construction of the other: of Asia and more specifically, of Japan.

Western Construction of Judo as Japanese Martial Art

The image of Japan in the early twentieth century is characterized by its exoticism. Japan was seen as place for spirituality, of mysteriousness, as a paradise long lost to the highly technological West. Embedded within the concept of Japan was the image of the small Japanese body (which certainly holds true when compared to the average size of Europeans). However, this image of the small Japanese was also connected to the idea of the 'weak Japanese'. Therefore we see the fascination with a martial arts system that apparently gave these 'small people' the power to fight against bigger and stronger enemies. When the first ju-jitsu fighters such as Tani Yukio came to Europe, it was exactly this image that predetermined the reception of the discipline, [47] and when Japan defeated Russia in 1905, it was a deep shock to Western nations. Sports writers of the time claimed that Japan's military success was connected not only to a hygienic way of living and vegetarian nutrition but also to *jûjutsû*. Ludwig Bach, for example, argues in his book, *Verteidige dich selbst* ('Defend Yourself') written in 1928, that the Japanese were able to 'compensate for the physical characteristics of their race' by employing ju-jitsu. [48]

This approach to Japanese culture, which was still predominant in the 1950s and 1960s, was based on a general dichotomy between Western technology and Eastern spirituality. In a speech Avery Brundage gave in Tokyo during the 54th Session of the IOC he remarked:

> Undoubtedly the East has gained from its association with the West in the Olympic Movement and its adoption of Western methods of physical training, in a stronger and healthier people. But, what about the West? What will the West gain from this meeting on the fields of sport, with people of different ideas of life, different customs, and different viewpoints? Well, if the East gains in a physical sense, perhaps the West will gain intellectually and spiritually. The wisdom of the East is proverbial, and Asia, after all, was the birthplace of all the great religions. Fair play and good sportsmanship are a part of all religions as well as of the Olympic Code. [49]

The question of the Western perception of Asia in general and judo in particular is mirrored in the struggle for the international recognition of judo within the Olympic Movement.

The emergence of the new international body meant an economic threat to the existing ju-jitsu clubs in Europe. But only when the IJF started its initiative to have judo included in the Olympic programme did we see resistance from the International World Judo Federation (IWJF), which encompassed under its wings different forms of *jûjutsu* and judo, like judo-do, developed by Julius Fleck in the late 1940s in Austria. The IWJF also wanted to be recognized by the IOC. The arguments against the recognition of the IJF put forward by the representatives of the IWJF reflect the sport's political controversies of the time as well as an ideological frame in which the dominance of the Kôdôkan was seen as a threat to the cultural and religious identity of the West.

In February 1955, Jack Robinson, president of the IWJF and president of the Johannesburg-based Jûdôkwai, asked for affiliation of the IWJF and for the inclusion of judo into the Games of 1956. [50] Robinson, a self-awarded tenth *dan*, had immigrated to South Africa from Britain and started to teach his own form of judo. He had founded the South African National Amateur Judo Association (SANAJA) and worked as instructor for the police and the military. [51] Already in this first letter to the IOC, Robinson connects the choice of the international body that will present judo to an ideological choice between West or Far East (Japan). Robinson argues that in judo 'the Western World [is] superior to Japan' and that the Japanese are avoiding 'combat' because their defeat 'is a moral certainty' and moreover, 'there [*sic*] principles and rules could never be accepted by the Western world, who refuses to bow on there [*sic*] knees'. [52] Robinson literally refers to the ritual of greeting but metaphorically transfers this ritual to an ideological level: the West will not surrender to the East.

The matter was handed over to Otto Mayer who informed Robinson that the IJF was already registered with the IOC and therefore his application could not be accepted. Additionally, Mayer advised Robinson to get into contact with the IJF and form one international body. [53] But the IJF did not want to merge with the IWJF, an organization that was too diffuse in its administration as well as its sporting aims. In his response letter, Robinson turns towards a more or less openly 'racist' vocabulary; he refers to the 'white men' and expresses his hope 'that every country will be officially recognized, and not only the yellow race'. [54] Robinson's approach certainly has to be seen from the perspective of the tense relationship between South Africa and the IOC during the late 1950s and 1960s. The problem of apartheid and racism in South Africa was a sensitive issue for the IOC, and the pressure to exclude the South Africans from the Games intensified from both inside and outside the IOC. [55]

Robinson resurfaces in 1961 and claims again that the Japanese organizations are not willing to form one body and ascribes this to a 'fear of defeat'. [56] Robinson, however, is not aware of the fact that in the meantime, the 'sporting liberal' [57]

Ira G. Emery, who was general secretary of the South African Olympic Association and president of the South African National Olympic Committee (SANOC), had written to the IJF describing the situation of judo in South Africa. In his letter, Emery distanced the South African Olympic Association from Robinson and his organization, seeing them as professionals. [58]

Emery's letter certainly weakened the position of Robinson and his attempt to remain an international sport official despite the growing international isolation of South African sportsmen and sport officials that in 1970 ultimately resulted in the expulsion of South Africa from the IOC. Robinson tried to maintain his image as that of a international sport administrator writing on behalf of the IWJF; [59] he became more insistent and even used the media. In an interview to the Johannesburg *Star* on 6 June 1961, he announced that he would go to Athens in order to participate in the meeting of the International Olympic Committee and 'demand' that the members of the IWJF also be allowed to compete. [60] Because Robinson was not a member of an organization that was affiliated to the IOC, he was not allowed to participate. In his answer to Robinson, Mayer is seemingly annoyed and makes clear that he regards 'Robinson's organization' as professional, 'which renders any contact between the IOC and [his] body more difficult if not impossible'. [61] Mayer is thus taking the position of Emery and Kanô Risei, who stated in a letter from May 1961: 'Except the IJF, there are some bodies whose substance is professional, such as the International World Judo Federation, but serious amateur sportsmen are taking no notice of such bodies'. [62] The accusation of not being a amateur organization had to be taken seriously.

During the presidency of Avery Brundage (1952–72), the attempt to keep the ideal of amateur sportsmen was one of the major issues within the IOC. Brundage, like de Coubertin, saw the Olympic Movement as a religion: 'A religion, whose ethical component Brundage summed up in the single word: amateurism'. [63] The question of amateurism thus was also a welcome argument for the IWJF representatives. Not only Robinson but also Stefan Aschenbrenner and Knud Janson, a Danish judo pioneer as well as secretary and later president of the IWJF, accused the IJF of being a professional and commercial organization: 'Can CIO recognize a body (IJU) which as its presidium has a professionel [sic] Judohighschool (Kôdôkan)?' [64] However, personal and political ties within the IOC were strong and Mayer turned toward Azuma, the former judomen and supporter of Kôdôkan judo, to ask for clarification. In Mayer's answer letter to Janson, we read: 'There is no professional amongst the leaders of that Federation in Tokyo. There are of course some teachers, but who are not leaders of the Federation'. [65] The Kôdôkan had in fact already in 1909 been transformed from a private enterprise into a foundation. [66] And Kanô Risei could thus state in a letter to Brundage: 'The International Judo Federation is naturally an amateur organization, and we will at this time renew the spirit of amateurism'. [67] Yet the existence of professional judo teachers could not be denied and in the previously mentioned IJF letter to the IOC from 5 June 1961, we subsequently read: 'It is absolutely clear that judo professors cannot take part in the Games'.

A second issue that was discussed around the recognition of the IJF is connected to the question of religious teachings in judo. The reverse diffusion of judo implied an exotification of judo because in the West it was inextricably connected to spirituality and Zen Buddhism, elements not found in the writings of Kanô Jigoro on judo. Kanô himself, as a typical intellectual of the Meiji period, was not interested in religion but in science. We also witness a promotion of state Shinto during the Meiji period, whereas Buddhism was suppressed by the Japanese government. A martial art based on Zen Buddhism could not have received governmental support to the extent that judo did. The identification of judo with Zen Buddhism should be seen as a process that took place concurrently with the diffusion of judo into the West. Even in sport history, the unity of Japanese martial arts and Zen Buddhism was taken for granted and a secularization of judo was observed. [68] The question of this esoteric perception of judo is mirrored in the IWJF's struggle to be internationally recognized to represent judo as a governing body in the Olympic Movement: 'Judo for the Japaneses [*sic*] and their followers is not only a sport, but a "bodily way" for working with Zen Buddhism (Buddhism of Samurai etc.) and code of Bushido'. Janson accused the IJF of 'working on a cocktail of Zen Buddhism, mysticism, Bushido'. [69]. The following letters show that the IWJF saw the dominance of Kôdôkan judo as a threat to the Western world and that it had to protect the Christian world from Buddhist infiltration and indeed from *religious imperialism*: 'We in IWJF like Judo as a fine sport, therefore we are trying to save it from the grip of mysticism and aggressive Budhism [*sic*] missionary work'. [70] In order to solve the question of a religious background in judo, Mayer consulted with the Japanese representative on the IOC, Ryôtarô Azuma, who denied the presence of any kind of religiosity in judo. [71]

Correspondence between the IWJF and the IOC stopped in the following years but was to be resumed after the IJF applied again to include judo in the 1960 Olympic programme. Subsequently, the issue of Zen Buddhism also surfaced again. In August 1960, Otto Mayer was pressed by Knud Janson to recognize the IWJF, repeating his accusation that the IJF was 'infiltrated' by Zen Buddhist ideology. [72] Mayer repeated that there was no connection between Judo and Zen Buddhism in a letter on 12 August 1960. But Avery Brundage, who himself looked 'with favour on some of the Zen-Buddhism principles', requested more detailed information about any connection between Zen Buddhism and the 'Kodokan Group'. [73] A connection between judo and Zen Buddhism was again categorically denied by Kanô: 'It is quite clear that Kôdôkan Jûdô has no connection with any religion'. [74] Janson agitated the problem further when he visited Mayer in Lausanne and handed over a memorandum on the issue, in which he warned that 'the united Buddhism these years is trying to make a great push inside the Christian Western culture' with its 'main weapon', Zen Buddhism.

The fact that the members of the IOC might not have heard about the synthesis of judo and Zen Buddhism was in Janson's view 'because a Japanese – f.i. a highgraduated Jûdôka – does not speak much about Zen Buddhism...he lives Zen instead of speaking it'. [75] The attempts of the IWJF to be recognized and to discredit the IJF by attacking the Kôdôkan were without success; however, the position of the Kôdôkan inside the IJF was certainly weakened. Inside the IJF, Europeans and Americans moved strongly towards a universal culture of judo and in 1965 the presidency was taken over by the British Charles Palmer, ending the hegemony of the Kôdôkan for the next 14 years.

Conclusion

This paper has argued that Kôdôkan judo became a metaphor for the Japanese nation in the post-war years in so far as Olympic judo helped to reinvent Japanese tradition and serve as the cultural foundation for rebuilding Japan in the post-war years. When judo was assimilated by the West, it incorporated the outer characteristics of Western sporting traditions. The Western perceptions of judo as a cultural phenomenon did not often correspond to any factual reality in Japan. This paper has attempted to analyse how Western responses to judo were deeply rooted in the modes of perceiving and exotifying the East in general. That is to say, the West often ascribed a spiritual and a religious dimension to judo that cannot be found in the writings of the founder of modern judo, Kanô Jigorô. Kanô's concept of judo was pragmatic and based on its moral and physical educational value to Japanese youth in early 1900s Japan. Based on its erroneous perceptions, the IWJF saw the inclusion of Kôdôkan judo into the Olympic programme as not only a threat to Christian sporting traditions but also as a tool of religious imperialism that promoted Buddhism throughout the world by means of sport. Although judo incorporated Western sporting traditions and rules and was often exoticized by the West, for the most part Olympic judo helped to internationalize the Olympic Movement for many spectators.

Acknowledgements

Thanks to all the staff of the Olympic Studies Centre located in the Olympic Museum in Lausanne and to the Postgraduate Research Grant Programme which made this paper possible.

Notes

If not marked otherwise, all letters cited can be found in the IOC Archives, IJF-Jûdô Programme 1960–84/IJF-Jûdô Correspondence 1951–73.
 [1] MacAloon, 'The Turn of Two Centuries', 42.
 [2] 'Invitations will be sent out by the Organizing Committee to participate in the 1948 "Games" early in the New Year. Germany and Japan will not be included'. *Bulletin du Comité International Olympique* 4 (April 1947), 15. The *Bulletin* is available online at http://www.aafla.org:8080/verity_templates/jsp/newsearch/search.jsp.
 [3] Already in January 1947, an 'Olympic Preparatory Committee' was established. Cf. Guttman and Thompson, *Japanese Sports*, 193. Nagai Matsuzo notified the IOC about the

re-establishing of a Japanese Olympic committee and that information was already announced in the *Bulletin du Comité International Olympique* 8 (January 1948), 1. So actually the Preparatory Committee de facto became the national Olympic committee.

[4] *Bulletin du Comité International Olympique* 21–2 (June–Aug. 1950), 14.

[5] Tsurumi, *A Cultural History*, 4.

[6] Guttmann and Thompson, *Japanese Sports*, 193–4. The other candidates seeking to host the 1960 Olympic Summer Games were Brussels, Budapest, Detroit, Lausanne, Mexico City and Rome. Cf. *Bulletin du Comité International Olympique* 50 (April 1955), 11 and *Bulletin du Comité International Olympique* 52 (Nov. 1955), 44.

[7] Tagsold, *Die Inszenierung der kulturellen Identität*, 61–3.

[8] Seki, *Sengo Nihon no supôtsu seisaku*, 87–170, esp. 152–4.

[9] *Bulletin du Comité International Olympique* 53 (Aug. 1958), 45.

[10] *Bulletin du Comité International Olympique* 67 (Aug. 1959), 76–7.

[11] Guttmann, *Games and Empires*, 138.

[12] Kanô Risei to Avery Brundage, 18 March 1953. Kanô sent this letter first to Mon Repos, but decided then to send it also to Brundage's address in Chicago (cf. Kanô Risei to Avery Brundage, 26 March 1953). Obviously Kanô wanted the issue to be discussed in the April meeting of the IOC in Mexico that year, and therefore could not afford to lose time. On 14 September 1954, Brundage wrote a letter to Kanô in which he – in more a personal judgment – mentions three reasons that speak against a successful application: (1) the general tendency to reduce the programme; (2) the notion that judo is 'too new a sport internationally'; and (3) that judo has 'too few participants'. Avery Brundage to Kanô Risei, 14 Sept. 1954.

[13] *Bulletin du Comité International Olympique* 39–40 (June 1953), 28. A general reduction of the programme had been proposed by Erik von Frenckell, president of the organizing committee of the 1952 Games in Helsinki, during the Rome Session 1949. He lists three important measures of which the second is 'Not to admit any new sport'. *Bulletin du Comité International Olympique* 15 (May 1949), 31.

[14] *Bulletin du Comité International Olympique* 46 (June–July 1954), 37.

[15] Ibid., 51. The IJF was supposed to provide more material, especially on the affiliated countries, but at this point it was already too late to include judo in the 1956 programme, as Mayer explained in a letter to Kanô on 25 February. Therefore Mayer advised Kanô to apply for the inclusion of judo on the list of optional sports. Otto Mayer to Kanô Risei, 25 Feb. 1955. See also below.

[16] Extract from the minutes of the 51st Session of the International Olympic Committee, Paris, 13–18 June 1955, *Bulletin du Comité International Olympique* 52 (Nov. 1955), 45–6.

[17] Kanô Risei to Avery Brundage, 14 May 1960.

[18] Shoriki Matsutarô to Otto Mayer, 6 June 1961.

[19] Extracts from the minutes of the 58th Session of the International Olympic Committee, Rome, 22–23 Aug. 1960, *Bulletin du Comité International Olympique* 72 (Nov. 1960), 63.

[20] Ibid. Already on 19 May (thus five days after Kanô had written the official petition), Azuma had written a letter to Otto Mayer to ensure that he was supporting the candidature. Azuma wrote not in his capacity as representative of the JOC, but as governor of Tokyo and the letter-head is that of the Tokyo Metropolitan Government, thereby putting his political power behind the candidature. Azuma Ryôtarô to Otto Mayer, 14 May 1960. Azuma was able to utilize his success in the bid for the Games for his political career. He ran as LDP candidate for the post of the major of Tokyo. After winning the election, he resigned from his position as president of the JOC.

[21] *Bulletin du Comité International Olympique* 72 (Nov. 1960), 63.

[22] Ibid.: 67. Already in the 57th IOC Session Avery Brundage had stressed the necessity to be more precise on the maximum number of sport events. Minutes of the 57th Session of the

International Olympic Committee, San Francisco 1960, *Bulletin du Comité International Olympique* 70 (May 1960), 50.

[23] Extracts from the minutes of the 58th Session of the International Olympic Committee, 22–3 Aug. 1960, *Bulletin du Comité International Olympique* 72 (Nov. 1960), 69. However, a final decision was not yet reached as M. Bolanaki proposed some minor adjustments. Ibid. A final text that limited the sports to 18 was agreed upon only in 1962. Extract from the minutes of the 60th Session of the International Olympic Committee, Moscow 1962, *Bulletin du Comité International Olympique* 80 (Nov. 1962), 50. This change of rule goes in hand with the general tendency to reduce the Olympic programme, but does not take into account the decision to include judo into the next programme; subsequently the IOC eliminated judo from the Games in 1968.

[24] Minutes of the 59th Session of the International Olympic Committee, Athens, 1961, *Bulletin du Comité International Olympique* 75 (Aug. 1961), 77.

[25] Ibid., 79.

[26] Minutes of the 61st Session of the International Olympic Committee, Baden-Baden Kurhaus, 1963, *Bulletin du Comité International Olympique* 85 (Feb. 1964), 72; see also the letter from Otto Mayer to the Kôdôkan, 9 Nov. 1963.

[27] The article entitled 'The Phenomenal Development of Judo' was published in *Bulletin du Comité International Olympique* 71 (Aug. 1960), 28–9. Otto Mayer to Azuma Ryôtarô, 24 May 1960.

[28] Kano Risei to Otto Mayer, 23 Aug. 1960.

[29] Kanô, 'Jûdô ippan narabi ni', 97.

[30] Kanô, 'Waga orinpikku hiroku', 369. Also, Kanô Risei in a letter to Brundage (8 May 1961) mentions that it was a 'long-cherished wish of the late Prof. Jigoro Kano to see judo as a Olympic discipline'. Kanô's wish to see judo as an Olympic sport, as well as his contributions to the Olympic Movement served also as important arguments for the supporters of an Olympic judo. See Eric Jonas, 'The Phenomenal Development of Judo', *Bulletin du Comité International Olympique* 71 (Aug. 1960), 28–9.

[31] Inoue, 'The Invention of the Martial Arts', 164.

[32] The song text is by Sekizawa Shinichi. The film *Sugata Sanshirô* is based on Tomita Tsuneo's 1942 wartime novel. See also Kurosawa, *Autobiography*, 121–32 and 135–7. For the full song text see Murata, *Golden Best*, 6. For more background on *enka* see Yano, *Tears of Longing*.

[33] Text by Hoshino Tetsurô, 1963. See Murata, *Golden Best*, 5.

[34] Maguire, *Global Sport*, 179.

[35] Roche, *Mega-Events and Modernity*, 219–20.

[36] Bickford, *Sumo and the Woodblock Print Masters*, 144. For examples of prints see ibid., 53 and 145.

[37] Jûdô Daijiten Henshû Shûinkai, *Jûdô Daijiten*, 186; Baseball Magazine-sha, *Nihon puroresu zenshi*, 17–18. For the consequences at the Kôdôkan as well as Kanô Jigorô's reaction see Kôdôkan, *Kanô Jigorô Taikei* vol. 2, 234–43.

[38] Buruma, *Inventing Japan*, 5.

[39] Tagsold, *Die Inszenierung der kulturellen Identität in Japan*, 73–85.

[40] Frühstück and Manzenreiter, 'Neverland Lost', 77.

[41] Kanô Risei remained president until 1965. He held the office of the head of the Kôdôkan from 1946 to 1980. Cf. Jûdô Daijiten Henshû Shûinkai, *Jûdô Daijiten*, 109.

[42] World Championships 1956: 1, Natsui Shokichi (JPN); 2, Yoshimatsu Yoshihiko (JPN); 3, Anton Geesink (NED); 3, H. Courtine (FRA). World Championships 1958: 1, Sone Koji (JPN); 2, Kaminaga Akio (JPN); 3, Yamashiki Noriyoshi (JPN); 3, B. Pariset (FRA). For detailed descriptions of the programme as well as all fights see Kôdôkan, *Kanô Jigoro Taikei, Betsumaki* 1127–34.

[43] World Championships 1961: 1, Anton Geesink (NED); 2, Sone Koji (JPN); 3, Koga Takeshi (JPN); 3, Kim T.P. (KOR). Kôdôkan, *Kanô Jigoro Taikei, Betsumaki*, 1134–7.

[44] Frühstück and Manzenreiter, 'Neverland Lost', 80.

[45] Letter from the IJF (P. Bonet-Maury; Kano R.; A. Ertel) to IOC, 5 June 1961. Already one month earlier the European Judo Union (EJU) had informed the IOC about the changes adopted by the EJU that were to become the guidelines for the IJF. See letter from EJU to IOC dated 30 May 1961.

[46] Guttmann, *Games and Empires*, 138.

[47] Niehaus, 'Miushinawareta Kanô Jigorô', 42.

[48] Bach, *Verteidige dich selbst*, 3–4; see also Niehaus, 'Miushinawareta Kanô Jigorô', 41–6.

[49] *Bulletin du Comité International Olympique* 63 (Aug. 1958), 44.

[50] Jack Robinson to Avery Brundage, 16 Feb. 1955.

[51] The letterhead from 16 February 1955, actually shows two different abbreviations: SAJJA and SAAJA. In his text he uses the term National Amateur Judo Association. Later with the South African Amateur Judo Association (SAAJA) a second body emerged; this organization was recognized by the government of South Africa and taught a judo based on the Kôdôkan judo. In the late 1970s and the 1980s, judo in South Africa was controlled on and off by a governing body comprising of members of both SAAJA and SANAJA. This committee was called the South African Judo Union (SAJU). Only in 1992, under the guidance of the National Olympic Committee of South Africa, did all judo organizations in Africa unite into one association called Judo South Africa (JSA).

[52] Jack Robinson to Avery Brundage, 16 Feb. 1955. The trustworthiness of the organization is certainly undermined by the fact that the letterhead of the Jûdôkwai reads like the family register of the Robinsons: president Jack Robinson; chairman J.W. Robinson; publicity manager A. Robinson; courses and display secretary D.B. Robinson. Additionally, of the six-member grading panel, five carry the family name Robinson (the names of the Robinsons in the letterhead are also underlined in the original letter, most likely by Brundage himself).

[53] Otto Mayer to Jack Robinson, 25 Feb. 1955. The same day Mayer also wrote a letter Kanô in which he advises Kanô how to further proceed in his application to have judo accepted into the programme of the Games and to ask for information about the IWJF. Letter from Otto Mayer to Kanô Risei, 25 Feb. 1955.

[54] Jack Robinson to Otto Mayer, 2 March 1955.

[55] However, Avery Brundage remained supportive towards the South African government despite growing concerns inside and outside the IOC. Keech, 'The Ties That Bind', 73.

[56] Letter from 23 Feb. 1961.

[57] Keech, 'The Ties That Bind', 76.

[58] Ira G. Emery to IJF, 20 Feb. 1961. In fact, Robinson in his letter to the IOC dated 2 February 1955, had already characterized himself as a professional judo teacher for the police and military.

[59] However, the president of the IWJF, Knud Janson, most likely being aware of the isolated position of Robinson, wrote to Mayer: 'It is many years ago Major Robinson left us' (7 Aug. 1960).

[60] This article was sent to Mayer by Emery with a letter dated 7 June 1961. However, Mayer had already received a letter from Robinson dated 5 June 5 in which he announced his arrival. The letter was answered by Mayer on 8 May, in a letter where he makes sure that Robinson will not be received. In this letter Mayer also raised the question of professionalism again. To keep Kanô Risei informed about the moves of the IWJF, Mayer made sure that Emery's letter as well as the newspaper clipping were forwarded to Kanô Risei (Otto Mayer to Jack Robinson, 8 June 1961 and Otto Mayer to Ira G. Emery, 9 June 1961).

[61] Otto Mayer to Jack Robinson, 8 June 1961 and Ira G. Emery to Otto Mayer, 7 June 1961. In a letter dated 26 September 1961, Robinson denied that the IWJF was a professional organization: '[T]his is entirely untrue, it is more than likely that a number of Clubs affiliated

to the IJF are professionals, but as far as I am concerned and I feel with my 50 years experience of judo, there is [*sic*] no professionals at all in the world, for there is nothing on record of any Judo exponents fighting and competing for money, since 1923, in the days of Yukio Tani' (26 Sept. 1961).

[62] Kanô to Mayer, 13 May 1961.
[63] Guttmann, *The Games Must Go On*, 116.
[64] Knud Janson to Otto Mayer, 7 Aug. 1960. See also the letter by Janson to Mayer from 20 August 1962. The issue of education was also delicate inside the IJF. The Europeans were moving towards a clear definition of judo as a sport, whereas the Japanese stressed the educational value of judo.
[65] Otto Mayer to Knud Janson, 12 Aug. 1960.
[66] Niehaus, *Leben und Werk Kanô Jigorôs (1860–1938)*, 219.
[67] Kanô Risei to Avery Brundage, 8 May 1961.
[68] E.g. Pfister, 'Die Faszination des Exotischen?', 311–29. For Kanô's judo concept cf. Niehaus, *Leben und Werk Werk Kanô Jigorôs (1860–1938)*.
[69] Knud Janson to Otto Mayer, 5 Aug. 1955.
[70] Letter from Knud Janson to Otto Mayer, 21 Jan. 1956, and Janson to Mayer, 3 Jan. 1956. Stephan Aschenbrenner (general secretary IWJF) and Julius Fleck (Disziplinpräsident IWJF) also argue from the standpoint that judo is promoting religion. However, in their letters the argument is based on the notion that what is called education in judo is nothing more than religious education. Stephan Aschenbrenner to Comite International Olympique, 2 Aug. 1956, and Julius Fleck to Avery Brundage, 10 Aug. 1956.
[71] Otto Mayer to Knud Janson, 14 Feb. 1956.
[72] Knud Janson to Otto Mayer, 7 Aug. 1960.
[73] Avery Brundage to Kanô Risei, 16 July 1962.
[74] Kanô Risei to Avery Brundage, 30 Aug. 1962.
[75] Letter from Knud Janson to IOC, 20 Aug. 1962.

References

Bach, Ludwig. *Verteidige dich selbst. Gymnastik, Boxen Jiu-Jitsu. Ein Kurs in Bildern*. Köln: Rufu-Verlag, 1928.
Baseball Magazine-sha, ed. *Nihon puroresu zenshi*. Tokyo: Baseball Magazine-sha, 1995.
Bickford, Lawrence. *Sumo and the Woodblock Print Masters*. Tokyo: Kodansha International, 1994.
Buruma, Ian. *Inventing Japan, 1853–1964*. New York: Random House, 2003.
Frühstück, Sabine and Wolfram Manzenreite. 'Neverland Lost: Jûdô Cultures in Austria, Japan and Everywhere'. In *Globalizing Japan. Ethnography of the Japanese Presence in Asia, Europe, and America*. edited by Harumi Befu and Sylvie Guichard-Anguis. London: Routledge 2001: 69–93.
Guttmann, Allen. *Games and Empires; Modern Sport and Cultural Imperialism*. New York: Columbia University Press, 1994.
——. *The Games Must Go On: Avery Brundage and the Olympic Movement*. New York: Columbia University Press, 1984.
Guttmann, Allen and Lee Thompson. *Japanese Sports: A History*. Honolulu: University of Hawaii Press, 2001.
Inoue, Shun. 'The Invention of the Martial Arts. Kanô Jigorô and Kôdôkan Jûdô'. In *Mirror of Modernity. Invented Traditions of Modern Japan*, edited by Stephen Vlastos. Berkeley, Los Angeles, CA and London: University of California Press, 1998.
Jûdô Daijiten Henshû Shûinkai, ed. *Jûdô Daijiten*. Tokyo: Atene Shobô, 1999.

Kanô, Jigorô. 'Jûdô ippan narabi ni sono kyôiku ue no kachi 1889'. In *Shiryô. Meiji Budo-shi.* edited by Ichirô Watanabe. Tokyo: Shinjinbutsu Ôrai, 1971.

——. 'Waga Orinpikku Kiroku'. In *Kanô Jigorô Taikei.* vol. 8, edited by Kôdôkan. Tokyo: Hon no Tomosha, 1988: 366–78 [Orig. pub. in *Kaizô* 20, no. 7 (1938)].

Kurosawa, Akira. *Something like an Autobiography.* New York: Vintage, 1983.

Keech, Marc. 'The Ties That Bind: South Africa and Sports Diplomacy 1958–63'. *The Sports Historian* 21, no. 1 (May 2001): 71–93.

Kôdôkan, ed. *Kanô Jigorô Taikei,* vol. 2. Tokyo: Hon no Tomosha, 1988.

——. *Kanô Jigorô Taikei,* vol. 13. Tokyo: Hon no Tomosha, 1988.

——. *Kanô Jigorô Taikei, Betsumaki.* Tokyo: Hon no Tomosha, 1988.

MacAloon, John. 'The Turn of Two Centuries: Sport and the Politics of Intercultural Relations'. In: Sport – The Third Millenium. Proceedings of the International Symposium (Quebec, 21–5 May 1990). Quebec: Les Presses de l'Université Laval, 1991.

Maguire, Joseph. *Global Sport. Identities, Societies, Civilizations.* Cambridge: Polity Press, 1999.

Murata: Hideo. *Golden Best* (CD). Japan: Nippon Columbia 1999.

Niehaus, Andreas. *Leben und Werk Kanô Jigorôs (1860–1938). Ein Forschungsbeitrag zur Leibeserziehung und zum Sport in Japan.* Würzburg: Ergon Verlag 2003.

——. Miushinawareta Kanô Jigorô – Doitsu ni okeru jûdô no dôka no kanten kara ['Why Kanô Jigorô Got Lost on his Way to Germany – Aspects of Assimilation in the German View of Judo']. *Taiikushi kenkyû* [Japanese Journal of the History of Physical Education] 22 (2005): 41–6.

Pfister, Gertrud. 'Die Faszination des Exotischen? Zur Entwicklung von Jiu-Jitsu und Judo in Deutschland'. In *Japan. Reich der Spiele.* edited by Stanca Scholz-Cionca. München: Iudicium 1998.

Roche, Maurice. *Mega-Events and Modernity. Olympics and Expos in the Growth of Global Culture.* Routledge: London, New York, 2000.

Seki, Harumi. *Sengo Nihon no supôtsu seisaku. Sono kosoku to hatten.* Tokyo: Daishukan Shoten, 1997.

Tagsold, Christian. *Die Inszenierung der kulturellen Identität. Das Beispiel der Olympischen Spiele Tôkyô 1964.* München: Iudicium, 2000.

Tsurumi, Sunsuke. *A Cultural History of Postwar Japan 1945–80.* London, New York: Kegan Paul International, 1994.

Yano, Christine R. *Tears of Longing. Nostalgia and the Nation in Japanese Popular Song.* Cambridge, MA and London: Harvard University Press, 2005.

Revisiting South Africa and the Olympic Movement: The Correspondence of Reginald S. Alexander and the International Olympic Committee, 1961–86

Maureen Margaret Smith

As colonial rule ended across much of Africa in the 1950s and 1960s, newly independent African nations sought to establish themselves with national identities and governments no longer connected to their imperialist landlords. Within the arena of sport, these independent nations sought to establish themselves as legitimate members of the international community through their close proximity with larger sporting bodies, most notably the Olympic Movement. Simultaneously, there was a concerted effort on the part of the International Olympic Committee to encourage such associations. [1] As leaders of the African continent worked to remove the shackles of colonial power, the IOC exerted tremendous political and financial power and influence on these newly independent countries and in trying to shape their sports facilities. As new African countries were joining the Olympic Movement, the apartheid government of South Africa was beginning to encounter opposition to its participation in the Olympic Games from the new members.

South Africa had been an early member of the IOC, participating in every Olympic Summer Games from 1904 until the country was barred from Olympic competition after the 1960 Games, as a result of the 1956 sporting policies that barred interracial competitions. Apartheid became the rule in both sport and society and was a clear violation of the Olympic Charter, which stated that no type of discrimination was to be tolerated. An IOC commission visited South Africa in 1967 to examine the country's sporting and societal practices, before their ultimate expulsion in 1970. [2] After debating South Africa's membership status for over 30 years, the IOC only recently readmitted the country in 1991, and a year later it participated in the Barcelona Games. [3]

Reginald S. Alexander of Kenya, elected to the IOC in 1960, wrote hundreds of letters to the IOC during his tenure addressing the status of Africa, and specifically South Africa, within the Olympic Movement. [4] Representing a continent that was struggling for recognition and status in the international sporting movement, Alexander established himself as a trusted figure within the Olympic Movement through his efforts as an IOC member and through his correspondence with IOC employees, members and presidents. As one of the few African members of the IOC, Reggie Alexander often took it upon himself to travel to South Africa to observe its practices and offer his assessments to the IOC. He believed that South African politics should not bar the country's athletes from participating in the Olympic Games and argued that their exclusion was a violation of the Olympic Charter, which stipulated that no type of discrimination should be tolerated. Because Alexander was a white African, other IOC members considered him to be an imperialist, including IOC President Avery Brundage, who admitted this in their exchanges. [5] For over two decades, Alexander corresponded with three IOC presidents – Avery Brundage, Lord Michael Killanin and Juan Antonio Samaranch – on the topic of South Africa. The election of Samaranch in 1980, as well as changes in South African society and sport, prompted an increase in the volume and intensity of letters from Alexander related to the continued exclusion of South Africa. Alexander argued against Samaranch's policy of isolation. Alexander was particularly upset that Samaranch was unwilling to initiate an inquiry into the matter to reassess any progress South Africa may had made in the decade since the last commission visited the country.

This article examines the correspondence of Alexander with three IOC presidents between 1961 and 1986. These written exchanges related to the status of South Africa in the Olympic Movement illustrate the primary issue debated within the movement from its inception – the role of politics within sport. [6] This correspondence demonstrates the immense powers of the IOC in choosing which countries could be recognized by the international sport community and who would be the beneficiaries of much-needed financial aid to establish and develop their Olympic programmes.

Alexander and Brundage: Early IOC Responses to South Africa's Apartheid Policies

Born in Nairobi, Kenya on 14 November 1914, Reginald Stanley Alexander was active in soccer, hockey, rugby, tennis, golf and athletics throughout his youth. Educated at the Prince of Wales School in Nairobi, he later served as a member of the Royal Air Force during the Second World War before entering a career in accounting. In 1954, he was a founding member of the Kenyan Commonwealth Games and Olympic Association. Within a year of his 1960 election to the IOC, Alexander lobbied President Avery Brundage to have the African continent host an IOC session, which would 'show all of Africa in a positive way that it really is wanted and fully recognized by the Olympic Movement'. Alexander wanted IOC members to 'experience and see personally what is happening in Africa before coming to conclusions'. He explained that the 'new Africa', as part of its 'growing up' process was 'inclined to throw off connections with the old world', which he viewed as 'part of the psychological process' of independence. In his view, hosting an IOC session in Africa would help demonstrate that they were 'equal members of the family'. [7] Alexander's early letters were largely focused on his efforts to have the African continent recognized by the international sporting community.

The IOC agreed to hold their 1963 session in Nairobi, but Kenya refused to grant visas to the South African delegation, forcing the IOC to relocate the meeting to Baden-Baden. [8] The Kenyan refusal made Alexander wonder which African countries would attend if South Africa and Portugal were invited. [9] Clearly, Alexander was aware of the politics within the continent and early in his membership he volunteered his services to the IOC leadership in the examination of South Africa, offering to visit the country, or accompany the IOC leadership on a trip given his 'experience in this part of the world'. [10] Brundage, in response to Alexander's letters, professed that he did not view the South African situation as 'entirely hopeless' and he thought with 'careful and intelligent handling' a solution would be found. From the evidence submitted, Brundage felt that 'as much or more is being done for the colored sportsmen in South Africa as in any other African country'. [11]

At the Madrid session in 1965, Alexander was elected the chairman of the IOC's subcommittee on relations with new African national Olympic committees, further establishing his position in African sport and the IOC. [12] He frequently sent newspaper clippings to the IOC to keep them abreast of various situations in African countries. Letters from Brundage indicate that he saw Alexander as a trusted source and Brundage often revealed a more human element in his responses, one that showed him to be a man concerned with his own image, power and legacy within the Olympic Movement. On the issue of South Africa, Brundage and Alexander shared a common belief that politics should not infringe on participation in the Games, echoing the sentiments of de Coubertin. Brundage clearly wanted to keep South Africa in the Games and argued his case before the executive board in April 1966. The South African delegation stated that they would adhere to IOC regulations, having a multiracial committee of officials, which went against their government policy. Brundage admired their stand and suggested that 'to suspend the National Olympic Committee would serve to drive it from the Olympic Movement', resulting in the punishment of athletes for the actions of their government. [13] A year later at an executive board meeting in Copenhagen, Brundage expressed his belief that the most important problem facing the IOC was 'how to maintain the authority and prestige of the IOC in connection with the increasing importance of the Olympic Movement and the growing threat of political interference'. He urged all to 'adhere' to the rules and 'not to tolerate deviation from Olympic principles and regulations'. Later in the session, he reiterated his stance on South Africa. He acknowledged the struggle the IOC faced in the delicate and complex matter, wanting to 'welcome all the youth of the World', while not wanting 'any discrimination within sports'. Still, Brundage believed apartheid was a government policy 'with which we have nothing to do', viewing the 'difference in principles' as something that needed to be taught to many of the new NOCs. [14]

In October 1966, Brundage established a fact-finding commission to visit South Africa. It was understood that no decisions would be made on the inclusion or exclusion of the country until the commission submitted a report of its visit. [15] Alexander, along with Ade Ademola of Nigeria and Lord Michael Killanin of Ireland, comprised the IOC's three-man commission designated to investigate South African sport. [16] In September 1967, the three men visited the country for ten days, checked facilities and interviewed over a hundred individuals who were part of various South African sport bodies. Based on their findings, the commission recommended to the IOC that South Africa be invited to compete in the 1968 Olympic Games in Mexico City. The IOC members approved the recommendation. [17]

Despite the commission's recommendation to invite South Africa to compete at the 1968 Games, the invitation was withdrawn after other African countries threatened to boycott the Games. [18] A year later, the status of South Africa remained in limbo. This time, Brundage adopted a new tactic and demanded that African delegates who favoured the expulsion of South Africa draw up a list of charges and evidence. A South African committee could then argue against the charges. [19] The IOC thus continued to waffle on what to do with South Africa. At its May 1970 session, two alternatives were presented: the withdrawal of the South African NOC, or that recognition be given to SANOC but permission to participate in the 1972 Games be withdrawn. [20] The result was that South Africa was officially expelled from the Olympic Movement, although the IOC member from South Africa, Reginald Honey, was permitted to remain a member of the IOC. [21]

Brundage continued to influence the actions of the IOC as they related to South Africa, even as his presidency neared its end. In February 1972, at the executive board meetings in Sapporo, Japan, Brundage suggested that the board withdraw the expulsion of South Africa and institute a suspension, a punishment that most members, he believed, would have preferred. This would entitle South Africa to recognition by the IOC. Though the executive board agreed with Brundage, the country remained expelled. [22]

Alexander and Lord Killanin: A New President and Little Progress for South Africa

Just as Alexander had been a trusted source and sounding board for Brundage, he served in a similar capacity for Brundage's successor, Lord Killanin. [23] Alexander continued to send newspaper clippings from African newspapers to the new president, who appreciated such information, even closing one letter referring to the African NOCs and New Zealand, with 'Do you know anything confidentially on this?' [24] With the passage of time, Alexander's desire to reconsider the role of South Africa in the Olympic Movement became more urgent. In August 1976, Alexander circulated a letter to all IOC members entitled 'Political Interference against the Olympic Movement'. He asked members to submit signatures in support of his efforts to call a special session to deal with his concerns. In his memo to Killanin, Alexander explained that his 'approach and attitude is one of objectivity'. He felt that Killanin knew the depths of his convictions on the subject and his determination to push the issue. By this time, Alexander believed that the IOC was in danger from the influence of politics that 'only determination of the most brutal kind' would 'save the Olympic Movement for the world'. [25]

Thus Alexander's persistence continued. Changes were taking place in South Africa – the Autonomous Sports Policy was enacted in 1979, which provided sports organizations with the right to administer their affairs independent of the government. [26] As evidence of progress, Alexander routinely sent press clippings, which reported on the exclusion of the Group Areas Act and the Liquor Licensing Act from sport. Such exclusions allowed for a white team to compete against a black team in a black township without a permit. Players from the competing teams were also allowed to drink together after a game. Killanin suggested they 'watch and see what will become of the action following the resignation' of South Africa's prime minister. He continued to rely on Alexander for his insight, closing with 'Naturally, any information you can obtain would be much appreciated'. [27]

Alexander's frustration with Killanin's diplomacy on the South African issue came to a head during the May 1978 IOC session in Athens, Greece. Alexander demanded that the membership discuss the issue of IOC credibility. Referring to Killanin's opening remarks, Alexander asked the president 'to confirm he was referring to countries which introduced racial discrimination by law', which Alexander felt 'amounted to institutionalizing discrimination'. 'If racial or other discrimination was not enforced by law', then, Alexander contended, 'the President believed it should be ignored'. It was Alexander's opinion that 'discrimination in practice was more sinister and insidious than discrimination by law' and he reminded the membership that they had remained silent on the atrocities committed by Idi Amin, the ex-head of state in Uganda, only a few years earlier. [28] He reiterated his belief that the credibility of the IOC was at stake and pressed for the formation of a committee to determine the meaning of discrimination. [29] As he had done with Brundage, Alexander cited discrimination in other countries as evidence that the IOC needed to be consistent with all nations, and that if such practices resulted in the expulsion of South Africa, investigations needed to occur in a number of other countries. The ensuing discussion revealed the split among the members. Killanin was able to table the issue by reminding the members that it had already been agreed to send a commission to South Africa after the 1980 Games. The commission's report would be tabled after the Moscow Olympics, at which point Killanin would no longer be president.

Such disagreements did not deter Alexander's letter-writing campaign. In another note accompanying a news clipping, Alexander lamented to Killanin: 'There are signs that the battle against politics is winning in Kenya; Oh! if you really knew of the extent of the disease in the remainder of Africa!' [30] Killanin responded that he wished everyone shared Alexander's view of keeping politics out of sport and reminded him there had been politics in the Olympic Games since the ancient Games, when they declared an Olympic truce. [31] Much to the consternation of both Killanin and Alexander, politics continued to influence the Olympic Games. Alexander's Kenya was one of the 65 nations to boycott the 1980 Moscow Games. [32]

Alexander and Juan Antonio Samaranch: A Reexamination of South Africa in the Olympic Movement

After Killanin's term ended in 1980, Juan Antonio Samaranch of Spain, an IOC member since 1966, was elected as the seventh president of the IOC. Alexander's primary mission throughout his correspondence with Samaranch was to have a commission of inquiry sent to South Africa to examine the changes in sport and society since the last IOC commission in 1967. Several themes dominate the letters exchanged between the two men from 1980 to 1986. Alexander routinely used the Olympic Charter to support the inclusion of South Africa and often referred to discrimination occurring in other member countries to justify a renewed look at South Africa. Samaranch stalled the appointment of a commission of inquiry and believed that the fate of South Africa rested in the hands of Africans, though he seemed to exclude Alexander from this group.

Initially, Samaranch was able to use Alexander as his predecessors had done – as an informant from a continent where chaos and constant change reigned. [33] Samaranch established a collegial relationship with Alexander, and with a closing that was reminiscent of his predecessors, the president ended one letter with a tone of appreciation and confidence: 'I am most grateful to you for keeping me informed about the situation in South Africa, and value your advice as one who is familiar with this continent. I look forward to receiving further details from you after your next trip to South Africa'. [34] Two weeks later, Samaranch echoed his thanks: 'Thank you very much for...the information you provided on South Africa.... I am in fact studying the formation of new commissions...as always, I should appreciate your collaboration'. [35] The new president nurtured his relationship with Alexander with personal requests for information and advice on issues.

After a trip to South Africa in which he met with the Minister for National Education and Sport as well as the South African Olympic and Games Association, Alexander reported to Samaranch that he was 'satisfied that there is genuine desire and willingness to comply with the *universal code of conduct in sport* as required by the IOC' and that in his view, it would be 'most unfortunate for all sport in South Africa if the IOC by words or actions, *in any way*, discouraged the Sports Administrators and/or Politicians from progressing as they are doing now'. Alexander concluded that the trip had solidified his belief that before a commission was sent the 'the IOC *must*...clearly establish that its concern *is only* with Olympic Sports', and refuse to 'be tainted or involved with the wider political questions'. To achieve this, the commission must 'clearly and unequivocally state that Sport and only Sport is to be examined'. Alexander felt that 'whatever racial progress [was] achieved *in sport*' would have a 'profound influence...on other aspects of human relationships', in South Africa, as well other parts of the world. He even believed that eventually the IOC would be able to 'claim a place for its statesmanship and leadership in South Africa'. Alexander, in a statement that would resonate throughout his writings, explained: 'We must be mindful, always, that racialism persists in most countries of the world; the mistake in South Africa is that they made laws about it; and in many parts of the world TRIBALISM is worse that racialism'. Reminding the president of Rule 24 of the Olympic Charter, that NOCS must resist pressures of a political nature, Alexander felt that the IOC had to set an example to the world. Boycotts, in Alexander's mind, were indications of failure to defeat politics. [36]

As Alexander became more confrontational, Samaranch maintained a neutral approach that neither encouraged nor discouraged Alexander's efforts. In response to Alexander's challenge to the IOC, Samaranch politely responded that Alexander understood better than the president the 'delicate problems which exist in South Africa', and explained that the IOC's relationship with South Africa was 'a little difficult' due to its expulsion. [37] Alexander continued to travel to South Africa and worked with its sports bodies to gain readmission into the Olympic Movement. [38] Despite the agreement to send a commission to South Africa, Samaranch routinely put off the commission, suggesting the timing was not right. [39]

Alexander's letters increased in their frequency and intensity in 1982. October was an especially prolific month, with the Kenyan writing Samaranch at least 11 letters, sometimes writing two days in a row. [40] He often referred to the politics in the Olympic Movement. In one letter, Alexander noted the irony, as well as the hypocrisy, of the IOC in applauding teams that defied their governments by participating in the 'boycotted' 1980 Moscow Games. At the same time, the IOC condemned some of those same teams who wanted to compete against South Africa. Reiterating his desire to re-examine South African sport, Alexander believed an inquiry would 'encourage them to improve quickly on such progress', and would allow the IOC the opportunity to guide the rogue nation back to civilization. Alexander viewed the IOC as a humanitarian force in international politics through sport. [41] He asked the president if he agreed that 'the wishes of the sports persons *within* any country must always *be paramount*?' In the case of South Africa, he asked if they should 'refuse to listen to the sports persons amongst some 18 million Blacks', the ones who were suffering from the denial to compete internationally. He urged Samaranch to meet with black sport leaders such as George Thabo, the supremo of soccer, who administered 'Black, White and Brown soccer'. Alexander urged the president to enlist the aid of the IOC '*inside* South Africa', noting that 'condemnations and criticism from *outside* South Africa' were a 'spent force'. He closed with a plea for the president to extricate the IOC 'from a 'failure' label before it is too late'. [42]

Samaranch usually responded to Alexander within days. He responded that Alexander was ignoring one 'extremely important point', namely the 'regional and international impact of this question'. Noting the divisiveness of the African continent, Samaranch viewed the South African issue as one point of unity. [43] This would be Samaranch's common response; Africans would be the ones to determine the issue, with the exception of Alexander.

In his correspondence, Alexander routinely challenged Samaranch's position on South Africa and often used the Olympic Charter to support the inclusion of South Africa. In one letter, Alexander asked the president what he believed were four basic questions. He asked if it was the ambition of the IOC 'to embrace in the Olympic Movement all the sportsmen and sportswomen of the world that comply with our Charter', which included 25 million South Africans. He wondered if the IOC acknowledged that 'complete "freedom in sport" is inhibited in some countries because of Government interference', and suggested that the IOC be able to help countries 'where there is clear proof that sport is striving positively to resist political interference'. Lastly, Alexander asked if the IOC should 'itself resist pressures to involve it and sport in attempts to change Governments or political systems'. Alexander proposed that if South Africa was able to meet IOC conditions for readmission by 1986, they be able to participate in the 1988 Games. He believed that '*Failure of such a lead now from the IOC*' would only help '*ultraconservative forces in South Africa*' who had declared that if they were elected to public office sport would return to being played and administered in racial terms. The ultraconservative forces argued that the IOC had ignored the progress made in South African sport. Alexander urged that the IOC '*move NOW to minimise the influence of such forces*', who pledged to halt progress. He truly believed that the IOC could lead the world and 'influence the whole structure of human relationships and basic human dignity'. [44]

Despite his desire to invite South Africa back into the Olympic Movement, Alexander often expressed his opposition to the practice of apartheid, as well as racial discrimination that was practised in other countries. To the president, he condemned apartheid as a political philosophy and said that he expressed these views on his frequent visits to South Africa. But, he reminded Samaranch, he also condemned the 121 countries that Amnesty International had recently 'identified for blatantly abusing basic human rights!' He explained that he was 'very conscious of the "politics" of Africa', as he lived with it every minute of every day. [45]

Samaranch responded by referring to the need for Africans to make the decision, explaining that for two years the IOC had been able to 'reinforce and strengthen' African unity on the topic. He did not want to put that unity in danger without considering the consequences. He reminded Alexander that the 42 African NOCs, as well as IOC members from Africa, agreed on this point. [46] A week later, Alexander replied to Samaranch, asking the president if the IOC was to be 'influenced only or mainly by politics' – or rather was the IOC to adhere to its Charter? It was, Alexander believed, the fundamental question the IOC needed to 'answer within ourselves', for until then, he felt it pointless to voice his opinions to the IOC membership. [47] Perhaps in a show of good faith to Alexander, or bowing to pressure from other IOC members, he did agree that he would present a proposal to the executive board, though he had little hope it would be accepted because of the African unity on the topic. [48]

Despite Samaranch's decision to seek input from African members, Alexander continued to critique the president's lack of decisive action on the issue. Alexander did not believe that invited opinions from members in Africa would result in any change, as he thought most members would be pressured by their governments to follow the anti-South Africa line. [49] On the other hand, Samaranch was adamant that it would be a decision made by Africans. The president explained to Alexander that he was 'convinced that this problem cannot be solved without the advice of people from the same continent and not purely by outsiders'. He felt the opinion of the 42 African NOCs and 13 IOC members in Africa was of 'paramount importance' since they knew better than anyone else the situation in Africa. [50]

In January 1983, Samaranch met with the South African delegation, who urged the president for an inquiry into South African sport for the sake of black sports organizations, reporting that even Africans were not united on the topic. As was his practice, Samaranch decided to send the decision to the executive board. [51] In February, Alexander asked Samaranch about a rumoured decision by the European Parliament to oppose sanctions on South Africa and to resume sporting ties. To Alexander, such a decision merited a renewed investigation into South Africa. [52] By March of that year, Samaranch announced he would not request a commission to study the South African situation. [53] Angry and frustrated, Alexander wrote to Samaranch expressing his disappointment, again reminding him of the Charter, even pointing out relevant page numbers. He wondered how the president could reconcile his decision with principle 3, which stated that no discrimination was allowed against any country on the grounds of politics. He also reminded the president that at this point only an inquiry was being requested. [54]

Perhaps to calm him, as well as to keep him in check, at the end of March, Samaranch had two private meetings with Alexander in New Delhi, India. Alexander thanked him for the 'frank exchange of words' and explained to the president that he believed 'entirely in straight, frank and open talking', which he viewed as the only way to 'achieve sincere and honest understanding'. He looked forward to future meetings when the two men would 'know one another from the inside considerably better and, hopefully, to our mutual advantage'. [55] Samaranch encouraged Alexander, responding: 'I am always open for any discussion, especially with persons such as yourself, who have so much experience within the IOC'. [56] In June, Samaranch indicated to Alexander that he did not want to raise the 'South African question' before the Los Angeles Games. He said a decision had already been made that the possibility of an inquiry mission would be re-examined after the Games. [57] The next day he sent Alexander a *Sports Illustrated* article about South African sport, and reminded the Kenyan that he did not want to raise the question before or during the LA Games. In subsequent letters, Samaranch reaffirmed his belief that Africans had to solve the issue. [58] Perhaps because he was firm about not wanting to address the South Africa issue prior to the Los Angeles Games, Alexander's letter-writing campaign slowed after the president's decision. Still, Alexander occasionally reminded the president of the topic and his willingness to be of assistance, offering to lead a 'Kenyan team to South Africa, Black, White and Brown, to travel in the same train and show how it is possible for different races to behave together naturally'. [59]

In the months preceding the LA Games, the South African issue remained at the forefront despite Samaranch's desire to not address it. In a report to the executive board in February 1984, Anani Matthia, president of the Association of National Olympic Committees of Africa, presented a 'truthful picture of sport in Africa', which was underdeveloped and suffered from a lack of funds, facilities and technical expertise. According to Matthia, most of the 42 African NOCs were financially dependent on their governments. [60] Alexander was worried that the IOC would be linked with the African National Congress, who had vowed to overthrow the South African government with violence. He thought that whoever wrote the principle – 'perhaps it was de Coubertin himself' – that outlawed discrimination on the grounds of politics, must have anticipated that politics and violence were so often 'bed fellows'. Because of its links with the ANC, it would be very difficult for the IOC to deny that 'political influences' determined the continued boycott of South Africa. Again, citing his citizenship as an African, born and bred in the continent, he claimed his 'dedication has always been as a humble contributor towards change and progress by peaceful means only!' In his mind, there had already been too much bloodshed, and sport was the 'best influence in the world for peace!' [61]

Leading up to the Los Angeles Games, a major issue of contention was the participation of South African runner Zola Budd. [62] The Zola Budd affair was complicated, but served Alexander's arguments and echoed Avery Brundage's earlier desires to not punish individual athletes. Born in South Africa, Budd was not allowed to compete at the Games because her nation was not invited. Rather than punish the individual athlete, the IOC allowed Budd to claim British nationality, which paved the way for her participation. Another issue related to the Games that caught

Alexander's attention was the refusal of the IOC to sell the television rights to South Africa. Alexander believed that televising the Games would be an effective way of educating South Africans by viewing 'Blacks, Whites and Browns participating in the Olympic Games'. Disseminating ideals of the Olympic Movement, Alexander believed, was a prime responsibility of the IOC. [63]

Alexander was not alone in his belief that the exiled nation's status should be re-examined. In the month prior to the Los Angeles Games, both of the IOC's US members, Julian Roosevelt and Douglas Roby, made statements in support of the country's inclusion at the Games. In an argument similar to Alexander, Roosevelt said: 'My personal position is that they should be readmitted. People are confusing politics with sports'. He believed that apartheid had been all but eliminated from sports in South Africa, and thought that there was probably less discrimination in sports in South Africa than in the US or the Soviet Union. [64] In anticipation of the issue arising at the LA Games, Samaranch sent Peter Ueberroth a telegram stating the IOC's position on the issue, ironically using the Olympic Charter as support. Noting that the South African NOC had been expelled in 1970 and that the nation would not be readmitted until apartheid was abolished, Samaranch stated that this was a time when the Olympic Movement 'must stand together respecting our principles', writing that no racial, political or religious discrimination can be tolerated in accordance with the Charter. [65] Samaranch desperately wanted to avoid the issue at the Los Angeles Games.

As the Games got under way, Alexander penned a three-page letter to Samaranch. He explained that he was observing the oath he took as an IOC member was being violated, 'keeping myself free from any political influence' an oath he viewed as 'sacred'. Foremost, he acknowledged that he was only 'a small, a very tiny part of an ideal, the OLYMPIC IDEAL, and whatever the circumstances, *at anytime*, it is protected and preserved'. He gave Samaranch his 'personal and solemn undertaking' that he would do his utmost to play his part in upholding the Charter and loyally following the president in its application. In an organized list of points, Alexander spelled out his arguments. He felt the IOC was 'guilty of violating one of its own fundamental principles', specifically not allowing for discrimination on the grounds of politics. Again, citing discrimination in other countries, he pointedly asked the president if it is was the denial of basic human rights that he sought to correct in South Africa, then why did the IOC not show a similar concern for the Tamils in Sri Lanka, the Basques in Spain, the Roman Catholics in Northern Ireland, the Sikhs in India or the Ndebele Tribe in Zimbabwe. Alexander acknowledged that the two men had differing approaches to achieve the ultimate goal of racially integrated sport in South Africa. His was 'by example, dialogue or persuasion', he wrote, while Samaranch's method was one of confrontation, namely a boycott, 'with the possibility of an implied association with the forces of violence'. He asked the president what 20 years of sports boycott achieved for sport in South Africa. Referring to the president's policy of allowing the Africans to determine South Africa's Olympic fate, Alexander expressed his disagreement and argued that the 'answer has to be *inside* South Africa' with the guidance of the IOC. In Alexander's assessment, the problem was for all South Africans to solve and for '*all* IOC members to judge'. He did not think it appropriate to pass the responsibility for such an important decision to one section of the membership. [66]

After the Games, Alexander continued to lobby for the South Africans. [67] In an interview with *The Standard*, a Nairobi newspaper, Alexander explained that South Africa should be invited back into the Olympic Movement. His statements created quite a reaction among the other Africans. The Hon. K.S.N. Matiba, Kenya's Minister for Culture and Social Sciences, sent a letter to Samaranch reporting that the Kenyan government 'categorically dissociates itself' from the views of Alexander. Matiba found it 'regrettable that a man who holds such contrary views from his national Government should remain a member' of the IOC. [68] Amadou Lamine Ba, the secretary-general of the Supreme Council for Sport in Africa, also sent a letter to Samaranch, explaining that Alexander was 'a major cause for concern for Africans on account of the theories he defends'. [69]

Despite the increased opposition from other African members, Alexander persisted in arguing that boycotts of any kind were wrong. In one letter, he stated, 'NO BOYCOTTS! by or against the IOC!' Reminding Samaranch of a statement the president had made in the most recent issue of *Olympic Review* – 'If I have learned one thing in my Life, it is that only through human contact can our differences be overcome and dialogue opened. Perhaps that is what our world lacks the most' – Alexander wondered if dialogue and contact with South Africa were the only exception. He closed with 'Invade South Africa with sport, not guns!' [70] The executive board addressed Alexander's statements at their meeting in November 1984. [71]

Realizing that he was the topic of controversy, Alexander expressed his concerns to Samaranch. He feared that a visit to Kenya from an IOC vice-president, as was planned by Samaranch, would be interpreted by some members as confirmation that Alexander had violated the Charter. According to rule 13, Alexander wrote, 'a member may be expelled by resolution of the IOC if in the IOC's opinion he has betrayed or neglected its interested or has been guilty of unworthy conduct'. Alexander explained that his controversial comment to the newspaper was exactly what he had expressed to Samaranch for the past three years, as well as being similar to those expressed by two US members the summer before. For those reasons, he thought it would be unfair if he were the only one judged, and requested that he be cleared by the IOC. Samaranch sympathized with Alexander, who as the year came to a close, looked forward to the New Year, and what he hoped would be better days. [72] In a handwritten note to the president only a few days later, Alexander noted with gratitude that the upcoming year would mark his 25th anniversary as a member, stating that 'the ideals are so worth while and have such personal meaning'. He hoped his health would enable him to continue to make contributions for years to come. [73] As the year came to a close, the tone of Alexander's letter reflected some relief as well as a desire to retain his dignity. [74]

Alexander's letter-writing campaign seemed to slow in early 1985 enough for Samaranch to send Alexander a telex that read: 'Not having heard from you for some time, I should be happy to have the latest news'. [75] The tone of Alexander's letters over the next two years reflects a shift in his approach, though not in his desire. His letters acknowledge the disagreement between himself and Samaranch and his desire to have an honourable dialogue about the Olympic Movement. Perhaps the shift was a result of his reflection on his lengthy career as an IOC member and his desire to make an impact on international sport, specifically in his home continent. Encouraged by Samaranch, who expressed confidence that the dialogue between the two men would 'would prove highly beneficial for the development of the Olympic Movement and Sport...throughout the whole of Africa', Alexander wrote back 'convinced that there is now a timely opportunity for positive "education" in what is required by the Charter and particularly the creation of a convention accepted by Governments'. [76] Alexander persisted in his attempt to change the tone of his efforts to re-examine South Africa, expressing his pleasure that they had been able to agree to disagree on the issue of South Africa while maintaining dignity and mutual respect. [77]

After finishing a tour of the 45 African NOCs, Samaranch reiterated to Alexander the unity shared by the Africans on the subject of apartheid, the one topic that all the African NOCs agreed on. [78] Alexander responded that he also had strong feelings about apartheid, noting 'the whole world has strong feelings about apartheid'. He believed that as an African, he had 'experience of living with and fighting and destroying apartheid within their own country', making him one among the small percentage of the world population 'who have *personal* experience of belonging in countries with multiracial communities'. Alexander held Kenya up as an example. He went on further, saying 'Apartheid is abhorrent, an insult to human dignity and it must go!' but admitted that the real issue was how to destroy apartheid. That solution would require 'wise, realistic and *reasoned* answers'. Continuing with his philosophy that the IOC should take the lead in helping South Africa, and again hammering the point that discrimination existed around the globe, Alexander reminded the president that 'it is well to remember that racial and tribal discrimination *in practice* is often worse than that of legalized apartheid'. As Alexander saw it, the IOC needed to be consistent in the application of its principles, citing the Asian victimization in Uganda. In an argument that he had used before, Alexander noted the two competing approaches: sanctions or boycotts, which he categorized as negative; and participation and example, his personal approach. As he closed his letter, Alexander pleaded with the president, offering to serve as 'your valet, your clerk and your skipping rope attendant', on a trip to South Africa where they would travel 'not as a VIP but just as ordinary you and me'. Such a trip would give Samaranch the opportunity to 'listen to other African feelings in Kenya and South Africa, Black, White and Brown'. Unlike the African NOCs and IOC members, Alexander explained that these Africans would tell him the truth, not what they think he wanted to hear. [79]

Months later, in an admission that politics had indeed influenced Olympic sport, Alexander professed to Samaranch his disappointment that political influences haD dominated attitudes and decisions on sport in and with South Africa. The Charter was being ignored, argued Alexander. [80] Returning to a familiar theme, Alexander reminded Samaranch that sometimes racial discrimination by practice was worse than that by law, this time pointing out racial discrimination in Brazil. [81]

In June 1986, Alexander recognized that perhaps the time was not right for an Inquiry, due to the current state of emergency in the country. Though he admitted that the state of emergency would make it difficult for a commission to function effectively, Alexander felt that to 'manifest the credibility of the IOC', it should send an commission of inquiry as soon as the emergency was lifted; believing that such a positive move would encourage South Africans. [82] After the IOC session, Alexander sent Samaranch a telex which revealed his fervent belief in his convictions related to the Olympic Movement. Noting that it was the best session of his 26 years of membership, he felt privileged to 'experience 3 crucifixions for my convictions'. He recognized that he was a dreamer, and that he envisioned a renaissance of Olympism. According to Alexander, 'every famous institution needs a careful and serious look at itself at least every 100 years. A self-analysis, the renaissance now begins'. [83]

Two months later, the Kenyan member summed up their six years of correspondence in a response to the president. Alexander thanked him for his frankness, which he had found 'most refreshing'. Stating that he had been waiting for several years for such honesty, Alexander wrote 'outspokenness with dignity is the way to understanding between humans'. Responding to what he termed 'the serious remark in your letter' (Samaranch had written 'However, I do believe that we must all be cognizant of the fact that when you were elected, Kenya was still a British Colony'), Alexander, while he understood the remark, also felt deep sorrow at the comment. Noting that the world had been fed 'emotionally potent and rhetorical slogans on "Colonialism", "Imperialism" etc'. for over 30 years, he felt it difficult for anyone without 'intimate experience of Africa to accept that there are White Natives in Africa who are as loyal and as committed as Black Natives'. Alexander explained that when Samaranch had been elected to the IOC in 1966, he had accepting the Spaniard as he was 'a Gentleman dedicated to the ideals of our Olympic Charter without any suggestion that ... you were part of a ruthless Fascist regime, appointed by a Dictator, Franco, to the position of President of the Barcelona "Diputacion"'. Alexander wrote: 'You had to live some 40 years in such undemocratic atmosphere!, this does not "label" you as a Fascist for the rest of your life' and marvelled at the way Spain had progressed to democracy in such a short time. Finally, after so many years of writing, Alexander confronted Samaranch with his view of the Kenyan as a colonial. He had hoped that the president would visit Africa to '*really* study Black Africa and try to understand White Natives such as myself'. Of the 'White Natives' in Kenya, he did not think they had much to be ashamed of, with the exception of 'manifestations of smugness and arrogance in the past', which he had publicly condemned. Noting the tremendous progress of the continent over the last hundred years, Alexander admitted to having moments of 'silent pride' in his contributions over 50 years of public service. He explained that when he had been elected Mayor of Nairobi, it was the result of a free democratic vote 'of Blacks, Whites and Browns'. Alexander closed his letter with an honest observation and perhaps a slight challenge to the president, noting that the subject raised in the president's letter 'opens up a hornets nest' or, more graphically, 'a can of worms'. He closed with hope that his reply would serve as some 'food for thought' for both. [84]

Conclusion: Goodbye Reggie Alexander, Hello South Africa

While this is not where the correspondence ends, it marks the end of the accessibility to the written exchanges between Alexander and the IOC due to the IOC's recent 30-year embargo on archival materials. [85] Alexander died in 1990, a year before South Africa was readmitted to the Olympic Movement and then invited to participate in the 1992 Olympic Games in Barcelona, Samaranch's hometown. [86]

After being named chair of the Apartheid and Olympism Commission in 1988, Keba Mbaye, an IOC vice president, led a delegation to South Africa in March 1991. Mbaye said the issue of political rights was not and never was on the IOC's agenda; 'democracy is desirable but it is not our role to insist on a universal franchise'. Echoing a sentiment expressed by Alexander a decade earlier, Mbaye said:

> the difference between South Africa and other countries which are not democratic is that there is racist legislation in South Africa.... If we remove all this legislation now, what is left? There is perhaps a country where not everyone has what they want, where democracy is not total. But there are a lot of countries like this in the world. [87]

Ultimately, readmission in 1991 was based on similar principles expressed by Alexander; that sport would assist in changing the laws and practices of the nation, and that the IOC would be in the lead. [88]

What makes the correspondence of Reggie Alexander noteworthy? For years, he shared the confidence of three IOC presidents and was an influential African neighbour to South Africa and the efforts to readmit the exiled nation into the Olympic Games. His efforts were steadfast and rooted in his belief that politics had no role in sport, echoing a value shared by every IOC president leading up to Samaranch. His rhetoric was categorized by others as colonial, and his citizenship as an African was often in question because of that. As the IOC 'decolonized' South African sport, Samaranch used Mbaye, a black African, to echo the same 'colonial' attitudes. The IOC's narrative of South Africa's readmission into the Games omits any efforts made by Alexander and is built upon the foundation that the actions of Samaranch's IOC were rooted in humanitarian principles. [89] The correspondence of Alexander provides us with a valuable perspective on one man's efforts to influence the sporting community in Africa and the larger Olympic Movement, and offers

insight into the presidencies and politics of Avery Brundage, Lord Killanin and Juan
Antonio Samaranch.

Acknowledgements

The author would like to acknowledge the staff at the IOC Olympic Studies Centre,
located in the Olympic Museum in Lausanne, and to the Postgraduate Research
Grant Programme, especially Cristina Bianchi and Sabine Christe of Archives, for
their assistance with the project. Dr Robert K. Barney provided helpful comments on
an earlier version of the paper.

Notes

[1] The International Aid Commission was established in the early 1960s and sought to
offer financial aid to new African countries in developing their sport programmes.
Reggie Alexander was among the first members of the group. See Summary of the Sporting
Situation and Needs in New African countries, Oct. 1963 (36-page document), CAIO Files,
IOC Archives, Lausanne, Switzerland. In December 1968, the commission was reestablished as
the Aid Commission and eventually evolved into Olympic Solidarity, which currently provides
countries with millions of dollars for sport development, coach training and travel.

[2] For a good account of South African sport history, see Booth, *The Race Game*. Also see Baker
and Mangan, *Sport in Africa*; Booth, 'The Antinomies of Multicultural Sporting
Nationalism'; Booth, 'South Africa's "Autonomous Sport" Strategy'; Jarvie, 'Sport, Popular
Struggle and South African Culture'; Kidd, 'From Quarantine to Cure', Nauright, '"Like Fleas
on a Dog"'; Rees, 'The NOSC and the Non-Racial Sports Movement'.

[3] For evidence of the lengthy debate around South African sport, see Mbaye, *The International
Olympic Committee and South Africa*, 271–7; letter from Transvaal Indian Youth Congress to
the IOC, 26 May 1955; response from Otto Mayer, 1 June 1955; Brundage to Ira Emery,
General Secretary, SAOCGA, 27 Sept. 1958, 24 Oct. 1958 and 7 April 1958; press clipping
from 21 Nov. 1958.

[4] Kenya joined the Olympic Movement in 1955. Kenyan independence from the United
Kingdom came on 12 December 1963.

[5] See Mbaye, *The International Olympic Committee and South Africa*, 279; reprint of a letter
from Brundage to Alexander, 3 May 1966: 'The African question remains and it is a most
thorny problem.... Please give me your views on this subject.... Incidentally I find that you
are, despite your record, considered as a "colonial" in certain quarters. How much this will
interfere with your activities is difficult to say but you must be aware that this view exists in
some places'.

[6] For more on the presidencies of Brundage, Killanin and Samaranch, see Guttmann,
The Games Must Go On; Killanin, *My Olympic Years*; Miller, *Olympic Revolution*; Ratner, *The
Seventh President*; Simson and Jennings, *The Lords of the Rings*. For one perspective on the
relationship of the IOC and politics, see Hoberman, 'Toward a Theory of Olympic
Internationalism'. For more on the origins of de Coubertin's philosophy of sport, see de
Coubertin, *Olympism*.

[7] Alexander to Brundage, 7 April 1961, responding to Brundage, 29 March 1961. Alexander
wrote a similar letter to Otto Mayer, Chancellor of the IOC. See Alexander to Mayer, 29 May
1961, Folder: Reginald S. Alexander, File: Correspondence 1960–69, IOC Archives, Lausanne
(hereafter Alexander Correspondence 1960–69).

[8]   Despite the efforts of Alexander, Kenya refused to grant visas to the South African delegation. See Guttmann, *The Games Must Go On*, 234, 302; Mbaye, *The International Olympic Committee and South Africa*, 96. The Baden-Baden meeting was held 14–20 October 1963. At that session, a resolution was passed by 30 votes to 20 stating 'That the South African Olympic Committee be told that it must make a firm declaration of its acceptance of the spirit of the Olympic Code and in particular of Principle 1 and Rule 24 read together, and must get from its government by 31 December 1963 a change in policy regarding racial discrimination in Sports and competitions in its country, failing which the South African National Olympic Committee will be debarred from entering its teams in the Olympic Games'. Minutes of IOC session, Baden-Baden, 14 Oct. 1963, Item 27.

[9]   Alexander to Mayer, 29 Aug. 1963, Alexander Correspondence 1960–69. African nations were upset with the inclusion of Portugal because it still held colonial rule over some African countries.

[10]   Alexander to Mayer, 15 Nov. 1962, Alexander Correspondence 1960–69.

[11]   Brundage to Alexander, 22 Nov. 1963, ibid.

[12]   IOC to Alexander, 22 March 1966, ibid.

[13]   Minutes of meetings of the IOC Executive Board, Rome, 21–4 April 1966, 2, Item 18, The Current Situation of the South African Olympic Committee.

[14]   Minutes of meeting of the IOC Executive Board, 11 and 12 Feb. 1967, Copenhagen 1, Item 1, Welcome by President Avery Brundage; ibid., 4, Item 11, Committee for South Africa.

[15]   Historian John Nauright states that South Africa made slight modifications to its sport policy in 1967 in an attempt to gain readmission, and made a 'myriad of reformist measures' over the next 20-year period. See Nauright, '"Like Fleas on a Dog"', 60.

[16]   For an overview of the commission's visit, see Guttmann, *The Games Must Go On*, 235–8. Alexander replaced Dutch member Herman van Karnebeek. The commission's lengthy report is in the South Africa file, IOC Archives, Lausanne.

[17]   Minutes of meeting of IOC Executive Board, Lausanne, 26 and 27 Jan. 1968; Grenoble, 29–31 Jan. 1968, 4, Item 4, Agenda for the 66th Session of the IOC (Annex IV). The report was released on 20 January 1968 and discussed on 2 February 1968.

[18]   Telegram from Brundage to Alexander, 21 April 1968, related to unanimous decision to withdraw invite to South Africa. Alexander Correspondence 1960–69.

[19]   Minutes of meetings of the IOC Executive Board, Dubrovnik, 23–7 Oct., 1969, 2, Item 6, Matters arising from the Warsaw Session, (c) SANOC.

[20]   Minutes of meetings of the IOC Executive Board, Amsterdam, 8–16 May 1970, 9, Item 23 (b) South Africa.

[21]   Alexander, as a protest against the expulsion, submitted a resolution on China, making an issue of the role of politics in Olympic sport in another country besides South Africa, a rationale that he would frequently rely on for two more decades. See Brundage to Alexander, 27 June 1970; Alexander to Brundage, 6 July 1970, Alexander Correspondence 1960–69. These exchanges reveal the growing rift between the two men, but also Alexander's willingness to use any tactic to call attention to his pet cause of South Africa, or more broadly, the intrusion of politics into the Olympic Movement, even if it meant being bullied and pressured by the president.

[22]   Minutes of Executive Board Meetings, Tokyo, 28 Jan. 1972; Sapporo, 29 Jan. – 1 Feb., 1972, Item 20, Other business – South Africa.

[23]   Killanin served as IOC president from 1972 to 1980.

[24]   Killanin to Alexander, 26 April 1976, Folder: Reginald S. Alexander, File: Correspondence 1974–78, IOC Archives, Lausanne (hereafter Alexander Correspondence 1974–78).

[25]   Alexander to Killanin, 23 Aug. 1976, ibid.

[26]   For examples, see Booth, 'Accommodating Race to Play the Game', 184.

[27] Killanin to Alexander, 16 Oct., 1978, Alexander Correspondence 1974–78.

[28] Idi Amin, president of Uganda between 1971 and 1978, was responsible for the massacre of between 300,000 and 500,000 Ugandans.

[29] Minutes of the 80th Session of the IOC, Athens, 17–20 May 1978, 31, Item 14, National Olympic Committees. The President commented that as he had stated in his opening speech, there were few countries where full human rights and liberty existed, adding that with the change of regime in Iran, the IOC had requested re-examination of the Iranian constitution. Alexander's letter, dated 18 April 1979, was partly a response to *Olympic Review* 137 (March 1979), 139.

[30] Alexander to Killanin, dated 4 Sept. 1979. The news clipping was from *The Standard*, dated 29 Aug. 1979. While most of their correspondence was amicable, there were disagreements. Alexander Correspondence 1974–78. On 8 June 1983, in a letter to Samaranch, Alexander confided that he often disagreed with Killanin. 'Towards the last 4 years (1976–80) Michael and I were in serious disagreement on several issues; at least, at Montreal in 1976, I told him "Michael, you have lost my confidence!"' Folder: Reginald S. Alexander, File: Correspondence 1983, IOC Archives, Lausanne.

[31] Killanin to Alexander, 5 Sept. 1979. Folder: Reginald S. Alexander, File: Correspondence 1979, IOC Archives, Lausanne.

[32] In 1976, Kenya was one of the 20 African countries who, along with Iraq and Guyana, boycotted the Montreal event: Press Statement, R.S. Matano, Office of the Minister for Housing and Social Services, 14 June 1980. Matano commended Kenyan athletes for taking such a stand. He also asked that no Kenyan attend any part of the Games, including meetings; 'We have taken a firm decision that all Kenyans should refrain from traveling to Moscow in any capacity whatsoever during the Games'. However, as Mbaye states, *The International Olympic Committee and South Africa*, 112, Alexander resigned in protest after Kenya decided to boycott the Games. Later that summer, boycott already decided, Alexander took on the role of agitator, continuing to argue for the Chinese as part of his effort to include South Africa, making an issue of the IOC's inconsistency with the use of the Olympic Charter to include and exclude countries. See Alexander to Killanin, 24 July 1980, 'China – Postal Ballot – Credibility'; Killanin to Alexander, 25 July 1980, 'China – Postal Ballot – Credibility; Berlioux to Killanin, 25 July 1980. Folder: Reginald S. Alexander, File: Correspondence 1980, IOC Archives, Lausanne.

[33] One of Samaranch's first requests of Alexander was to have him investigate Zimbabwe's women's field hockey team, who were scheduled to compete against a South African team. Zimbabwe's field hockey team had planned a tour of South Africa; Alexander felt that the 'question of teams to South Africa is ultimately the internal politics of any country' and that the IOC should not get involved. The hockey team's visit was cancelled. Samaranch to Alexander, 26 Sept. 1980; Alexander to Samaranch, 30 Sept. 1980; IOC Secretariat to Alexander, 3 Oct. 1980; Alexander to Samaranch, 6 Oct. 1980; Alexander to Samaranch, 10 Oct. 1980; Samaranch to Alexander, 15 Oct. 1980. Folder: Reginald S. Alexander, File: Correspondence 1980, IOC Archives, Lausanne.

[34] Samaranch to Alexander, 15 Oct. 1981. Folder: Reginald S. Alexander, File: Correspondence 1981, IOC Archives, Lausanne.

[35] Samaranch to Alexander, 28 Oct. 1981, ibid.

[36] Alexander to Samaranch, 24 Nov. 1984, identified as strictly private and confidential, ibid. Underlining and use of capital letters is Alexander's.

[37] Samaranch to Alexander, 23 Dec. 1981, ibid.

[38] Telegram, Mr Rudolph W.J. Opperman, President of South Africa Olympic and National Games Association, to Samaranch, 13 Sept. 1982. Opperman was requesting a meeting with Samaranch proposed by Alexander. Folder: Reginald S. Alexander, File: Correspondence 1982, IOC Archives, Lausanne (hereafter Alexander Correspondence 1982).

[39] Minutes of meetings of the IOC Executive Board, Baden-Baden, 20, 22, 27 and 30 Sept. 1981; Minutes of the meetings of the IOC Executive Board, Rome, 25, 26 and 28 May 1982, 18; Minutes of meetings of IOC Executive Board, Lausanne, 10–13 Oct. 1982.

[40] Alexander sent Samaranch letters on 5, 6, 11, 12, 18, 19, 22, and 29 Oct. and received a response from Samaranch on 19 Oct. 1982. Folder: Reginald S. Alexander, File: Correspondence 1982, IOC Archives, Lausanne.

[41] Alexander to Samaranch, 6 Oct. 1982, ibid.

[42] Alexander to Samaranch, 19 Oct. 1982, ibid. Underlining is Alexander's.

[43] Samaranch to Alexander, 19 Oct. 1982, ibid.

[44] Alexander to Samaranch, 2 Oct. 1982, ibid. Underlining is Alexander's. At the end of his lengthy letter, Alexander included an appendix of individuals he had met with on his recent trip to South Africa.

[45] Alexander to Samaranch, 29 Oct. 1982, ibid. Alexander's views on apartheid did not make him popular with whites in South Africa. See Guttmann, *The Games Must Go On*, 239.

[46] Samaranch to Alexander, 8 Nov. 1982, Alexander Correspondence 1982.

[47] Alexander to Samaranch, 17 Nov. 1982, ibid.

[48] IOC member Richard W. Pound of Canada, also supported an inquiry into South Africa. See Pound to Samaranch, 12 Nov. 1982; Samaranch to Pound, 1 December 1982. Samaranch decided to poll African members on the topic. See Samaranch to IOC members in Africa, 29 Nov. 1982. Samaranch wrote to Alexander on 2 December 1982 informing him of his letter to the African members: Alexander Correspondence 1982.

[49] Alexander to Samaranch, 4 December 1982, 14 December 1982, Alexander Correspondence 1982.

[50] Samaranch to Alexander, 8 December 1982, ibid. A.D. Touny, IOC member, United Arab Republic, responded to Samaranch on 7 December 1982, and was in support of a commission. Bashir M. Attarabulsi, IOC, Socialist People's Libyan Arab Jamahiriya, to Samaranch, 7 Dec. 1982, did not support a commission. Other responses were not located in the file. Although not part of the African contingent, Julian K. Roosevelt, US (to Samaranch, 29 Dec. 1982), also supported a commission. South Africa file, IOC Archives, Lausanne.

[51] The South African delegation included Rudolph Opperman, chairman of the South African Olympic Committee, Denis McIldowie, vice-president, E. Sethsedi, vice-president, South African Athletic Union, R. Legwale, president, Black School Sport, and J.B. du Plessis, director of the International Liaison Committee: Memorandum of the meeting of the IOC President with a South African delegation, 11 Jan. 1983. South Africa file, IOC Archives, Lausanne.

[52] Alexander to Samaranch, 23 Feb. 1983, 'South Africa – European Parliament'. Folder: Reginald S. Alexander, File: Correspondence 1983, IOC Archives, Lausanne (hereafter Alexander Correspondence 1983).

[53] Berlioux to Alexander, 3 March 1983: 'The President asked me to transmit to you the decision taken by the Executive Council of the ANOC: "The ANOC Executive Council, with the unanimous approval of the General Assembly meeting in Los Angeles, requests you to not send an IOC commission to South Africa"'. Alexander Correspondence 1983.

[54] Alexander to Samaranch, in response to 3 March letter, ibid.

[55] Alexander to Samaranch, 28 March, 1983, ibid.

[56] Samaranch to Alexander, 8 April 1983, ibid.

[57] Samaranch to Alexander, 15 June 1983, ibid.

[58] Samaranch to Alexander, 16 June 1983. In July 1983, Denis McIldowie contacted Samaranch asking for his assistance with African countries. Admitting that he realized the way for South Africa to be readmitted was through other African countries, McIldowie wrote of his lack of success in getting African countries to visit South Africa to assess their sport. Samaranch

replied to his letter on 2 August 1983, but not to his request for aid. Samaranch response to Alexander, 12 Sept. 1983 (Alexander letter, 18 Oct. 1983): 'As I have already told you, I believe that the problem in South Africa is an African question, to be solved between Africans. Therefore, I must also listen with the same interest and attention to the opinion of all other African members'. Alexander Correspondence 1983.

[59] Alexander to Samaranch, 14 December 1983, ibid. After Alexander copied Opperman and McIldowie, both of the South African delegation, into a letter he had sent to Samaranch, the IOC president closed one letter with consternation and concern: 'Until now I was under the impression that our correspondence on this subject was to remain private. Should this not be the case, I could no longer express my opinion freely to you'. Despite the chilly response from Samaranch, the two men remained friendly and their correspondence continued; see Samaranch to Alexander, 21 Dec. 1983. Alexander promptly apologized; 'I considered it was proper and honourable that Opperman and McIldowie should know my candid reactions on an incident of worldwide publicity and that they should be aware of what I had written to the President of the IOC. On reflection it might have been wiser for me to address them and copy to you. It's only this sort of dialogue that will help the South Africans to solve their racial problems'. See Alexander to Samaranch, 4 Jan. 1984, Folder: Reginald S. Alexander, File: Correspondence 1984, IOC Archives, Lausanne (hereafter Alexander Correspondence 1984).

[60] Executive Board minutes, 2, 3, 5, 6 and 18 Feb. 1984, Sarajevo, 21–2, Item 25, Sports Organisation in Africa, Comment on position of IOC as far as government control of sport.

[61] Alexander to Samaranch, 5 March 1984, Alexander Correspondence 1984. Though South Africa was foremost in his efforts, Alexander was primarily concerned with the intrusion of politics into Olympic sport and felt it his duty to address the issue. See Alexander to Samaranch, 19 April 1984, 'The Koreas and Politics'; Samaranch to Alexander, 26 April 1984, Alexander Correspondence 1984.

[62] Executive Board minutes, Aug. 1984, 36–8. Also see *SANROC News*, Nov. 1984 for SANROC's (South African Non-Racial Olympic Committee) views on Budd's citizenship, as well as her own refusal to comment on apartheid. Budd was not the only South African to seek citizenship somewhere else to compete in the 1984 Games. Joao de Silva (Portugal), Sydney Maree (US), Mark Handelsman (Israel), Matthews Motshwaratecu (Botswana) and Koos van der Merwe (Germany) were among the other South Africans to successfully compete for other teams. See letter from Sam Ramsamy to Samaranch, 4 July 1984. Also see Brian Vine, 'Zola Cuts Ties with South Africa', *Daily Mail* (London), 16 May 1984; 'South Africa's Unofficial Olympic Team', *The Star* (South Africa), 21 April 1984; Molefi Mika, 'Loop en Val wants a place in the Olympics', *The Sowetan*, 24 May 1984; Barry Streek, 'Zola Not the Only "Bok" Aiming for Olympics', *Cape Times*, 29 March 1984; 'Zola Budd Athletic Marvel', *South African Panarama*, March 1984, 42–5. Alexander addressed Budd in a letter to the Rt. Hon. Denis Howell, House of Commons, London, England, 20 June 1984, and sent a copy to Samaranch: 'By any logic, the "attack" on Zola Budd is discrimination of the worse kind, the indiscriminate abuse of an individual who is in a somewhat defenceless position (her Parents may have been at fault?, but that is not her mistake, it's another question). If I was advising her I could prompt her to the reply of my Wife, who was born in India, and when asked "but you don't look like an Indian", she always replies "if I was born in a stable does that make me a donkey"!' As for Budd's ability to get a British nationality, Alexander explained that though both he and Budd were born in Africa, the 'kith and kin' policy of the British government gave them both claims to dual nationality: Alexander Correspondence 1984.

[63] Alexander to Samaranch, 16 Aug. 1984. A similar handwritten letter was written on 25 July 1984. Both were in response to the IOC's decision to refuse the sale of television rights of the LA Games to South Africa. Alexander Correspondence 1984.

[64] *LA Times*, 3 July 1984. Lance Cross, the member from New Zealand, was also in favour of sending an inquiry, an opinion he expressed in a 22 Aug. 1984 letter to Samaranch. South Africa file. IOC Archives, Lausanne.

[65] Telegram from Samaranch to Peter Ueberroth, 5 July 1984. South Africa file. IOC Archives, Lausanne.

[66] Alexander to Samaranch, 2 Aug. 1984. Italics (underlining in original) are Alexander's. Alexander closed his letter with a suggestion that Samaranch's planned meeting with the Kenya Minister of Sport should be accompanied by the newly elected IOC Vice President, Mr Mbaye, from Africa, rather than the president of the Kenya NOC. Other letters written around this time: Alexander to Samaranch, 11 Aug. 1984; Samaranch to Alexander, 12 Aug. 1984; Alexander to Samaranch, 15 Aug. 1984 (Title: Boycotts – the IOC is winning – 'Now that we are winning, by example over boycotts *against* the IOC we must, with honour, win over any boycott *BY* the IOC, we too need education and realism!'); Alexander to Samaranch, 15 Aug. 1984 (Title: Sports Travel – Special Discounts on Air Fares); Alexander to Samaranch, 16 Aug. 1984 (Title: Boycotts); Alexander to Samaranch, 16 Aug. 1984 (Title: Television Boycott – South Africa); Alexander statement to IOC Session, 25 July 1984, 88th IOC Session; a copy was mailed to Alexander from Berlioux on 19 Oct. 1984. Delivered during 'Report by the President on the on-participation of some NOCs': Alexander Correspondence 1984.

[67] 'Reconciliation, is I believe one of the foremost responsibilities for the IOC to promote.... How much longer are we to run away from, 'to sweep under the carpet' the South African problem? Is the IOC to wait until the holocaust ("blood bath") commences, when it will be too late, or are we prepared to move now and be one of those influences whereby sport helps *now*, whilst there is some little time left to solve some of the other fundamental problems in that country, such as for example my current concerns with Schooling and Conservatism in the Rural Areas': see Alexander to Samaranch, 28 Aug. 1984, Alexander Correspondence 1984.

[68] Letter from Hon. K.S.N. Matiba M.P., Minister for Culture and Social Sciences to Samaranch, 30 Aug. 1984. Matiba had sent a previous letter (9 July 1984) in which he wrote to Samaranch, that his 'views on sports policy are at variance with Reggie'. South Africa file. IOC Archives, Lausanne.

[69] Letter from Mr Amadou Lamine Ba, Secretary General, Supreme Council for Sport in Africa, 11 Sept. 1984. South Africa file. A reply was sent on 8 Oct. 1984. For press coverage of the response to Alexander's support of including South Africa in the Olympic Movement, see Benson Riungu, 'Alexander Challenged to Renounce Citizenship', *Sunday Nation* (Nairobi), 2 Sept. 1984; 'We Won't Link with SA – Moi', *Sunday Nation*, 2 Sept. 1984; 'Call for SA Ties Riles Matiba', *The Standard* (Nairobi), 1 Sept. 1984; 'Alexander is Disowned by the KOA!', *The Standard*, 1 Sept. 1984; James Kimondo, 'Policy on SA Reiterated', *The Standard*, n.d. In this article, Alexander was quoted: 'the sight of Black athletes beating Whites on track and field would do a lot to undermine racism'. The statement that generated the protest read: 'I believe that if we could lead the world in sport reconciliation with South Africa, indeed it would prove the influence of the IOC and sport and would have a deep influence on the other aspects of life in that country which are of no direct or immediate concern to the IOC'. The Kenyan Government responded: 'This statement is not only utterly contradictory to the policy of the Kenya Government regarding any contacts and links with the racist regime of Pretoria, but it is also out of tune with the aspirations and stand taken by the OAU'. See 'KOA Shocked – Chairman', *The Standard*, n.d.; Pius Nyamora and Lucy Oriang, 'Govt Condemns SA Link-up Call', *Daily Nation*, 1 Sept. 1984; Charles Kulundu, 'Alexander Now in Hot Soup – MP', *The Kenya Times*, 4 Sept. 1984; letter from Amadou Lamine Ba, secretary-general for Supreme Council for Sport in Africa, sent to Samaranch, 11 Sept. 1984 condemning remarks by Alexander; Samaranch response, 8 Oct. 1984; Samaranch to Alexander, 10 Sept. 1984. In this

three-page, seven-item letter, Samaranch maintains a pleasant tone and requests a copy of Alexander's statement to the *Standard*. Alexander to Samaranch, 21 Sept. 1984: 'At a time when I am admiring much of what you say and do it is unfortunate that we have to "agree to disagree" on the sports boycott of South Africa'. Alexander Correspondence 1984.

[70] Alexander to Samaranch, 25 Oct. 1984 (Title: Boycotts), referring to quote in *Olympic Review* 203 (Sept 1984), 598. Other letters that month included Alexander to Samaranch, 11 Oct. 1984 (Title: Boycotts); Alexander to Samaranch, 12 Oct. 1984 (Title: Rule 13 – Cessation of Membership). Alexander Correspondence 1984. Simultaneously, South Africa requested a fact-finding mission. Samaranch said that the time was not right. A letter from Opperman, Annex 29, indicates that Samaranch had hoped to send a commission before the end of 1984. See Executive Board minutes, 7 and 8 Nov. 1984, 22; Other Business, (b) South Africa, 23.

[71] Executive Board minutes, 7 and 8 Nov. 1984, 3; Executive Board minutes, 30 Nov., 1 Dec. 1984, 12; Other Business, (a) IOC member in Kenya, 2.

[72] Alexander to Samaranch, 28 Nov. 1984; Alexander to Samaranch, 24 Nov. 1984, Alexander Correspondence 1984.

[73] Handwritten letter from Alexander to Samaranch, 3 Dec. 1984. Alexander sent a telex the next day. Alexander Correspondence 1984.

[74] Alexander to Samaranch, 6 Dec. 1984 (Title: Independence of IOC Members – looking to close the matter with honour). Alexander Correspondence 1984. Things were shifting with South African sport. Tennis, cricket, the British Sports Council and the French Parliamentary Delegation had all resumed sporting ties with South Africa. See Letter from Opperman to Samaranch, 30 Nov. 1984. Bishop Desmond Tutu had even chimed in on the changes happening in South Africa, saying 'We have got a very good example of pressure succeeding. It happened with the sports boycott where apartheid has been stood on its head. The South African Government has done something that they said they would not do. We have got multiracial sport precisely because of that pressure'. See Letter from McIldowie to Samaranch, 16 Dec. 1984. South Africa file. IOC Archives, Lausanne.

[75] Telex from Samaranch to Alexander, 30 Jan. 1985. Folder: Reginald S. Alexander, File: Correspondence 1985, IOC Archives, Lausanne (hereafter Alexander Correspondence 1985).

[76] Alexander telex to Samaranch, 31 Jan. 1985, referenced in Alexander to Samaranch, 1 March 1985; Samaranch to Alexander, 21 Feb. 1985. Alexander Correspondence 1985.

[77] Alexander to Samaranch, 4 April 1985; Alexander to Samaranch, 25 March 1985. Alexander persisted in arguing for the ideal of Olympism, the fundamental principle the Olympic Games founder Baron de Coubertin believed would sweep across the world, and a principle which Alexander believed was worth fighting for. He maintained his view that the Charter provided a guide for the Olympic Movement. In an October 1985 letter he expressed his concern about the Pan Islamic Games. He reported to Samaranch that he was vehemently opposed to any Olympic patronage of the proposed Games because it was a 'violation of our ideals and of our Charter which, at Fundamental Principle 3, states: "No discrimination ... is allowed against any ... person on grounds of ... religion"'. Alexander saw religion as a divisive issue for Olympic sport, similar to politics. See Alexander to Samaranch, 31 Oct. 1985 (Title: Pan Islamic Games). Other letters written during this time period include Alexander to Samaranch, 19 Aug. 1985 (Title: The Executive Board and IOC Members); Alexander to Samaranch, 28 Aug. 1985 (Title: Autonomy of NOCs); Alexander to Samaranch, 3 Sept. 1985 (Title: Independence of Sport); Alexander to Samaranch, 21 Nov. 1985 (Title: Commercialism of Sport); Alexander to Samaranch, 21 Nov. 1985 (Title: Strong Feelings of All Africans). Alexander Correspondence 1985.

[78] Samaranch to Alexander, 2 Dec. 1985, ibid.

[79] Alexander to Samaranch, 9 Dec. 1985 (Title: Apartheid); refers to letters from Samaranch, 12 Nov. and 2 Dec. 1985. Italics (underlining in original) are Alexander's. Alexander Correspondence 1985.

[80] Alexander to Samaranch, 13 May, 1986 (Title: South Africa), enclosing 'Reinventing South Africa', *The Economist*, 10 May 1986. Folder: Reginald S. Alexander, File: Correspondence 1986, IOC Archives, Lausanne (hereafter Alexander Correspondence 1986).

[81] Alexander to Samaranch, 21 May 1986 (Title: Racial Discrimination). Samaranch to Alexander, 28 May 1986. Samaranch asked if Alexander wanted to put Brazil on the next agenda. Alexander Correspondence 1986.

[82] Alexander to Samaranch, 16 June 1986 (Title: Racial discrimination), enclosing two articles: Chris Cairncross, 'Mixed Sport at School Level to be Fostered' and 'De Beer Seeks School Sport', *Business News* 16 May 1986; Alexander to Samaranch, 2 Aug. 1986, enclosing brochure that discussed sport as a major influence for reform in South Africa, after Samaranch asked for ethnic divisions in total population; Alexander to Samaranch, 18 Aug. 1986, enclosing Hector Wandera, 'Delegation Fails to Secure More Money', *The Daily Nation*, n.d., related to financing of All-African Games. Alexander Correspondence 1986.

[83] Telex from Alexander to Samaranch, 18 Oct. 1986; Alexander to Samaranch, 31 Oct. 1986 (Title: All Africa Games 1987), enclosing 'Muliro's Daughter Marries', *Sunday Nation*, 16 Nov. 1986; Samaranch to Alexander, 25 Nov. 1986; Alexander to Samaranch, 1 Dec. 1986 (Title: Eligibility: 'Athletes Code'); Samaranch to Alexander, 18 Dec. 1986. Alexander Correspondence 1986.

[84] Alexander to Samaranch, 17 Dec. 1986 (Title: Confidence in IOC Members). Response to Samaranch letter, 25 Nov. 1986, which had been marked 'personal'. Ibid.

[85] Recently, President Jacque Rogge increased the embargo from 20 years to 30 years, making most documents related to South Africa's re-entry into the Olympic Movement unlikely to be examined until 2020.

[86] After his death, Alexander was identified as 'defender of a cause that some might regard as reactionary in a sports world undergoing change . . . the strength of his convictions could not but demand respect from those whose opinions differed from his own'. See Obituaries, *Olympic Review* 271/272 (May/June 1990), 254.

[87] Booth, 'Accommodating Race to Play the Game', 195. Due to the embargo, letters from Alexander after the creation of the Apartheid and Olympism Commission are inaccessible. It would be interesting to read his reactions and thoughts related to the IOC in the late 1980s.

[88] Mbaye was unable to explain why Samaranch initially decided to hold the Olympism and Apartheid meeting in June 1988; see Mbaye, *The International Olympic Committee and South Africa*, 127. On page 263, Mbaye explained that the IOC 'used all available means to support the anti-apartheid campaign. . . . However, the IOC did not hesitate to reopen the doors of the international sports community to the athletes and sports leaders alike. It did so when the time was right, when it sensed, thanks to the intuition of Samaranch, that the final countdown for the demise of apartheid had begun . . . the IOC also succeeded in making clear that, in pursuing its anti-apartheid action, it was neither jumping on the bandwagon nor displaying any kind of animosity towards South Africa, but simply implementing a humanist sports policy, initiated by Pierre de Coubertin and pursued by Samaranch'. Historian Douglas Booth detailed the readmission of South Africa into the IOC and revealed how the Olympic Movement pre-empted the efforts of other sport organizations, though when all was said and done, apartheid in practice remained. Booth suggests that Samaranch was motivated by personal ambition to host the first complete Olympic Games in Barcelona, his home city, and to receive a Nobel Prize nomination. See Booth, 'South Africa's "Autonomous Sport" Strategy'. This assertion is supported in Simson and Jennings, *The Lords of the Rings*. Booth also suggests that the sole objective of the boycotts was to integrate sport, not a humanitarian concern with government policies; see Booth, 'Accommodating Race to Play the Game', 183. In addition, see Nauright, '"Like Fleas on a Dog"', 55. Nauright contends that the expulsion from the Olympic Movement was not the most crucial event in the attempt to isolate South

Africa; rather, the campaign to eliminate South Africa from international rugby competitions had a greater impact on white South Africans. Despite Mbaye's claim that the IOC led the way for the dismantling of apartheid, even the back of his book admits that progress did not occur for two years after the participation of South African athletes at the 1992 Barcelona Games. Written by Michel Clare, the back of Mbaye's book, *The International Olympic Committee and South Africa*, notes: 'The world was witness to South Africa's astonishing progress toward full democracy only two years after its athletes' return to Barcelona'.

[89] Mbaye was provided full access to the IOC documents, allowing his book to be the only account of South Africa's readmission into the Olympic Movement based on the archival materials. Not only does the book omit any of Alexander's contributions, it diminishes his input. On page 110, Mbaye claimed that Alexander was a British citizen living in Kenya who later took on Kenyan nationality. Alexander was born in Kenya and identified himself as a Kenyan and as an African.

References

Baker, W.J. and J.A. Mangan, eds. *Sport in Africa: Essays in Social History*. New York: Africana Publishing Company, 1987.

Booth, D. 'South Africa's "Autonomous Sport" Strategy: Desegregation Apartheid Style'. *Sporting Traditions* 6 (1990): 155–79.

——. 'Accommodating Race to Play the Game: South Africa's Readmission to International Sport'. *Sporting Traditions* 8 (1990): 182–209.

——. *The Race Game: Sport and Politics in South Africa*. London: Frank Cass, 1998.

——. 'The Antinomies of Multicultural Sporting Nationalism: A Case Study of Australia and South Africa'. *International Sport Studies* 21 (1999): 5–24.

De Coubertin, P. *Olympism: Selected Writings*. Edited by N. Muller. Lausanne: IOC, 2000.

Guttmann, A. *The Games Must Go On: Avery Brundage and the Olympic Movement*. New York: Columbia University Press, 1984.

Hoberman, J. 'Toward a Theory of Olympic Internationalism'. *Journal of Sport History* 22 (1995): 1–37.

Jarvie, G. 'Sport, Popular Struggle and South African Culture'. In *Sport, Racism and Ethnicity*, edited by Grant Jarvie. London: Frank Cass, 1991: 175–89.

Kidd, B. 'From Quarantine to Cure: The New Phase of the Struggle against Apartheid Sport'. *Sociology of Sport Journal* 8 (1991): 33–46.

Killanin, Lord. *My Olympic Years*. London: Secker & Warburg, 1983.

Mbaye, K. *The International Olympic Committee and South Africa: Analysis and Illustration of a Humanist Sport Policy*. Lausanne: IOC, 1995.

Miller, D. *Olympic Revolution: The Biography of Juan Antonio Samaranch*. London: Pavilion, 1994.

Nauright, J. '"Like Fleas on a Dog": Emerging National and International Conflict over New Zealand Rugby Ties with South Africa, 1965–74', *Sporting Traditions* 10 (1993): 54–77.

Ratner, A. *The Seventh President: Juan Antonio Samaranch, the True Story*. Moscow: Olympic Panarama, 2001.

Rees, R. 'The NOSC and the Non-Racial Sports Movement: Towards Post-Apartheid Sport in South Africa'. In *Critical Reflections on Olympic Ideology: Proceedings, First International Symposium for Olympic Research*. London, Ontario: Centre for Olympic Studies, 1992: 40–54.

Simson, V. and A. Jennings, *The Lords of the Rings: Power, Money and Drugs in the Modern Olympics*. London: Simon & Schuster, 1992.

When North–South Fight, the Nation is out of Sight: The Politics of Olympic Sport in Postcolonial India

Boria Majumdar

The Balinese cockfight is – or more exactly, deliberately is made to be – a simulation of the social matrix, the involved system of crosscutting, overlapping, highly corporate groups – villages, kingroups, irrigation societies, temple congregations, 'castes' – in which its devotees live. And as prestige, the necessity to affirm it, defend it, celebrate it, justify it, and just plain bask in it ... is perhaps the central driving force in the society. [1]

By transposing the terms 'cockfight' with hockey or cricket and 'Bali' with India, one may in essence capture the significance of sport in the subcontinent; perhaps the only realm where 'India' exists on the international stage. India's cricket, hockey and football teams represent India; and not Bengal, Maharastra or Tamil Nadu. Sport is perhaps the only site where being Indian still matters. This has become marked in recent years with the passionate display of the tricolour during international sports tournaments. [2] If only for a few weeks every year, Indian sports fans, from home and the diaspora, celebrate the cardinal truth of being 'Indian'. For a country obsessed with history and transformed by its well-spread postcolonial diaspora, this may seem unlikely. But is it widely visible.

Indians across the country, it is known, learn weird variants of their history in school textbooks. While for schoolkids in the east it is Subhas Chandra Bose who led the nation to freedom; in pockets of the west dominated by certain caste groupings it may be Ambedkar or Phule; in the north Indian heartland it is Gandhi. In stark contrast to this peculiar situation, most discussions of 'Indian' hockey/cricket and issues governing their fortunes are still common tropes, mentioned almost daily in the national/local media. Sport in India is continually influenced by the intersecting vectors of politics and commerce. Yet in the vast literature on Indian history, sport, one of the most important cultural practices of the twentieth and twenty-first century, finds little mention. The reason behind this absence, not only in the Indian case but worldwide more generally, scholars such as Dipesh Chakrabarty and Brian Stoddart have pointed out, are varied and complex. For Chakrabarty, the contours of the (British) social history or 'history from below' movement, which influenced much of the writing of Indian social history and into which sport scholars wanted to have themselves integrated, had certain intellectual priorities built into them. Sporting events, he argues, were seen as less important than strikes or some other act of overt class conflict or class resistance. [3] Chakrabarty is thus of the opinion that even though the defenders of sports history in the 1970s and 1980s perceived it as central to the business of social history, it 'never quite became a mainstream subject to historians who saw themselves as engaged in that trade'. [4]

Brian Stoddart, one of the torchbearers of the initial movement to mainstream sports history, however, argues that 'from the start, much of the better sports history was explicitly cross-disciplinary in focus, drawing upon anthropology and sociology in particular and therein lies at least one of the strands to be followed in the "why did not History departments take on sports history?"'. [5] He goes on to suggest that many of the standard approaches followed by historians did not adequately explain social stories and behaviours associated with sport. This evolves from Stoddart's earlier contentions that even as

> the decolonization process gathered momentum following India's independence in 1947, the contradiction of sport representing the ideals of a vanishing empire on the one hand and becoming a no longer apolitical ideal on the other proved

to be an important postcolonial problem.... In Pakistan, the control of sport became an increasingly political occupation, as demonstrated by Air Vice Marshal Nur Khan, who from the 1950s while a member of government was also prominent on the national boards of several major sports. But there were more subtle problems as postcolonial states came to realize that, while the former and institutional trappings of power could be readily taken over, the principles of cultural power, especially sport, were not so easily shifted, particularly as a number of states sought to use that cultural power themselves for nation building purposes. [6]

Stoddart uses the 'difference' marker, i.e. the fact that sport is often not influenced by dominant political trends, to explain the situation in the Caribbean islands in the early 1950s:

By the early 1950s in the West Indies, for example, the bulk of the political power had been shifted to black responsibility in a prelude to full independence, with men such as Norman Manley, Sir Grantley Adams, Forbes Burnham and Eric Williams proving to be formidable and talented architects of their people's futures. Yet, until 1960 no black player captained the West Indies on a regular basis; the captain was the only white player on the team, a symbol of continuing white cultural domination during a period in which nonwhites were becoming increasingly influential in other areas of political and economic life. [7]

Just like the 'blacks' in the West Indies, the southern states in India had emerged as major players in the nation's political scene by the early 1970s. Central to this ascendancy was the success of the DMK, a front-ranked South Indian political party in the general elections of 1967.

Yet, when it came to sport, and in the case of the country's leading Olympic sport, hockey, the south was still subservient to the stranglehold exerted by the north. As a result, southern sports administrators were soon determined to challenge the well-entrenched northern supremacy even if that entailed the sacrificing of national interest in the long run. In the fight with the north for the control of Indian hockey, the south bloc led by M.A.M. Ramaswamy enlisted the support of the International Hockey Federation. [8] In doing so, they pre-empted the possibilities of a strong Indian protest when the shift to artificial turf was proposed in the mid-1970s. As a close ally of the International Hockey Federation and its president Rene Frank, Ramaswamy, having assumed presidency of the Indian federation, had little choice but to offer tacit consent to the move to AstroTurf. [9] A fight for supremacy between the north and south blocs, this paper will demonstrate, was at the root of the Indian apathy towards stemming the move to AstroTurf, central to the subsequent decline of India's leading Olympic sport. It follows that more than the shift to AstroTurf, it was regional power play provoked by the peculiar nature of sport as a cultural practice that resulted in the disappearance of hockey from its position of centrality in the Indian sporting landscape.

Indian Hockey: A Brief History

> Hockey, more than any other game, is etched in the Indian psyche. It is hockey that brings out the magic and mystery, the poetry and prose in Indian sport. [10]

One of the world's oldest sports, hockey predates the ancient Olympic Games by a little more than 1,200 years. However, the modern game of field hockey (for those distinguishing it from ice hockey) evolved in the British Isles in the middle of the nineteenth century. The British helped spread hockey globally, promoting it in parts of the empire as part of the civilizing process, and subsequently its popularity became especially visible in the Indian subcontinent by the early twentieth century. In colonial India, especially in the early decades of the twentieth century, hockey was equally as popular as cricket and football, the country's other passions. Even school and college magazines of the period are replete with descriptions of hockey matches, and they specifically draw attention to India's spectacular performance in the Olympics. [11]

Men's hockey first appeared at the 1908 Olympic Games in London. It reappeared in Antwerp in 1920, returning to stay from the 1928 Amsterdam Games onwards. Women's hockey waited much longer, finally debuting in 1980. India won six straight Olympic gold medals and 24 consecutive matches between 1928 and 1956, a record likely to stand for the foreseeable future. Indians have won two more gold medals since, in 1964 and 1980.

In contrast to the above description of the upbeat nature of hockey in colonial and immediately postcolonial India, the period since the late 1970s presents a rather dismal picture. India has performed miserably in the Olympics and the Champions' Trophy in the 1980s and 1990s, and in the eight-nation tournament in Holland in August 2005, the Indian hockey team finished a dismal seventh. [12] Since the late 1970s hockey has languished (bronze medals in Mexico in 1968 and Munich in 1972 notwithstanding), hardly comparable in popularity to cricket, which has gained in reputation since. With cricket reigning as the national passion, mass spectatorship in hockey in contemporary India is a rarity. Often, hockey spectatorship is less than five per cent of the spectator base for cricket in the country.

Hockey's failure to retain its earlier glory has been the primary reason for the game's decline. The Indian Olympic Association (IOA) and the Indian Hockey Federation (IHF) blame the corporate world and the media for unfair stepmotherly treatment, but poor marketing strategies, internal politicking and the myopic views of officials who run these institutions have also accounted for the regression of the sport.

Further, hockey continues to be regarded as a male domain, taboo for respectable middle-class women. In contrast to other Asian nations such as China and Korea, women hockey players in India try their hands at the game with no other means of livelihood in sight. Hockey associations continue to stagnate, financial crisis a permanent companion of the women's game. Leading stars are hardly ever given due recognition, and jobs on offer are never higher than the clerical grade. It is commonplace to see noted women hockey players languishing in penury after retirement, often rescued from such plight by welfare organizations and sports enthusiasts. Under such circumstances, women are often forced to give up hockey, while in many other cases they hardly ever attempt to take up the game seriously in the first place, having grown up to understand that hockey is something reserved for men only.

Sadly enough, the Indian Olympic Association and the Indian Hockey Federation have both contributed to this plight. Most measures undertaken to develop hockey were in the colonial period; in post-independence India, neither the IOA nor the IHF have considered it relevant to make attempts to match cricket and football, relegating the glories of hockey to India's sporting folklore. Such apathy, aggravated especially by the attitude of the Indian Hockey Federation, has contributed to converting hockey into a lower-class vocation in contemporary India. This ambivalence, as mentioned earlier, is best evident from the lack of protest on the part of the IHF when field hockey was moved from grass to AstroTurf in the mid 1970s. Being the only sport where the Indians could flex their muscles at the Olympic stage, the IHF and the IOA's lack of initiative to pre-empt this manoeuvre is revealing. However, the conversion to AstroTurf simply cannot explain the sad plight of Indian hockey. This is because Pakistan, a nation economically worse off than India and one which has far fewer artificial turf fields, has done particularly well in recent times, even winning the eight-nation unofficial world championships at Amstelveen in August 2005. The argument very simply then becomes: if Pakistan can, why can't the Indians?

This paper aims to use the sudden decline of Indian hockey as an entry point for commenting on the functioning of the IHF and the IOA since the 1970s. The story of sports administration in 1970s India, it will transpire, was but a small segment of a far more important story of regional assertion, of the contest for supremacy between the north and the south of India. [13] It is an irony that the Indian hockey team, which has performed miserably in recent times, has often blamed its plight on the poor administration of the sport. [14] The recent recourse to a government ruling passed in 1975, which specifies that no official can stay at the helm of a sport for more than two terms, [15] marks the completion of a cycle of administrative anarchy that started three decades ago when the country's Hockey Federation was fractured down the middle between the north and south lobbies.

This paper is based on the premise that a full history of India's Olympic sporting experience must be framed within the broader themes of south Asian history and should not be restricted to the history of Olympism in general or Indian hockey in particular. The paper is part of the growing academic concern to locate sport within the broader socio-economic processes that have shaped colonial and postcolonial societies in South Asia. Throughout this history, hockey is used as the prism/ metaphor to analyse the workings of sports administrators in India. Studying this will help us understand the complexities of modern Indian society, while bringing to light the role played by 'sport' in creating and moulding such complexities. It will be evident from this study that hockey was, and remains, a cultural form adopted by

Indians to fulfil social, political and economic aspirations and imperatives. The prime intention here is also to assess how hockey has defined and continues to define sporting relations in India, to delineate the interrelationship between those who support, promote, play and view the game, to comment on the nature of Indian sports administration and finally to emphasize that a study of Indian hockey in the 1970s goes beyond the playing field and shifts focus to the growing menace of regionalism in a seemingly united, independent nation state.

When It All Went Wrong

Things had been going well for Indian hockey until 1973 when Ashwini Kumar, the president of the Indian Hockey Federation, was forced to step down from his post due to burgeoning opposition against him. His resignation was followed by a long spell of anarchy within the ranks of the IHF and conflict between the north and south blocs as P.N. Sahni and M.A.M. Ramaswamy engaged in a bitter and arduous struggle for the presidency. [16] While Sahni had the backing of Kumar, Ramaswamy, an extremely influential Madras businessman, had the backing of some in the union ministry in Delhi. The feud turned murky when the group led by Sahni made every effort to stall Ramaswamy's assumption of the IHF presidency by dragging things to court when the election had been overseen by a reputed judge of the Supreme Court. [17] At the time when the dispute was raging, the IOA had cancelled the affiliation of the IHF and had taken over the administration of hockey in the country. This decision by the IOA was resented by the Ramaswamy faction, evident from a confidential letter written by Raja Bhalindra Singh, then president of the IOA, to Rene Frank, president of the International Hockey Federation. In his letter, Raja Bhalindra Singh expressed resentment over the actions of the Ramaswamy faction in taking the IOA to court and suggested that such actions might have prevented the Indian Olympic Association from selecting a team for the forthcoming Tehran Asian Games: 'This, you will agree, was a very cruel blow to our efforts in sending a representative team and went a long way in demoralizing the selected team, which, at the moment is under training'. [18] He went on to suggest that the IOA had been able to obtain a temporary injunction from the High Court against the restraint imposed by the lower judiciary on team selection.

A year after participating in the Asian Games at Tehran, the Indian hockey team, still under the stewardship of the IOA, won the Hockey World Cup for the first and only time in its history at Kuala Lumpur under the coaching of Balbir Singh Jr. The coaching camp before the tournament and the tour itself had to be funded by the Punjab government in the absence of funding from a dysfunctional IHF. [19] The camp, as Balbir Singh writes,

> was held on the campus of Punjab University, Chandigarh. A newly constructed girls' hostel was given as the residence for the trainees. This being in front of

another girls' hostel across the road, some girls started making courtesy calls at our visitors' lounge. This was discouraged by having the front gate locked, and advising the girls to watch the players in action on the field. That prompted the players to give their best during practice sessions to impress the girls. [20]

Internal squabbling within the IHF temporarily seemed to come to an end in 1975, when Ramasamy was duly recognized as president. However, even when this happened there were numerous affiliated units that were opposed to the move and thus refused to participate in activities of the IHF. In fact, Ramaswamy was aware of the unhappy situation and promptly announced his intention to bring under one roof all those affiliated units and individuals who had stayed away from the meeting that elected him president. The meeting was held, strangely enough, under the auspices of the Ministry of Education in New Delhi. [21] The IOA also approached the newly elected president with a request that in the interest of cordiality and to ensure that a sense of confidence prevail among all affiliated units of the IHF, he should take action to give, as far as possible, equitable representation to the affiliated members. [22] Unfortunately nothing was done to fulfil the promise, and for some time the IHF continued to function as a preserve of individuals from the south.

Contentious issues between the IOA and the IHF flared up once again in mid-1977 on the eve of the meeting of the IOA general assembly. At the meeting, on 2 July, 1977 members of the IOA general council expressed dissatisfaction with the working of the IHF and it was 'desired that the IOA must make concerted moves to remedy the situation and if necessary place the entire situation before the Government'. [23]

As a follow-up, General O.P. Mehra, who had succeeded Raja Bhalindra Singh as the president of the IOA in 1975, sent a letter to Ramaswamy on 19 July 1977 inviting him to a meeting in August that year to address the growing ill-will. [24] Ramaswamy, soon after, informed General Mehra that he was out of the country in August but would meet the IOA president in early September 1977. On receipt of this letter, a tentative meeting between the presidents of the IOA and the IHF was set up for 3 September in New Delhi. However, this meeting never materialized and the IOA executive council, which met on 24 September 1977, expressed deep resentment at the conduct of the IHF and its president. In a letter of 6 October 1977 addressed to M. Dayanand, secretary of the IHF, Vice Marshall C.L. Mehra, secretary-general of the IOA, alleged that the president of the IHF, despite having been in Delhi for meetings with officials of the Ministry of Education, had preferred not to get in touch with the president of the IOA. Accordingly, the IOA had reached the conclusion that the IHF was not interested in arriving at an amicable solution. In another letter addressed to Ramaswamy on 11 October 1977, the IOA congratulated him on his work in securing the rights to host the 1982 World Cup in India and assured him that the resources of the IOA were at all times at his disposal. The flurry of letter-writing did not abate and in another confidential letter written on 7 November 1977, the IOA repeated its long-standing request for a meeting. Finally, on 23 December 1977, the secretary of the IOA in a personal note to the president of the IHF almost pleaded for his intervention:

> As you may be aware, the IOA General Assembly meeting will be held in New Delhi on 14 January 1978 at 1400 hours. You will recollect that in the last General Assembly meeting held in July 1977, members of the IOA had raised certain issues connected with the workings of the Indian Hockey Federation.... Given that the meeting between yourself and the IOA has not materialised in spite of efforts made in that direction and given that the IOA General Assembly may raise issues relating to hockey, we request you to kindly attend this meeting along with your Secretary so that first hand clarifications can be given to all points raised. This will also avoid any decisions being taken by the IOA in your absence. You will agree that this is in the best interests of the IOA and the IHF. [25]

In the absence of any effort on the part of the IHF and its president to attend the meeting of 14 January 1978, and given that the IHF had done little in the interim to address the concerns raised against its functioning, the IOA had little option but to suspend the functioning of the IHF. The concerns against the IHF arose out of the following issues:

1. The IHF had not paid its dues to the IOA, amounting to approximately 45,000 rupees. Some of the amounts, it was observed, were outstanding for years. It was noted by the IOA general council that its president had made personal efforts to get the IHF to clear its dues and had convened a host of meetings with the treasurer and secretary of the IHF. And even when the IHF conceded to having defaulted, no action was taken to repay the outstanding dues.
2. Non-implementation of the ruling announced by the IOA that each state or affiliated member should be represented by 'one unit only'. This resolution had been adopted to prevent the mushrooming of dissident groups and had been implemented by all other national federations/associations. The IHF's refusal to accede to the ruling was perceived as creating a dangerous precedent for other national federations.
3. Non-implementation of the assurance given by the president of the IHF, M.A.M. Ramaswamy, to give equitable representation to those associations/individuals absent when he was elected president.
4. The acceptance of interference from a member of the government in the selection of the Indian hockey team and in the management of the day-to-day affairs of the federation. [26]

Of the concerns, the fourth and final one had deeper roots and went back to instances of interference by the union Minister for Works and Housing, Sikandar Bakht. Only a week before the meeting of the IOA general assembly, Bakht had attended the probables camp at Patiala and made statements contesting the rights and jurisdiction of the IOA. First, he had unilaterally foiled attempts to reinstate the three dissident stars, Surjit Singh, Virender Singh and Baldev Singh, declaring that 'discipline in sports was essential and there must be respectful distance between players and selectors'. [27] And when asked if his stand amounted to interference in the affairs of the IOA, Bakht was abrasive in declaring that the 'Government had every right to ensure that public funds were not misused by any sports body. In Socialist countries sports were totally run by the government and there was no objection to it'. [28] This was in complete disregard of a statement issued by the IOC President, Lord Killanin, on his visit to India in December 1977. [29] Speaking to the media, Killanin had declared that if any instance of willing submission by a national federation to government or outside dictates was brought before an international federation recognised by the IOC, that national federation could be suspended by the international federation concerned. He reiterated that the IOC had the right to authorize a national Olympic committee to run the affairs of a national federation in which dispute existed and which was adversely affecting the interest of the sportsmen concerned. [30]

The IOA's resentment against Bakht becomes evident from the finding of a confidential letter written by Raja Bhalindra Singh to the president of the International Olympic Committee.

> Unfortunately a minister of government who has no direct connection with sports has been using his official position to interfere in the affairs of the Indian Hockey Federation, and has gone so far as to influence the selection of the national team. This has been resented and has attracted a lot of adverse public criticism both in Parliament and outside. The official government stand, that of the Ministry of Education and Sports, is one of unhappiness. However, the minister continues to interfere and the President of the IHF, whose own position is not too secure, continues to flout all norms of behaviour by seeking help from this extra constitutional authority, and in a most authoritarian way flout both the autonomy of his Federation as well as the spirit of the constitution of the National Olympic Committee. He refused to listen to the National Olympic Committee and has not even cared to be present in the various meetings convened to set matters right. [31]

Despite having suspended the IHF at its meeting of 14 January, the president of the IOA did once again invite the president of the IHF to a meeting to resolve differences by a letter dated 17 January 1978. [32]

However, in total disregard for the efforts of the IOA president, the IHF once again dragged the IOA to court and obtained an injunction contesting the disqualification. [33] Also, in a personal letter to the president of the International Hockey Federation, Rene Frank, the IHF president outlined reasons for not attending the meeting of the IOA. While it is intriguing to wonder why reasons were cited to the International Hockey Federation and not to the IOA, the reasons themselves seem no less dubious. The three reasons cited by President Ramaswamy were as follows:

1. The 14th of January was Pongal Day – one of the most important feast days for us in South India and I had to respect my revered father's wishes and participate in the religious ceremonies at home.

2.   As Chairman and Senior Steward of the Madras Race Club, I had to be present at the Race Course to officiate the running of the South India derby.

3.   The first circular and second circulars convening the IOA meeting did not include any item on hockey affairs. [34]

He went on to state that sports in India was under the direct control of the union government and the Prime Minister, Shri Morarji Desai, had placed Mr Sikandar Bakht in complete charge of hockey. He also assured the international federation president that in the battle royal against the IOA, the IHF was assured of the support of Mr Bakht.

The letter ended with the assertion that the resolution suspending the IHF was illegal and the Madras High Court, on 18 January 1978, had already granted a temporary injunction against the suspension. [35]

He followed this letter with another long memo addressed to the president of the IOA on 31 January 1978 and declared that unless the IOA withdrew the order of suspension, any meeting between the two organizations would prove futile. [36]

The conflict turned ugly when Rene Frank, president of the International Hockey Federation, joined hands with the Indian Hockey Federation president supporting his claims in a memo to the IOC president. In his telegram, sent on 27 February 1978, Frank suggested that the opposition lobby, which had failed to check Ramaswamy's ascendancy to the presidency of the IHF, was using the instance of action taken against the three Punjabi players to resume the tussle.

> It must be noted that the players involved are most probably all Punjabis, three of them belonging to a team of which Kumar is the chief. As far as the suspension of the IHF by the IOA is concerned, we fully disapprove it. It must also be noted that all the people involved belong to the North. [37]

He concluded with an assertion that Ramaswamy, who was a member of his council, was an eminent personality in south India, was the director of a number of companies and had helped his association financially since becoming the president. [38]

Upon knowing that Frank had written a letter to the IOC president supporting Ramaswamy, General Mehra went to great lengths in trying to explain to the president of the International Hockey Federation the reasons behind the IOA's actions. He repeatedly made the point that had it been the intention of the IOA to take over the functioning of the IHF, it would not have allowed Ramaswamy to go ahead with the planning of the India-Pakistan hockey series for later in the year and would not have permitted the IHF to run a conditioning camp for the World Cup to be played in Argentina. [39]

Things came to a head when Frank's confidential letter to the IOC president found its way to the Indian press in June 1978. [40] On the one hand, Frank's views provoked a hostile reaction in the national sporting media. [41] On the other, it was perceived as a serious slur on the reputation of the IOA. Upset at the leakage, on 30 June 1978 General Mehra complained about Frank to the IOC president,

Lord Killanin. He suggested that the issue of north-south relations was a rather sensitive one and it was unethical on Frank's part to comment on such matters. He reminded Killanin of a letter he had sent on 27 March which mentioned that Frank had 'hurt our national sentiments by giving a political slant to the dispute by referring to personal interests and north versus the rest of India as factor'. [42]

He also drew attention to Frank's silence over a similar tussle in Pakistan, arguing that the Pakistani government's takeover of the nation's hockey affairs by disbanding the hockey federation had far more serious consequences for the international sporting fraternity.

He concluded with an affirmation that his letter was written more in anguish and hoped that the IOC would exert pressure on Frank to let the IOA handle its internal affairs without any extraneous influence playing a part. [43]

Bobby Talyarkhan, a veteran sportswriter, also made the point that Frank had overstepped his limits in declaring 'that the real trouble is between the north and the south of India'. Talyarkhan, who had earlier supported the IHF against the IOA and had argued against the IOA takeover of the functioning of the IHF during the 1975 World Cup, stated that

> Frank has gone so far as to mention the Sikhs as an entity and I assert this is none of his business. By stating what he has done Rene Frank is merely adding fuel to fire.... Frank has no business to go into any details calculated to turn India's hockey control into a burning cauldron.... India's sport has enough internal squabbles for a foreigner to step in and add to the troubles. [44]

The Past

Instances of regional conflict were hardly new to Indian sport. In colonial conditions for example, British recognition and support had proved pivotal in shaping the development of Indian soccer in the 1930s and 1940s. With the Indian Football Association (IFA) based in Calcutta unhappy with its role as a regional institution and aiming to govern the development of football in the whole country, it sought British support in posing as the governing body for soccer in India. It was as a mark of protest against such intentions of the IFA that other state associations for soccer formed the All India Football Association (AIFA) in the 1930s. The formation of the All India Football Association in September 1935 triggered the commencement of a bitter struggle between the Indian states – Bengal on the one hand and the western and northern Indian states on the other – to assert supremacy over the control of the game. In this struggle, Bengal at every stage drew upon British support, a factor that eventually contributed to the success of the Maharaja of Santosh, the president of the IFA, in combating efforts to establish a parallel governing body, the All India Football Association, to rival the IFA with its head quarters in Calcutta. Recognition granted by the English Football Association to the IFA was garnered by the Maharaja of Santosh to impress that the IFA was the only internationally recognized governing body for soccer in India. [45]

Just as in the case of hockey, Bengali dominance over soccer was unquestioned until the 1920s. However, this state of affairs underwent a transformation from the close of the decade. At the root of this transformation lay the changes in the status of the sport in the rest of the country, when other provinces, averse to soccer, shunned their earlier repugnance and emerged conscious patrons of the sport. This in turn marked the onset of a phase of crisis in Indian soccer that was to culminate with the formation of the All India Football Federation in 1937. [46]

The Sports-Politics Vortex

The point of proximity between the two instances of the politicization of sport, though located in completely different conditions and time frames, is difficult to miss. While in the case of soccer, Bengali sports patrons had sought to enlist British support, in the case of hockey almost half a century later the IOA and the IHF tried to garner international support – from the IOC and the International Hockey Federation. Such attempts to internationalize internal rifts have adversely affected India's international standing, although this has hardly been recorded in India's political history.

In the post-independence context, hockey was one sport where India had a resounding global presence. However, with the rise of regionalism at the national level concurrent with the move to AstroTurf, India's dominance soon gave way to subjection. Contemporary Indian hockey stagnates, with the glory days receding towards the horizon.

This paper has tried demonstrate how a cultural practice, here the case of 'hockey', created deep-rooted fissures between two regional cultures in the north and the south of India, when other causes of regional tension were often diplomatically resolved. The 'north-south' labelling of the conflict itself was problematic. It was only when the tussle was internationalized that the label was applied – in fact, it was introduced by the president of the International Hockey Federation. While the rupture had concrete form in some respects, it was more often a vague tension as the north and south regions use hockey in quite different ways.

The paper also demonstrated how 'sport' fashions the international standing of a nation, which is most evident when power and politics intersect in the sporting landscape as they did with Indian hockey. A cultural history of Indian hockey, I emphasize, is a political one and is not confined to the playing field but expands into the domain of regional politicking. Interestingly, while the controversy over the control of hockey reinforced the politics/sport connection and while there was a heightened sensitivity in India about what such control might symbolize, subsequent social science research suggests that there was no such sensitivity in the Indian academy to interpret the politicization of a well-entrenched cultural practice.

For India, then, hockey has been a vehicle to express both national and regional achievement and ambition, but in quite different ways. This paper has expanded the political analysis of hockey in arguing that even at periods when performances were at a low ebb (1970–80), the sport was a site to settle regional discord. This was an uneasy phase with the unwilling intervention of the central government in sport, evident from its apathy over checking Sikandar Bakht from intruding into the affairs of the IOA. Such apathy was part of the general official neglect of sport. With the government continuing to view sport as entertainment and leisure until the early 1970s, there were no incentives for bureaucrats or politicians to perceive a sporting portfolio as special. Such narrow underpinnings had their root in the government's difficulty in understanding the political significance of sport and changed only partly during the organization of the 1982 Asian Games, when India as a nation appreciated the popular appeal of sport.

Even today, the dynamics of how sport and contemporary Indian society influence one another seldom finds mention in histories of modern India. Suffice it to say that sport has globally become crucial to modern human existence, having made itself indispensable to a world infested by terror. Sport and politics are inextricably linked, and India is no aberration. The sooner Indian social science recognizes the reality, the better it is for the academy. To go a step further, bringing sport within the ambit will enable the academy to provide a more nuanced understanding of the complexities of our age.

Acknowledgements

This paper has been written on the basis of research conducted in the archives at the IOC Olympic Studies Centre, located in the Olympic Museum in Lausanne. I am grateful to the staff of the Olympic Studies Centre, especially Nuria, Ruth and Patricia, for their help during my stint there as fellow in December–January 2004–05.

Notes

[1] Geertz, 'Deep play'.
[2] In recent times Indian supporters have far outnumbered supporters from other nations in international sports contests. At both the 2003 Cricket World Cup in South Africa and the eight-nation hockey championship at Amstelveen in Holland, the Indians had great support, with the stadiums decked in the tricolour. Even when Sania Mirza had her dream US Open run in August 2005, Indians from all over the US flocked by the hundreds to Flushing Meadow, New York, to cheer their favourite tennis star.
[3] Chakrabarty, 'Introduction'.
[4] See the exchange between Dipesh Chakrabarty and Brian Stoddart in 'Feedback', *Biblio – A Review of Books*, Nov.–Dec. 2005, available online at http://www.biblio-india.com/feedbackrec.asp?mp= MJ05, accessed 15 Dec. 2005.
[5] Ibid.
[6] Stoddart, 'Sport, Cultural Imperialism and Colonial Response', 671.
[7] Ibid.
[8] File OU MO01 14 36, CIO CNO IND CORR, Olympic Studies Centre, IOC Museum, Lausanne. This file deals primarily with correspondence exchanged between the Indian

Olympic Association and the Indian Olympic Committee. Also, any document sent from India to the IOC – letters, pamphlets, constitutions etc have been retained in this file.

[9] Ibid.

[10] Rajdeep Sardesai, *Sunday Times of India*, 1992.

[11] Magazines of the Presidency and St Xavier's Colleges in Calcutta between 1920 and 1940 are full of praise for the Indian hockey team's performance at the Olympics.

[12] Even in the match for the seventh position, India got a lucky break against England, winning 2–1.

[13] See the confidential letters exchanged between the IOA and the IHF, File OU MO01 14 36, CIO CNO IND CORR, Olympic Studies Centre, IOC Museum, Lausanne.

[14] For details see; Pargat Singh, 'IHF destroying Indian Hockey', available online at http://www.indianhockey.com/phpmodule/view.php3?id=264, accessed 15 Dec. 2005.

[15] This was originally passed by Parliament in 1974 as a remedy for the nation's poor showing in international sports meets. There was severe protest by sports bodies soon after and eventually the ruling was disregarded, with the result that politicians have been at the helm of sporting federations for well over a decade.

[16] See file OU MO01 14 36, CIO CNO IND CORR, Olympic Studies Centre, IOC Museum, Lausanne. The file contains details of the ongoing dispute between the two rival blocs, including original letters and other correspondence.

[17] See File IDD CHEMISE 9404 CIO CNOINDE CORR, Olympic Studies Centre, IOC Museum, Lausanne. Correspondence between the IOC and the Indian Olympic Association is chronologically arranged. Sometimes things are organized thematically. This file mostly contains material on issues relating to Indian hockey.

[18] Letter from Raja Bhalindra Singh to IOC President, 14 Aug. 1974, OU MO01 14 36, CIO CNO IND CORR, Olympic Studies Centre, IOC Museum, Lausanne.

[19] For details see Singh, *The Golden Hat Trick*. The book contains fascinating material on how politicized Indian hockey was in the 1970s.

[20] Balbir Singh, 'Kuala Lumpur Has Always Been Lucky', available online at http://www.indianhockey.com/mcol3/1.php, accessed 15 Dec. 2005.

[21] OU MO01 14 36, CIO CNO IND CORR, Olympic Studies Centre, IOC Museum, Lausanne.

[22] Extracts from the minutes of the IOA General Assembly Meeting held on 2 July 1977, OU MO01 14 36, CIO CNO IND CORR, Olympic Studies Centre, IOC Museum, Lausanne.

[23] Ibid.

[24] OU MO01 14 36, CIO CNO IND CORR, Olympic Studies Centre, IOC Museum, Lausanne.

[25] Ibid.

[26] Ibid.

[27] *Hindustan Times*, 10 Jan. 1978.

[28] Ibid., 14 Jan. 1978.

[29] Ibid., 2 Dec. 1977.

[30] Ibid.

[31] Raja Bhalindra Singh, letter to Lord Killanin, 15 Jan. 1978, OU MO01 14 36, CIO CNO IND CORR, Olympic Studies Centre, IOC Museum, Lausanne.

[32] OU MO01 14 36, CIO CNO IND CORR, Olympic Studies Centre, IOC Museum, Lausanne.

[33] Injunction issued by the Madras Court on 18 Jan. 1978, OU MO01 14 36, CIO CNO IND CORR, Olympic Studies Centre, IOC Museum, Lausanne.

[34] Letter from Ramaswamy to Rene Frank, 21 Jan. 1978, OU MO01 14 36, CIO CNO IND CORR, Olympic Studies Centre, IOC Museum, Lausanne.

[35] Ibid.

[36] OU MO01 14 36, CIO CNO IND CORR 1977–78, Olympic Studies Centre, IOC Museum, Lausanne.

[37] Ibid.

[38] Ibid.

[39] Letter from General Mehra to Rene Frank, 16 March 1978, OU MO01 14 36, CIO CNO IND CORR, Olympic Studies Centre, IOC Museum, Lausanne.

[40] The letter was published in the *Hindustan Times*, 9 June 1978.

[41] The media were unanimous that Frank had overstepped his limits. Most reports expressed concern about the future of Indian hockey and lamented the gradual decline of a sport with a glorious tradition.

[42] OU MO01 14 36, CIO CNO IND CORR 1977–78, Lausanne, IOC Museum, Olympic Studies Centre.

[43] Ibid.

[44] Bobby Talyarkhan, 'When Rene gets too Frank', OU MO01 14 36, CIO CNO IND CORR 1977–78, Lausanne, IOC Museum, Olympic Studies Centre.

[45] See Chapter 4 of Majumdar and Bandyopadhyay, *Goalless*.

[46] Ibid.

References

Chakrabarty, Dipesh. 'Introduction'. In *Sport in South Asian Society – Past and Present*, edited by Boria Majumdar and J.A. Mangan. London: Routledge, 2005.

Geertz, Clifford. 'Deep Play: Notes on the Balinese Cockfight'. In *The Interpretation of Cultures: Selected Essays*. New York: Basic Books, 1973.

Majumdar, Boria and Kausik Bandyopadhyay. *Goalless: The Story of a Unique Footballing Nation.* New Delhi: Penguin-Viking, 2006.

Singh, Balbir. *The Golden Hat Trick: My Hockey Days.* New Delhi: Vikas, 1977.

Stoddart, Brian. 'Sport, Cultural Imperialism and Colonial Response in the British Empire: a Framework for Analysis'. *Comparative Studies In Society And History* 14, no. 3 (Winter 1987).

A Brief Historical Review of Olympic Urbanization

Hanwen Liao and Adrian Pitts

Introduction

For many people, the modern Olympics Games are seen as a great contest of sportsmanship and chauvinism; for others, they are a media extravaganza. It should also be stressed, however, that the Olympics are also about venues and cities. Cities themselves provide the platforms and backdrops for the Games, characterize each event with a specific identity and context and, at the same time, are affected in a direct and dramatic fashion by the Games. There are two major impacts: firstly the Olympics have sufficient momentum to intervene in the host city's short- and long-term development activities, placing unparalleled challenges and opportunities in the sphere of urbanization during the process of preparation; secondly the modern Games imply a certain standard of hosting milieu, such that cities need to rearrange their urban fabric and built environment to win the bid as well as to safeguard the success of Olympic events. According to one Olympic bidding manual, in hosting a summer Games a city needs to prepare 31 to 38 competition venues and up to 90 training sites for the 28 summer Olympic sports; one or more Olympic Village(s) for housing approximate 15,000 athletes and National Olympic committee (NOC) officials; broadcasting facilities and accommodation for more than 15,000 journalists; at least 40,000 hotel rooms and all kinds of other infrastructure – transport, logistics, telecommunications and entertainment facilities – to support the event. As Hiller points out, the Olympics represent both urban opportunities and urban liabilities: [1] an example might be the satisfaction of Olympic requirements in a way that is to the long-term detriment of local development and local need.

Over the last century, urban development in connection with the Olympic Summer Games has passed through a tortuous evolutionary course, from the *mono-stadium* model in the early years to an *Olympic quarter* model; from planning concentrated on competition facilities to a very broad scope of supportive construction. Olympic urbanization has clearly grown in terms of content, scale, form and complexity. The beginning of Olympic urban initiatives dates back to the fourth Games in London in 1908, with the construction of the White City Olympic Stadium. Yet even up to the post-Second World War period, the provision of sports venues and athlete Villages dominated Olympic preparation and the impact on the wider urban infrastructure was limited. It was not until 1960 that the dormant forces for large-scale development began to reveal themselves. From the Rome Olympics onwards, the Games began to have many far-reaching consequences on the local built environment – particularly in line with the needs of urban expansion in the 1960s and 1970s, of inner-city regeneration in the 1980s and 1990s and of sustainable urban form in the current decade. There is a constant intimacy between Olympic development and the evolution of host cities.

Recently, with sustainability issues having gained world attention, the International Olympic Committee (IOC) signalled the desire to promote the global campaign of building a positive environmental legacy for future generations by applying sustainable development concepts in the Olympic Movement. One of the challenges facing decision-making will therefore be to find ways of using Olympic planning as a vehicle for host cities to achieve more lasting and sustainable benefits. Although the Official Report of each Games is couched almost exclusively in the rhetoric of economic growth, social renaissance and environmental enhancement, its real effects can only be examined in a historical manner and the study of Olympic urbanization history can provide a useful starting point. It is important in this context to provide the historical timing of the introduction of the environmental element. This is because researchers often make the mistake of looking for environmental treatments in such Games as Atlanta and then produce a critique concerning the lack of initiative. This is a false critique, as 'environment' was not introduced as an element to be considered by the bid groups until the bid process related to the 2000 Games of the Olympiad.

This paper examines the different ways that Olympic facilities have been integrated into the host city's urban fabric. The main focus is on the post-war period when

Olympic planning to stimulate and justify large-scale urban improvements became commonplace. In reviewing the history of Olympic urbanization, there are several aims:

- to provide a panoramic view of Olympic urban practices and changes over time;
- to identify the influential factors which determined the ever-changing course of Olympic urban planning, and also their significance as an aid in contemporary decision-making;
- to examine various Olympic urban policies which reference twentieth-century town planning concepts;
- to evaluate, with the benefit of hindsight, Olympic urban legacies against their stated original intentions, and then to posit lessons for the planning and design practice for future Olympic preparation.

A substantial part of the paper is presented in chronological order so that the reader may easily follow the sequence of the changing patterns in Olympic urban development.

Olympic Games and Cities

The interdependency of the Olympic Games and the host city is reflected in the Olympic Charter, according to which the Games can only be awarded to a host city rather than a country. This is particularly central with regard to the Summer Games. Although the Olympic Winter Games are also awarded to a host city and not a country, the IOC introduced an additional winter-specific stipulation into the Olympic Charter in 1991. Since that time, the stipulation has opened the door to the possibility that certain events could be held in a bordering country when, due to geographic or topographic limitations, it was not possible for these events to be organized within the country of the host city. [2] Although the IOC never sets rigid physical, economic or social criteria in selecting host cities, convention indicates that the Summer Games are accommodated by large cities with more than three million inhabitants. [3]

The modern Olympics have grown to the point that their size suggests that they are on a different scale from any other major sporting event; the only sports extravaganza that might possibly challenge the Olympics influence is soccer's World Cup, even though statistical evidence indicates that its scale is substantially less. Nowadays, each Olympic Summer Games might involve more than 15,000 athletes and officials, at least the same number of media representatives, and from 400,000 to a million out-of-city visitors. This means the host city has a huge increase in temporary population, which places great demands on civic infrastructure and accommodation. Only the world's largest cities have the required resources to cope with such challenges and sufficient population thresholds to sustain the viability of the facilities in the long term after the Games are over. Further, the increasing pre-investment costs for the bidding stage and overall cost of the Games mean that only the key cities of concentrated regional economic power can afford the financial commitment. Most Olympic hosts have come from among the most influential *mega*-cities in the world. [4]

These factors have created geographic inequalities by leaving out potential smaller city hosts (such as Lausanne's candidature in 1948 and 1960; Baltimore's in 1948; and Minneapolis's in 1952 and 1956) and cities in the developing world. The increasing gigantism and polarization of the modern Olympics have raised concerns within the IOC; in 2002 the Olympic Games Study Commission was appointed to evaluate possible reduction in the number of events, participants, procedures and costs for future Games. It seems, however, that no matter the extent to which the Olympics may be moderated in the future, the Games will remain a high-profile event in promoting host cities on the world stage and attracting inward investment to these cities. As such, the Games will continue to be a focal point of competition among the world's major cities, as witnessed by the numerous cities bidding for the 2012 event.

That Olympic host cities are some of the world's largest and most cosmopolitan is an interesting point, because the evolution of these cities reflects the mainstream of urbanization processes in a modern, democratic and industrialized society. And this urbanization process, as will be mentioned later, can be used as an important reference to understand the ways that Olympic facilities are integrated into different urban contexts.

Olympic Urbanization History

Since 1896, 25 out of 28 planned Summer Games have actually been staged in 21 different cities spread over 17 countries. In order to review more clearly the evolution of Olympic urbanization, it is useful to identify four historical phases within which host cities carried out relatively homogeneous urban approaches to prepare for the Games. The first phase includes the first decade of Olympic revival, which corresponds to the three earliest, modestly prepared, low-key events, with minimal urban intervention. The second phase covers the period from 1908 to 1928 when the event began to attract more world attention, to be prepared in a planned manner and to involve sport-specific venues. The Olympic Games entered its third phase in 1932, which spanned to 1956. This period witnessed substantial development of Olympic-related urban elements with some, perhaps, modest, renovation activities. In the fourth phase, since 1960, Olympic urbanization has extended far beyond the boundary of sports and associated facilities, to a more comprehensive urban scheme with many projects perhaps not having visible connections with the Games' organization. In this phase, cities are no longer passive *containers* to serve the Olympic performances; rather, the Olympics become a pretext to trigger large-scale urban improvement and shape planning policy.

The Origins of Olympic Urbanism (1896–1904)

The origin of Olympic urbanism can be traced back to Pierre de Coubertin's concept of creating a 'modern Olympia', which has set the tone of the modern Olympic built environment, and still nourishes today's venue planning and design. Coubertin had perceived the long-term appeal of the ancient Olympic Games in the ancient Hellenic world as being deeply rooted in its unique festival form, a '*cult of human essence*', as well as being located in a solid, physical setting, the holy city of Olympia. [5] He believed that if the modern Games were to extend beyond being a pure sports event and to be felt as a sense of culture and belief, then the definition of a unique urban context was paramount. In this pamphlet, which was published in 1906, Coubertin revealed his vision of future Olympic settings. He wanted it to be a '*city*' that 'harmoniously linked with athletics, literature and art' and 'closely collaborated of man and nature'. He also gave details of his concept:

> First the Olympic city must be visible to the visitor if not in its entirety, then at least as a grandiose and dignified ensemble. Second, it is desirable for this first view of the city to be related to its role....Third, the shape of the city must clearly attempt to fit into the surrounding countryside, and to take advantage of it. Fourth, it would be a mistake to imitate the crowding of the ancient site. It would also be a mistake to take the opposite approach, spreading the site out too much. It seems to us that these are general principles regarding the setting of the city. [6]

Coubertin's idea was to some extent a parallel development with other contemporary urban utopianism in the nineteenth and twentieth centuries, such as the *phalanstère* of Charles Fourier (in the 1840s) and the *international city* of Ernest Hebrand (in the 1910s), and inspired by various avant-garde design practices for urban spectacles such as world expositions at the time. [7] Many of the above principles are still meaningful in guiding today's Olympic urban decision-making. The 'Modern Olympia' self-implies a site concentration approach, which has been favoured by the IOC for many decades. Pierre de Coubertin's preference for a more pastoral setting inspires the creation of numerous scenic Olympic parks in crowded urban contexts. Additionally, his insistence on the 'Modern Olympia' moving from one city to another instead of a permanent resort to spread the Olympic spirit makes it possible to capitalize Olympic preparation for various urban transformations.

However, during the first decade of Olympic revival, there were many more urgent tasks to be accomplished for the incipient movement; Coubertin's plea could only remain as utopian. Furthermore, the Games did not attract the general public's attention and were extremely financially constrained. Although Athens in 1896 did involve a limited provision of new facilities, including the restoration of the 2,000-year-old Panathenaic Stadium and the refurbishment of the Zappeion building in its downtown area, the following two Games, at Paris and St Louis, had few meaningful settings and left few urban legacies. In Paris (1900) the Games were exclusively held in natural settings, where swimmers had to negotiate the muddied Seine and hammer-throwers were impeded by trees. [8]

The Dominance of the Olympic Stadium (1908–28)

Although tethered to the Franco-British Exhibition of the same year, the London Games of 1908 were a milestone in the Olympic urbanization journey, where the first piece of Olympic architecture, the White City Stadium, was introduced. Aiming to showcase the technical achievements of the new century, the stadium was gigantic in size and was characterized by avant-garde industrial aesthetics, yet in function, it was found to be less than ideal due to the design attempting to reconcile too many – and often conflicting – functions for different sports through one architectural solution. Nonetheless, it placed Olympic urbanization on a more secure footing.

In a rethinking of London's approach, Stockholm 1912 developed a range of venues for separate sports at Djungarden in the northern suburb of the city. The centrepiece was the neo-classical athletic stadium, meticulously built in reddish stone to be in harmony with the context of Scandinavian cities. Stockholm's approach can still be considered a *mono-stadium* model because the Olympic Stadium remained the backbone of the Games where most contests and ceremonies were concentrated, and it used most (87 per cent) of the budget. [9] Commended by Coubertin himself, Stockholm's practice soon became a prototype for later cities to follow. Until the late 1920s, the pattern of Olympic urbanization can be summarized as: purpose built Olympic stadium (covering most of the competitions) + small rented halls (for a few essential indoor events) + improvised adapted water course (for aquatic sports).

From a town-planning perspective, Olympic urbanization in the 1910s to 1920s did not impinge greatly on host cities; yet purposefully created athletic stadiums effectively defined an Olympic *node* (if not a *quarter*) in urban fabric terms, stamping the location with new landmarks and identities. Further, there was in evidence a cultural diversity of the host society or the era through different architectural dialects, for instance, the industrial craftsmanship in London (1908) and Paris (1924), the gothic revival in Stockholm (1912), the *beaux arts* in Antwerp (1920) and the modernism of Amsterdam (1928). Aesthetic and symbolic expression subsequently became an important theme of later Olympic urban development.

The Rise of the Olympic Quarter (1932–56)

The Los Angeles Games of 1932 turned out to be another breakthrough for Olympic urbanization, where the first genuine Olympic Village, comprising 550 prefabricated wooden cottages, was set up in a 101-hectare compound on Baldwin Hill at the edge of the city. This allowed the last indispensable component of Coubertin's 'Modern Olympia' to come to life and extended the content of Olympic urbanization from sports premises to urban housing. William Garland, Los Angeles civic leader and the Games' chief organizer, was perhaps the first to perceive the potential benefits that could be brought to host cities by Olympic intervention. [10] Under his leadership, Los Angeles prepared an inventory of new facilities, including the epic 105,000-spectator-capacity Memorial Coliseum, a swimming arena and a fencing pavilion. These were located in a 160-acre site that had once been Exposition Park, and which would later become the city's after-hours amusement district. The Coliseum remained the largest Olympic arena built until the Sydney Games of 2000.

The Berlin Games of 1936 consolidated the trend for the development of substantial facilities in forming an Olympic quarter, and resulted in a 130-hectare site at Grunewald in western Berlin (later named as Reich's Sport Field) being developed as a sporting and cultural quarter. A further purpose of this effort was to showcase Hitler's propaganda for National Socialism. The site included a new stadium with 100,000 seats, a swimming centre, an open-air amphitheatre, a sports forum and large assembly fields and service buildings, all built in rigid neo-classic forms and linked by monumental axes. A 16-kilometre ceremonial boulevard, the 'Via Triumphalis', was specially routed to articulate the Olympic site and the city centre through the Brandenburg Gate. A self-contained Village encompassing 194 bungalows was created in a verdant 55-hectare site 14.5 kilometres west of the Olympic complex, with full training and leisure facilities. The Berlin Games have been seen as a turning point for the Olympics, moving from modest sports celebrations to sumptuous, multi-dimensional spectacles. Although controversially coloured by the Nazi regime, the urban settings of these Games were superb and were not surpassed for many years to come.

Due to post-war economic austerity, the London Games of 1948 had to rely on existing facilities and left little impact on the city's built environment. The following two Games in Helsinki (1952) and Melbourne (1956), however, continued the tendency to produce more facilities for the expanding Games and to integrate the planning procedure into the local urban agenda. Helsinki made two significant contributions: the creation of the first pastoral Olympic park in which 'buildings and landscape were perfectly harmonized in an expression of dignify and loftiness'; [11] and the combination of the Olympic Village development with the municipal housing scheme, which has become commonplace in later Games. Similarly, Melbourne concentrated most of its venues in a 20-hectare Olympic Park on the Yarra River two kilometres from the city centre and established a social-housing-oriented Village in the northern suburb of Heidelberg. There was some criticism of Melbourne's Olympic urbanization when several key venues were demolished or restructured after the Games, yet the Olympic Park remained the city's main sports resort and memorable legacy.

Up to the 1950s, the breadth and depth of Olympic urbanization remained moderate by modern standards. This was partly due to the limits of transport (with typically low private vehicle usage), stable urban population growth and the amateurism promoted by the Olympic Movement which limited over-commercialism and political interference. Since 1960, however, Olympic urban planning has become more ambitious with wider impacts.

The Age of Urban Transformation (1960–2012)

Due to rapid progress in the world economy, social mobility and communication techniques, the 1960s witnessed a wave of radical urban growth across all major world cities, creating great pressures on housing and civic infrastructures. Meanwhile,

Western planning ideas were heavily influenced by architectural modernism, leading to calls for urban transformation towards more rational and functional settlements. Inevitably, 1960s and 1970s Olympic urbanization was impacted upon by these zeitgeists.

The Rome Games of 1960 provided the first paradigm of the Olympics as a catalyst for major urban change, where the delivery of Olympic venues as key elements in urbanistic intervention gave way to a wider urbanistic programme. The main sporting facilities for the Rome Games were clustered in three separate sites, two in the northern and one in the southern outskirts of the city, stretching the built area in two directions. The main sites were connected by a new thoroughfare called the Olympic Way. Besides Games-related facilities, the city also developed a new water supply system, new hotels, a new jetport and improved public transport, street lighting and urban landscaping. The largest project involved the road network connecting Olympic venues to the rest of the city, occupying 75 per cent of the land used for the event. [12] The lavish developments even led to calls for the cancellation of the next Games because of the increasing scale and complexity of Olympic urban commitment. [13]

The role of the Olympics in triggering urban transformation was taken further in Tokyo for the 1964 Games. The Games provided a timely opportunity to remedy the city's poor civic infrastructure and to fast-track the already proposed ten-year development plan. Tokyo spent nearly US$2.7 billion in 1964, or 3.2 per cent of GNP in 1965, on an ambitious urban renovation plan, which included extensive road improvements, harbour expansion and developments of urban amenities, housing, tourist accommodation and waste and sewage disposal systems. [14] But at the plan's core was a carefully contrived, multi-hierarchy transport network that crisscrossed the whole city, embracing eight new expressways, 22 motor links of various kinds, 73 kilometres of subway, 13.2 kilometres of monorail and a 500-kilometre *Shinkansen* ('Bullet train') connecting Tokyo, Kyoto and Osaka. [15] Interestingly, among Tokyo's vast Olympic expenditure only a tiny portion (less than three per cent) went to the construction of purely competition-related facilities; the majority was invested to meet the city's short-term and long-term development needs. This sparked the IOC's view that the cost was 'the result of local interests, not Olympic interests at all'; [16] nevertheless, what had been planned and achieved in Tokyo did transform the city from congested, war-damaged chaos to a modern, prosperous metropolis.

Due to financial strictures and civic opposition, the Mexico City Games of 1968 could not afford developments on the scale of Tokyo; rather existing facilities were largely refurbished for Olympic use. The main investment included the giant Sports Palace, a swimming/gymnastics compound, some open-air stadiums and two self-sufficient Olympic Villages with combined capacity of 8,500 flat units. Described as a 'Games of long walks', Mexico City extended the decentralized approach to its limit and placed new urban developments strategically in areas where growth was expected. With new and refurbished venues heavily scattered over its sprawling urbanscape, the city's public transport was under great stress. The Olympics stimulated the construction of the city's metro but did not benefit from it – the first 12-kilometre line was inaugurated in 1969, one year after the Games. The most successful urban work that distinguished Mexico City from previous hosts was its 'Olympic Identity Programme', which introduced strong decorative elements and signposts to the whole city, particularly the Olympic routes, to create a carnival atmosphere. This strategy has been widely adopted by later Games organizers.

By comparison with the over-discrete Mexican scheme, the Munich Games of 1972 adopted a very centralized approach and located most Olympic venues and the Athletes' Village on one concentrated 280-hectare site of derelict land at Oberwiesenfeld only four kilometres north of the city centre. Munich's Olympic plan was characterized by land-use modification and urban renewal. Oberwiesenfeld had once been a pre-war airstrip and then a dumping ground for building debris. The 1963 city development plan had earmarked the site for the development of a sports and entertainment centre over a 15- to 20-year period yet, under the Olympic banner, the development speed increased. [17]

In order to efface the arrogant impression of the Berlin 1936 Games, Munich Olympic Park was designed to embrace an enchanting style and humanistic taste and to avoid any metaphor of monumentality. The site was enriched by a green landscape of hills, hollows, waters and woods, in the midst of which lay a set of venues unified by a wave-form, net-structured roof, giving a sense of freedom and flux. The Olympic Village was constructed in the immediate vicinity of the site with diverse building types and vivid spatial layers to echo the theme. Yet the hostage taking of Israeli athletes by terrorists in the Olympic Village placed its open character and tortuous layout under criticism and highlighted security as a crucial point in Olympic urban design.

At Munich, other improvements also took place, from new shopping complexes to renewed public transport infrastructures. Studies of the price index for cost of living in recent host cities during and after the Games suggest that Munich is one of those (along with Barcelona) that have successfully converted to service-based economy associated with high consumption/high income during the Olympic cycle. While this conversion might be caused by various factors, nonetheless Olympic urbanization certainly contributed a significant part. [18]

The pattern of centralized Olympic urban development continued with Montreal for the 1976 Games, where the local authority was keen to use *grand projects* to reshape the city, as had been the case with the 1967 Exposition. Yet due to the lack of federal financial support, the initial idea was to promote a 'modest, self-financing' Games. Existing facilities were widely used and Olympic construction was focused on the Olympic Stadium, the swimming arena, velodrome and the Athletes' Village, forming Maisonneuve Olympic Park in the proximity of Montreal downtown. Similar to Munich, the site had been earmarked for sports and recreational use by early urban plans and already contained some athletic facilities. The Olympic development package also included a 20-kilometre extension of the metro lines, a new air terminal as well as some improvements of urban roads.

Although Montreal's planning was as meaningful as previous cases, the implementation was, however, plagued with problems. Designed by Robert Tailibert, Montreal's Olympic facilities have been noted as 'among the most complex concrete structures ever attempted' [19] – the most striking features of which were colossal self-stabilizing roof shells and an 18-floor leaning tower designed to house a retractable fabric canopy overhanging the main stadium. The ambitious structure, new techniques and materials, interwoven with perhaps lax project management, global inflation and local labour relations disputes, resulted in a debt of C$ 1.5 billion. [20] The Games were nearly cancelled before the Opening Ceremony. The development of the Olympic Village was also problematic. The original proposal was to build five different residential compounds spreading over a radius of several kilometres from the Olympic park to be in line with the city's housing scheme. It was, however, rejected by the IOC, who by then preferred a concentrated approach in the wake of the Munich tragedy. The result was to locate the Village in the vicinity of the sports facilities and compress 980 suites into two giant pyramidal towers; the consequent use of 34 hectares of urban green reservation caused a wave of local protests.

Ironically, despite all the efforts made, the Games seem to have had little benefit for local communities. Now 30 years after the Montreal Games, the sports complex is having difficulty in being sustained for its original functions and the stadium has been suggested for demolition. [21] Montreal's Olympic urbanization shows the risk of creating 'white elephant' legacies and resulting in long-term debts.

The lessons from Montreal inevitably affected the planning of subsequent Games. Both Moscow (1980) and Los Angeles (1984) attempted to avoid the construction of over-extravagant projects. Nonetheless, Moscow's Olympic inventory still embraced more than 90 construction sites across the conurbation. [22] The Soviet planning philosophy had long been influenced by rationalism and the satellite-city theory stemming from the early modern movement. Moscow's master plan 1971–90 zoned the city into eight planning agglomerations with each centred on an economic, recreational and social-cultural core. Moscow's Olympic scheme was largely devised in line with this vision. Olympic venues were established in six different zones as part of the city's sub-centres identified in its tenth five-year development plan. The 107-hectare Olympic Village, now the home of 15,000 Muscovites, was built in an urban extension south-west of the city that had been earmarked as a residential quarter much earlier. The Olympics also boosted the city's underdeveloped hotel market and broadcasting and communication infrastructures.

The Los Angeles Games of 1984 represented a heterogeneous approach deviating from the mainstream of Olympic urban practice since the 1960s (where the whole concept was to create an 'ephemeral Olympic scene' rather than to bolster any substantial urban change). Due to local taxpayers' opposition, the 1984 Games became an entirely privately sponsored event. In order to minimize expenditure on installation, the organizers mobilized existing facilities as far as possible and provided the rest with makeshift structures. In the whole plan no meaningful Olympic precinct had been truly defined and venues were dispersed throughout the city's vast territory. Being the only candidate city and a city already possessing 24 of 31 venues needed to stage the Games, Los Angeles had unique advantages to realize its strategy.

The old Memorial Coliseum was once again refurbished as the main venue and the student dormitories at three local universities were temporarily converted to Athletes' Villages. The whole city was ablaze with colourful streamers, banners, balloons, signposts, light towers and all kinds of graphic design works. Yet behind these sparkling 'urban confetti' the Olympics brought little change to the urban fabric. Nonetheless, with a profit of US $225 million, the 1984 Games is remembered as a great commercial success and a renaissance for the Olympic Movement.

The theme of utilizing the Olympics for local urbanization was revived with the Seoul Games of 1988 and the Barcelona Games of 1992. From the late 1980s there were increasing needs for Western industrialized cities to regenerate their run-down areas associated with suburbanization, urban displacement or the decline of manufacturing; the Olympics provide opportunities for such operations. In the case of Seoul, Chamsil on the south bank of the Han River was a slum and flood-risk area that had been occupied by various low-quality housing projects suffering from various environmental problems. Seoul's Olympic organizers took over this site, designated 60 hectares for the development of Seoul Sports Complex and the remaining 63 hectares for an Athletes' Village. A further 260-hectare tract of land in nearby Kangdong-gu was also chosen to develop Seoul Olympic Park, containing supplementary venues and media premises. These exploitations were consistent with the city's long-term plan to extend the urban fabric towards the south of the Han River.

Other important themes of Seoul's Olympic urbanization included the showcasing of Korean culture to the world and the improvement of the city's general health and hygiene standards. Localism and Korean aesthetic identity were emphasized in the design of key Olympic architecture, and various cultural utilities, including museums, arts centres and historic monuments, were established in time for the Games. But the most visible change of the urbanscape was through the *environmental beautification programme*, which aimed to both improve the street scene and remove sources of physical pollution. Streets were decorated with flora, artworks and better paving. Many open spaces and parks were introduced throughout the city. Moreover, urban traffic was enhanced with the expansion of Seoul's light-rail network and the establishment of bus lanes and one-way systems.

Following Spain's joining the European Union in 1986, Barcelona took advantage of the 1992 Games to reform a local economy that had been in decline and to remedy infrastructural deficiencies left from the Franco period. Major developments were undertaken in four urban precincts: Montjuic Park, Vall d'Hebron, Diagonal and the seafront area of Poblenou. The Montjuic Stadium had been the site for the 1929 Exposition and the 1936 People's Olympiad; it was remodelled as the centrepiece of the 1992 Games and a symbol of local sporting heritage. Poblenou was an area consisting of derelict warehouses and railway facilities, cutting off the beach from the city and fragmenting the neighbourhood. Olympic development rehabilitated this area with stylish apartments, a new sewage system, a new costal ring road, a new marina (Olympic Harbour) and other amenities along the 5.2-kilometre barrier-free costal strip. Improvements in other supportive infrastructures, particularly the cultural aspects and telecommunications, were also carried out. The regeneration of Barcelona has been cited as one of the most successful Olympic urban initiatives, transforming the city from a decaying industrial port to a popular tourist terminal, and putting the city on the world urban map.

The Centennial Games of Atlanta in 1996, by contrast, represent a pause in Olympic urban transformation as it concentrated on the development of essential sporting facilities. Most venues were located within a three-kilometre circle of the Olympic Ring in the heart of the city; many others were constructed on a temporary basis at Stone Mountain Park site, 25 kilometres east of downtown Atlanta. The Olympic Stadium was designed as a combination of athletic ground and baseball diamond so that it could be converted into a ballpark after the Games. Many new and reused facilities were developed in cooperation with local colleges, including the Olympic Village that used the 130-hectare campus of Georgia Institute of Technology. To provide the Olympic concourse a commemorative legacy, the organizers set up an 8.5-hectare Centennial Olympic Park in the city centre with a rich collection of horticultural works.

Atlanta's general urban infrastructure, however, was less touched by the Olympics. The organizers self-consciously followed the Los Angeles model but did not appear to understand that the city lacked sufficient supportive facilities compared with those of Los Angeles, and neither was the Olympic Movement in the same situation as the late 1970s. The lack of substantial investment in the city's infrastructure resulted in wide criticism of transportation, logistics and security matters. Also, the intention to revive Atlanta's downtown through the development of centrally located venues does not appear to have been successful; recent studies suggest that the decline of many of the poorest communities in central Atlanta continues. [23]

The Sydney Games of 2000 was widely labelled as a 'green' event. Inspired by the IOC's new environmental policy, Sydney established a detailed set of sustainable development guidelines to govern the design, construction and maintenance of Olympic facilities. The main site for the Games at Homebush Bay, some 15 kilometres west of Sydney Harbour, was a neglected urban wasteland comprising unusable swamp, outdated industrial premises and noxious landfill sites, and had been earmarked for environmental rehabilitation. Homebush was also the demographic centre of the greater Sydney region, strategically linking two major central business districts (CBDs): Darwin Harbour in the east and Parramatta in the west. The Olympic development thus attempted to agglomerate Sydney's amorphous tissue and consolidate the connections between regional centres.

Consisting of 14 grand venues, the Homebush bay site formed the largest venue cluster in Olympic history. This included the 115,000-seat Stadium Australia, the largest Olympic stadium ever created. It featured retractable stands to support versatility and demountable stands to enable the venue to resize after the Games. Temporary overlays were widely used in Olympic facilities. Renewable energy sources, particularly solar panels, were demonstrated throughout the Olympic site and the Athletes' Village. In order to restore the ecosystem of the region, a 420-hectare site surrounding the Olympic venues was converted into Millennium Parklands with diverse landscaped topography. As with other host cities, the Olympics also brought forward improvements to Sydney's general built environment, particularly in the area of hotel stock, motorways, rail links and public domain in the central city. Sydney's tourism and convention sector were also boosted.

There were problems as well. Although Sydney was cited as a benchmark of eco-sensitive design for future Games, its green credentials in decontamination and various sustainability goals have been questioned in view of such a hasty Olympic timetable. In addition, many venues at Homebush Bay have experienced low usage in recent years, suggesting the after-use issue is still a pressing subject to be explored.

The Games returned to their birthplace Athens in 2004. Given the special meaning of the Olympics to Greece, local communities held high aspirations to showcase successful organization and to reinvent Athens as a thriving postmodern city embracing the new century. Olympic projects were carried out in almost every part of the city, but principally accumulated in four precincts. The main site was Athens Olympic Sports Complex, located in the city's north-eastern suburb nine kilometres from the Acropolis. The site already contained some quality venues and in preparing for the 2004 Games it was reshaped by the designer Santiago Calatrava incorporating his stunning – but also expensive – futuristic steel-trussed roofs. Other major developments took place at the Faliro coastal zone, Hellinikon, Goudi and Marathonas. The 530-hectare brownfield site at the obsolete Hellinikon airport was converted into Europe's largest park for sports and recreational use. [24] The 2,300-unit Olympic Village was built on a 124-hectare site at the foot of Mountain Parnitha, 25 kilometres north-west of the city centre, aiming to attract more migrants to this under-populated area in the longer term.

Likewise, Athens built new metro and tram lines to link main Olympic sites with other urban territories, strengthening the city's articulation along its north-east/south-west axis perpendicular to the sea. There were also new air terminals, new plazas and new hotels. Many archaeological remains were restored and supported with museum facilities. Athens's Olympic urbanization, however, was also over-shadowed by worrisome delays in construction and cost overruns. The expenditure for Olympic installation nearly quintupled from the original budget. The environmentally-sensitive design concept, such a promising focus in Sydney, was less meaningfully incorporated in Athens; and the problem of post-Olympic use of venues has already been raised as an issue.

Olympic urbanization continues with the Beijing Games to be held in 2008, which is in hectic preparation, and the development plan for the London Games of 2012 is close to completion. Beijing aims to use the Olympics to raise its international profile and remedy some severe environmental problems. Most venues are being constructed in a 405-hectare Olympic Park on the northern edge of the city's central mass and adjacent to the old Asian Games Park. The idea is to make full use of the existing sports premises left from the 1990 Asian Games and to reinforce, in a symbolic sense, the city's north-south axis, as a series of key Olympic buildings sit right on the northern end of this ritualistic axis lining up with the Tiananmen Gate at the city's geographic centre.

For the benefit of the Games bid, Beijing's Olympic urbanization does not follow the south-eastward strategy identified in the city's earlier master-plan. [25] Criticisms therefore emerged that this would further aggravate the current development imbalance and social inequity. Nevertheless, this deficiency may be made up to some extent by Beijing's ambitious ongoing initiative in expanding its metro and light rail network to the whole urban fabric, particularly the southern territory, over a 15-year period. Also, extensive infrastructural improvements and beautification endeavours are being made in the whole city beyond the Olympic precincts.

Comparatively, London's Olympic plan for 2012 is more consistent with the city's long-term efforts to regenerate its degraded eastern boroughs, which started with the redevelopment of Docklands in the 1980s and continues in the Mayor of London's 2004 plan. [26] Most of the new venues and the Olympic Village will be constructed in a 200-hectare site in the Lower Lea valley, 13 kilometres east of the city centre. New transport facilities are being conceived to serve this area including a high-speed 'Olympic Javelin' shuttle train. At present, London's Olympic preparation is still under detailed planning, but it can be foreseen that the impact will cover the entire 'Thames Gateway' area.

Planning in Olympic Host Cities: Successful Olympic Urbanization

In order to aid understanding, Figure 1 shows schematic drawing of the Olympic site planning in some host cities. Looking at Olympic history, urbanization has taken place with diverse breadths and depths at different times in various places, and consequently has left very different and distinct footprints in host cities' urban fabric. On the other hand, it is also consistent, being carried out for the same objective, on an equal timescale, and endowed with the common Olympic identity. To judge the success or otherwise of an Olympic urban approach is difficult, because the comparisons need to face a great diversity of urban contexts, social evolutionary stages, resource availability and built environment deficiencies. All these would naturally lead to heterogeneous decision-making.

Nevertheless, consensus exists in evaluating the changes in host cities after respective Games based on the first-hand experiences of local communities. It is true to say that in cities such as Tokyo and Barcelona, the Olympics have triggered profound urban revival while in some others, such as Los Angeles and Atlanta, the Games were only a passing phase. In Munich and Sydney, Olympic parks have been preserved as urban landmarks but in Melbourne and Montreal some well-conceived

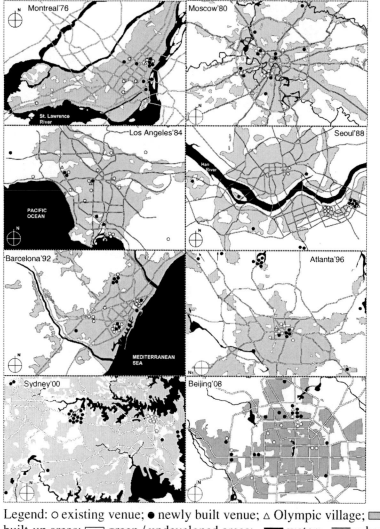

Legend: ○ existing venue; ● newly built venue; △ Olympic village; ▭ built-up areas; ▢ green / undeveloped areas; ■ water; ☰ urban road / public transit

Figure 1 Schematic drawing of the Olympic site planning in some host cities.

venues have failed to stand the test of time. Given such different outcomes, the question arises as to what makes a successful Olympic scheme in terms of urbanization. Several key aspects stand out as reference points for this investigation: the content and scale of Olympic intervention, the urban entity they define and the vision of urban integration they represent.

To some extent, the content and scale of Olympic urbanization can be examined by looking at the capital investment in Olympic construction at each Games. The variations are shown in Figure 2 where all values have been converted into US

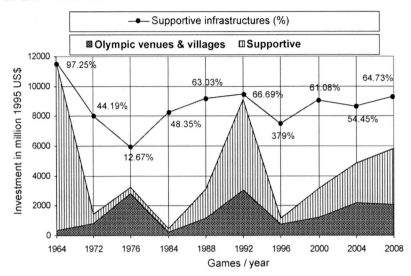

Figure 2 Investment in Olympic construction, Tokyo 1964 to Beijing 2008.

dollars for comparison. It shows that the highest investment, which was made by Tokyo in 1964, is approximately 24 times higher than that of Los Angeles in 1984. There are also striking differences in the development of supportive infrastructures: in Seoul (1988) and Barcelona (1992), about two-thirds of the total expenditure was spent on this component, and in the case of Tokyo, the ratio is as high as 97 per cent. By contrast, in Montreal (1976) only 13 per cent of the investment was made for indirect Olympic projects. In general, those Games with modest infrastructural investment or those over-concentrated on the development of competition-related facilities are unlikely to involve mass urban transformation and subsequent longer-lasting benefits.

Of course, this is not a simple story of 'spend more, get more'. As shown by the case of Helsinki and Munich, limited resources can still be well leveraged to improve urban amenities and create stylish spaces; or as shown by the case of Montreal, lavish investment does not guarantee wider urban improvement and sustainable legacies. What should be included and excluded from the Olympic development package requires wisdom in decision-making, and comes from a thorough understanding of the city's tradition, actuality, problems and needs; a sharp insight in predicting the local development trend; a holistic planning strategy with scientific analysis of pros and cons; a democratic consultation process to ensure the public interest; and sufficient economic capacity to enable the development to take place.

A successful Olympic urban scheme seems always to be associated with a suitable and linked long-term master-plan for the host city in terms of project determination, land usage, resource mobilization and development orientation. Emphasis on such may help to avoid over-ambitious initiatives triggered by infatuated enthusiasm, or any hasty decision-making because of the tight Olympic deadline. It also helps to rationalize the budgetary deployment so that Olympic projects do not overshadow the development of other essential facilities in the city.

A successful Olympic scheme also derives from a holistic planning concept that respects the distinct character of host cities in urbanization conditions, demographic change, socio-economic reality and environmental deficiencies. This is particularly reflected by the integration of major Olympic facilities into host cities' urban fabric as fundamental to the overall planning intervention. Historically Olympic sites have been integrated with cities in six models, with each having different advantages and limitations, and should be used or adapted based on local externalities (see Figure 3).

In general, the decentralized model is suitable for a city having good civic infrastructures, with no obvious environmental deficiencies to be redressed in a planning manner, yet needing a partial adjustment of its urban fabric to balance the holistic development. Inner-city clustering models are suitable for a city suffering from inner city decline, suburbanization and hence sprawl. They can help to re-nucleate an evenly dispersed urban form and introduced large green and public spaces to the city's central mass. The periphery clustering model is suitable for cities experiencing a considerable population growth, with outward development pressure and expansion needs. It can help to define the development orientation and convert an outspread urban form into a linear-shaped transit-oriented form. The satellite clustering model is suitable for large conurbations where internal development pressures need to be organically dispersed and multi-hierarchy settlements need to be reinforced in the whole region. The joint clustering model is suitable for the coordination of two closely located developing urban areas for a strategic development.

Conclusion

The Olympic Games have now travelled around the world and left a rich spectrum of urban heritages which, taken together, are a unique and indispensable contribution to the success of the modern Olympic Movement. The 'Modern Olympia' is not a truly geographic concept and the 'Olympic city' is not a distinct urban genre; rather, they are open-ended phenomena constantly enriched by the practice of host cities and reinterpreted through the preparation for every new Olympics. Mass Olympic urban development has always been a double-edged sword for both the Games and local communities. On the one hand it may bring desirable social changes and a global reputation; on the other financial disaster and a tempest of criticism. Each Olympic urban scheme therefore has to balance between sports, ritual, social, economic, environmental and symbolic considerations, and appreciate the long-term realities. Nevertheless, Olympic urbanization has emerged as an essential part of the modern Olympic Movement, which bridges the worlds of sport and urban environment where daily life takes place and different cultures meet each other, and extends the Olympic

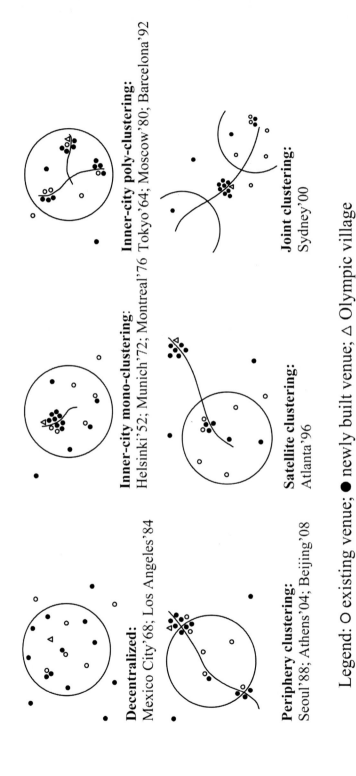

Decentralized:
Mexico City'68; Los Angeles'84

Inner-city mono-clustering:
Helsinki'52; Munich'72; Montreal'76

Inner-city poly-clustering:
Tokyo'64; Moscow'80; Barcelona'92

Periphery clustering:
Seoul'88; Athens'04; Beijing'08

Satellite clustering:
Atlanta'96

Joint clustering:
Sydney'00

Legend: ○ existing venue; ● newly built venue; △ Olympic village

Figure 3 The six theoretical models of Olympic site integration to the host city (Cf. Fig. 1).

footprint well beyond the simple '16 days of glory' over which the summer Games take place.

The Olympic Games can be seen as one extreme of a wide range of hallmark sports events. The implications of the Olympic Games for major world cities are amplified examples for other smaller cities with scaled-down sports spectacles, such as world championships and inter-continental Games. Parallel studies need to be introduced to non-Olympic contexts; such research would add to the understanding of sport-event-orientated urban development and enrich the findings of this study. The review of modern Olympic urbanization history, however, can provide a valuable starting point.

Notes

[1] Hiller, 'Towards a Science of Olympic Outcomes', 102. It is necessary, however, to assert that requirements for bid cities are not always uniform, nor do Olympic bid manuals remain the same across time. For example, in the 2008 version of the bid document the IOC provides estimates of required accomodation numbers. For the 2012 Games, by contrast, no numbers are specified.

[2] See International Olympic Committee, *Olympic Charter 1991*.

[3] Essex and Chalkey, 'The Infrastructural Legacy', 94.

[4] The Globalization and World Cities (GaWc) research group centred at Loughborough University produced a preliminary ranking of world mega-cities based on their size, population, scientific and cultural impacts, economic capacity and roles in the global service network. Most cities that have acted as the Olympic hosts are among those designated as 'world class nexus'. Cf. Sassen, *Global Networks, Linked Cities*, 68.

[5] Coubertin, 'Le Cadre, Une Olympie Moderne', 153–6.

[6] Ibid., 155.

[7] A *phalanstère* was a type of building cluster designed for a utopian community where people are working together for mutual benefits, which was conceived in the mid-1800s by French socialist Charles Fourier. The *international city* was proposed by French architect Ernest Hebrard after the Hague Peace Conference (1899) for creating a permanent Village where intellectuals could gather to solve 'the world's conflicts'. Cf. Greslery, *La Ciutat Mundial*, 164.

[8] Lucas, *The Olympic Games, 1904*, 19.

[9] Swedish Olympic Committee, *Official Report*, 46.

[10] International Olympic Committee, 'William May Garland', 12. It should be asserted here that an Olympic Village had been created for the 1924 Games in Paris and that the 1932 Olympic Village was only temporary, was only for the male competitors, and that the women were housed in hotel accommodation.

[11] Gordon, *Olympic Architecture, Building for the Summer Olympic Games*, 3.

[12] Munoz, 'Historic Evolution and Urban Planning Typology', 14.

[13] Chalkley and Essex, 'Urban Development Through Hosting International Events', 379.

[14] Tokyo Organizing Committee for the Olympic Games 1964, *Official Report*, vol. 1, 46.

[15] Gordon, *Olympic Architecture, Building for the Summer Olympic Games*, 94.

[16] In a speech at the University of Lausanne in 1928, Coubertin criticized many Olympic arenas that were 'the result of local, and too often, commercial interests, not Olympic interests at all' (Cf. Muller, *Pierre de Coubertin: Olympism – Selected Writings*, 184). And Lord Killanin (IOC president, 1972–80) commented on the Montreal Games: 'Who force the cities to take on excessive cost? They use the Olympic Games to develop their city and to create new sports

facilities...Mexico City, Tokyo, Munich and also Montreal used the Games as an occasion to develop their cities. Sport is not guilty for this'. Cf. Newfield, *Montreal–Innsbruck '76*, 11.

[17] Chalkley and Essex, 'Urban Development Through Hosting International Events', 381.
[18] Preuss, *Economics of the Olympic Games*, 66–8.
[19] Malouf, *Report of the Commission of Inquiry*, vol. 2, 58.
[20] Kidd, 'The Culture Wars of the Montreal Olympics', 156.
[21] Canadian Broadcasting Corporation, *The Big Woe* (video archive).
[22] Gordon, *Olympic architecture, building for the Summer Olympic Games*, 156.
[23] Stone, 'The Atlanta Experience Re-examined', 20.
[24] Plumb and McKay, *Reaching Beyond the Gold*, 9.
[25] Beijing Municipality, *General Plan of Beijing, 1991–2010*.
[26] Greater London Authority, *Mayor of London, the London Plan*, 39.

References

Beijing Municipality. *General Plan of Beijing, 19912010* (in Chinese). Beijing: Beijing Development and Reform Committee, 1991.

Canadian Broadcasting Corporation. *The Big Woe*. CBC News Archives, 22 Jan. 1999. Toronto. Available online at http://archives.cbc.ca, accessed 24 July 2006.

Chalkley, B. and S. Essex. 'Urban Development Through Hosting International Events: A History of the Olympic Games'. *Planning Perspectives* 14 (1999): 369–94.

Coubertin, P. 'Le Cadre, Une Olympie Moderne' ['The Setting, a Modern Olympia']. *Revue Olympique*, October 1909: 153–6.

Essex, S. and B. Chalkey, B. 'The Infrastructural Legacy of the Summer and Winter Olympic Games, a Comparative Analysis'. *Proceedings of the International Symposium on the Legacy of the Olympic Games, 1984–2000*. Lausanne: International Olympic Committee, 2003.

Gordon, B. *Olympic Architecture, Building for the Summer Olympic Games*. New York: John Wiley & Sons, 1983.

Greater London Authority. *Mayor of London, the London Plan: Spatial Development Strategy for Great London*. London: Greater London Authority, 2004.

Greslery, G. 'La Ciutat Mundial'. In *Visions Urbanes, Europa 1870–1993*. Barcelona: Centre de Cultura Comtemporania de Barcelona, 1994.

Hiller, H. 'Towards a Science of Olympic Outcomes: The Urban Legacy'. *Proceedings of the International Symposium on the Legacy of the Olympic Games, 1984–2000*. Lausanne: International Olympic Committee, 2003.

International Olympic Committee. *Olympic Charter 1991*. Lausanne: IOC, 1991.

———. 'William May Garland'. *Bulletin of the International Olympic Committee*, November 1948.

Kidd, J. 'The Culture Wars of the Montreal Olympics'. *International Review for the Sociology of Sports* 27 (1992): 156.

Lucas, C. *The Olympic Games, 1904*. St Louis, MO: Woodard & Tiernan, 1904.

Malouf, A. *Report of the Commission of Inquiry into the Cost of the 21st Olympiad*. 4 vols. Montreal: Canadian Commission of Inquiry into the Cost of the 21st Olympiad, 1980.

Muller, N., ed. *Pierre de Coubertin: Olympism – Selected writings*. Lausanne: International Olympic Committee, 2000.

Munoz, F. 'Historic Evolution and Urban Planning Typology of Olympic Village'. *Proceedings of the International Symposium on Olympic Villages*. Lausanne: International Olympic Committee, 1997.

Newfield, F., ed. *Montreal–Innsbruck '76: The Olympic Games*. Montreal: ProSport Canada, 1976.

Plumb, C. and M. McKay. *Reaching Beyond the Gold, the Impact of the Olympic Games on Real Estate Markets*. Chicago: Jones Lang LaSalle, 2001.

Preuss, H. *Economics of the Olympic Games, Hosting the Games 1972–2000.* Sydney: University of New South Wales Press, 2000.

Sassen, S., ed. *Global Networks, Linked Cities.* London: Routledge, 2002.

Stone, C. 'The Atlanta Experience Re-Examined: The Link Between Agenda and Regime Change'. *International Journal of Urban and Regional Research* 25 (2001): 20–4.

Swedish Olympic Committee. *Official Report of the Games of the V Olympiad.* Stockholm: Wahlstrom and Widstrand, 1912.

Tokyo Organizing Committee for the Olympic Games 1964. *Official Report of the Games of the XVIII Olympiad*, 2 vols. Tokyo: Tokyo Organizing Committee for the Olympic Games, 1964.

Epilogue

Sandra Collins

As is well known by now, born out of the Postgraduate Research Grant Programme of the Olympic Studies Centre (OSC), the eight essays of this groundbreaking collection focus on different historical aspects of the modern Olympic Games. Ranging from issues of women's studies, urban planning, national representation, Olympic diplomacy, postcolonial resistance, sports diffusion and the dismantling of amateurism, this interdisciplinary volume explores the compelling historical antecedents of the world's most successful sports spectacle. Studies that explore the complexity of the relationship between sports, geopolitics and nationalism are joined here with those that unravel the different philosophical debates that erupted within the Olympic Movement, with specific emphasis on the time period from the 1890s to the 1980s. Many authors present a more complex understanding of the people and events that were previously ignored or relegated to footnotes in the tomes of Olympic biographies. It can thus be claimed that these essays have attempted to represent within the context of Olympism and the Olympic Movement the scholarly balance between archival research and critical analysis in the writing of meaningful history. Further, this collection represents the most contemporary work on how excursions into the Olympic past provide a prism to understand the significance of the Olympic Movement in the present.

Situating these essays according to their historical timeframes helps contextualize these different encounters with the Olympic Movement. The first group of essays – the contributions of Torres, Carpentier and Lefèvre, and Collins – addresses the inter-war period between 1910 and 1940 and reveals the IOC's difficulty in universalizing the Olympic Movement and expanding the locus of its control. Different movements – in Latin America, in Japan, the Zionist movement and women's demands to compete – were compelling the IOC to adapt to new visions of the social and political milieu. Yet the authority of IOC remained a uniquely private affair. Informed by their individual opinions and their social networks, the members of the IOC retained moral authority over Olympism. These essays provide rich historical detail, key to understanding the inter-war debates that challenged the putative politics of IOC governance – from the cooption of Alice Milliat's FSFI; the strategic alliances formed with the YMCA in Latin America; to the conflicts of 'aggressive' Japanese Olympic diplomacy, which also included the first Olympic 'bribe' for a host city. These essays also reveal the degree to which the authority of the IOC came under increased scrutiny during the inter-war period.

In the second group, the essays by Wrynn and Niehaus analyse Olympism in the turbulent political decades of the 1950s and the 1960s. They demonstrate that worldwide movements that questioned established authority and custom also affected the Olympic Games. Niehaus examines how the inclusion of judo as the first non-Western sport affected not only discourses on Olympic universalism but also those on the cultural identity of modern Japan. In turn, the IOC was forced to question its definition of universalism when asked by Japan to include judo in the Olympic programme for the 1964 Tokyo Olympic Games. By tracing how Olympic judo became a metaphor for the normalization of post-Second World War Japan, Niehaus reveals the different misreadings of Olympic judo since judo was often tied to the question of national identity by Japan. Along a different axis, Wrynn resurrects the historical arguments on several controversial tensions that emerged within the IOC: amateurism and professionalism and the role of science and athletics. As scientific inquiry into athleticism increased, the impact of Mexico City's high altitude on Olympic performance forced the IOC to reconsider its definition of amateurism in order to facilitate the training period demanded by high-altitude. These two essays document how the IOC was forced to adapt to transformations in social and scientific understanding.

The impact of the many independence movements of former colonies on Olympism is described in the essays by Smith and Majumdar. Smith's contribution details how the IOC's self-reputed 'political neutrality' was often questioned by its own members. In the letters between IOC member Reginald Alexander and three IOC presidents, the IOC's exertion of political control in the expulsion of the South African NOC is constantly justified. Despite its appeals to logic and positive internationalism, the IOC exercised its own form of governance that was often dependent upon the IOC president's personal prejudices. In contrast to the locus of IOC control in the 1960s and 1970s, Majumdar's work looks at the tensions of Olympism at the local level, here between the north and south regions of India. The disputes that led to the demise of Indian Olympic hockey, he argues, were ultimately tied to the 'broader socio-economic processes that have shaped colonial and postcolonial societies in South Asia'.

Lastly, Liao and Pitts provide a succinct overview of the history of Olympic urbanization from 1896 (Athens) to 2012 (London). The dynamic relationship between Olympic host cities and Olympic development is detailed in their historical analysis. This essay is one of the first to expand the historical approach of Olympic studies beyond its economic, political or social frameworks; and one can eagerly anticipate future historical essays to be informed by the changing discourses of economics, film studies and even game theory on the Olympic Games.

Ultimately, the authors in this collection disclose that in different historical contexts the Olympic Games have played a critical role in shaping modern society. These histories expose different experiences of the Olympic past, which are of great relevance to understanding our Olympic present. [1] The institution of the IOC – which has managed the Olympic Games for over a century – emerges as a complex intersection of people, power and place. More often than not, the Olympic Movement emerges as the unforeseeable result of contingent events and quirks of individual IOC opinions, as Stephen Jay Gould once opined in another context. [2] And through the prism of the Olympic past, our suspicions on the current situation of the Olympic Games are confirmed: the Olympic Games continue to be meaningful to us today, for they continue to be of immense global significance politically, economically, socially and culturally. Finally, it is important here to introduce a caveat: the essays in this volume all stop in the 1980s. This is because of the 30-year embargo (recently increased to 30 from an earlier practice of 20) imposed on the Olympic archives by the IOC, which forces these essays (to their advantage) to be historical and retrospective. Thus we will have to wait for future work in Olympic studies to understand the myriad ways in which Olympism has changed since the 1980s. Until then, these essays will continually remind us of the magnitude of the Olympic Games and how its legacy is constantly recreated by each Olympic generation.

Notes

[1] Benjamin, 'Theses on the Philosophy of History', 684.
[2] Gould, *The Hedgehog*, 225.

References

Benjamin, Walter. 'Theses on the Philosophy of History'. In *Critical Theory Since 1965*, edited by Hazard Adams and Leroy Searle. Gainesville, FL: University Press of Florida, 1989.
Gould, Stephen Jay. *The Hedgehog, the Fox, and the Magister's Pox*. New York: Three Rivers Press, 2003.

Index

Page numbers in **bold** represent figures.